# ARIZONA
## IN YOUR FUTURE

### The complete relocation guide for job-seekers, retirees and Snowbirds

**By Don W. Martin & Betty Woo Martin**

*Third edition*

**DISCOVERGUIDES • Las Vegas, Nevada**

## BOOKS BY DON & BETTY MARTIN

*Adventure Cruising* • 1996
*Arizona Discovery Guide* • 1990, 1993, 1994, 1996, 1998
*Arizona in Your Future* • 1991, 1993, 1998, 2003
*The Best of Denver & the Rockies* • 2001
*The Best of Phoenix & Tucson* • 2001
*The Best of San Francisco* • 1986, 1990, 1994, 1997, 2003
*The Best of the Gold Country* • 1987, 1990, 1992
*The Best of the Wine Country* • 1991, 1994, 1995, 2001
*California-Nevada Roads Less Traveled* • 1999
*Hawaii: The Best of Paradise* • 2003
*Inside San Francisco* • 1991
*Las Vegas: The Best of Glitter City* • 1998, 2001, 2003
*Nevada Discovery Guide* • 1992, 1997
*Nevada In Your Future* • 2000
*New Mexico Discovery Guide* • 1998
*Northern California Discovery Guide* • 1993
*Oregon Discovery Guide* • 1993, 1995, 1996, 1999
*San Diego: The Best of Sunshine City* • 1999, 2003
*San Francisco's Ultimate Dining Guide* • 1988
*Seattle: The Best of Emerald City* • 2000
*The Toll-free Traveler* • 1997
*The Ultimate Wine Book* • 1993, 2000
*Utah Discovery Guide* • 1995
*Washington Discovery Guide* • 1994, 1997, 2000

**Library of Congress Cataloging-in-Publication Data**
Martin, Don and Betty —
Arizona In Your Future
Includes index.
1. Arizona—Description and travel
2. Arizona—Relocating, job-seeking, retiring

**ISBN: 0-942053-40-0**

COVER DESIGN • **Dave Bonnot**, Columbine Type & Design
  Sonora, California
PHOTOS • **Betty** or **Don Martin** unless otherwise credited
CHARTS AND GRAPHS • **Jil Weil**, Oakland, California

# CONTENTS
## PART ONE: THE STATE

# PART TWO: THE COMMUNITIES

# PART THREE: THE ATTRACTIONS

# ARIZONA: A STATE FOR EVERYONE

Is Arizona in your future? This comprehensive relocation guide gallops off in three directions. It provides useful information for job-seekers and their families, retirees looking for their special place under Arizona's sun and "Snowbirds" seeking to flee south for the winter. **Part I** covers "Arizona: the State," with essential information for new residents including state laws, taxes, public education, job-hunting, the best retirement areas and Snowbird roosts. We then offer detailed descriptions of most of Arizona's cities and towns in **Part II**, followed by lists of attractions throughout the state in **Part III**.

*Arizona in Your Future* contains no paid listings or advertising, so it's free of outside bias. No agency, organization or community listed herein has asked to be included. All of the information—and opinions—have come from our own research and observations. Of course, most of what we have to say about Arizona is positive, because it's a stimulating, growing, vibrant and attractive state.

Over the years, we've prowled every corner of the Grand Canyon State to research this relocation guide, plus two travel books—*Arizona Discovery Guide* and *The Best of Phoenix & Tucson*. We learned why Arizona has been, and will continue to be, one of America's fastest growing states. It's amazingly diverse, with every kind of landscape except a seacoast. It offers two major metropolitan centers with their cultural variety, fine dining and—yes—commute-hour traffic. Or, one can settle in a tiny hamlet where nothing changes but the weather.

Phoenix is America's sixth largest city, with a population topping 1.3 million, and Tucson has nearly half a million residents. By the turn of the century, Arizona had passed Washington to become the second most populous state in Western America, with more than five million residents. Yet overall, the state has a rather low population density, with only about thirty-two folks per square mile.

Many people think of Arizona primarily as a Sunbelt state. Indeed, 85 percent of its population resides in warmer climes. Yet, you can choose to live under the pines of Flagstaff and ski the slopes of the next-door San Francisco Peaks. Or you can play cowboy, or be a real one, on the high prairies of the state's southeastern corner.

You can run rivers, hike the high country, fish in crystalline streams and explore prehistoric ruins left by the very first Arizonans. On the flip side of the activity coin, you can attend opening night at the Tucson Opera or Phoenix Symphony, dine in style, prowl through fine museums, putter around golf courses and—obviously—laze at beside a swimming pool. Arizona is one of the few places on the planet where you can soak up both culture and toasty sunshine in winter. In Tucson, you can work on your suntan, then go skiing and catch an opera or a play—all on the same day!

Is Arizona in your future? Come and check it out!

# Surfing to Arizona

**S**everal useful web sites can help you explore Arizona even before you go there. The state's official internet site is ***www.state.az.us***, with links to various government departments. Another helpful site is ***www.piperinfo.com/state***, with access to state and local government agencies in Arizona and elsewhere.

Here are some other useful sites to help you surf Arizona:

***www.azcommerce.com*** is the web site of the Arizona Department of Commerce, which issues—on the internet—community profiles of most of Arizona's cities and towns. It also compiles reams of other data relating to the state's economic development.

***www.de.state.az.us*** is the site of the Arizona Department of Economic Security, which operates the state's Job Service offices, coordinates job training programs and compiles information on the state's economic outlook, wages and the most-needed job skills in the state.

***arizonaguide.com*** and ***arizonavacationvalues.com*** are the web sites of the Arizona Office of Tourism. You can request a free copy of the *Arizona Travel Planner* guide, or browse its pages on the net.

***www.ade.state.az.us*** is the Arizona Department of Education's site, with information on the state's public education system from kindergarten through its universities.

***www.revenue.state.az.us*** is your source for information about personal income, corporate and other taxes in the state.

Other internet sites and some e-mail addresses are listed elsewhere in this book.

# A BIT ABOUT THE AUTHORS

**D**on and Betty Martin have written more than twenty travel books, mostly under their *DISCOVERGUIDES* banner and its predecessor, Pine Cone Press. When not tending to their publishing company in Las Vegas or retreating to in their second home in an historic California mining town, they explore America and the world beyond. Both are members of the Society of American Travel Writers. They are gold medal winners in the Best Guidebook category of the annual Lowell Thomas Travel Journalism Awards, North America's most prestigious travel writing competition.

Don, who provides most of the adjectives, has been a journalist since he was 16, when classmates elected him editor of his high school newspaper. (No one else wanted the job.) After graduating, he left his small family farm in Idaho, wandered about the country a bit, and then joined the Marine Corps. He was assigned as a military correspondent in the Orient and at bases in California. Back in civvies, he worked as a reporter, sports writer and editor for several West Coast newspapers, then he became associate editor of a San Francisco-based travel magazine. In 1988, he left to establish Pine Cone Press, Inc. He now devotes his time to writing, travel, sipping decent Zinfandel and—for some odd reason—collecting squirrel and chipmunk artifacts.

Betty, a Chinese-American whose varied credentials have included a doctorate in pharmacy and a real estate broker's license, does much of the research and editing for their books. She also has written travel articles for assorted newspapers and magazines and she has sold travel photos through a major New York stock agency. When she isn't helping Don run their publishing company, she wanders the globe—with or without him. Her travels have taken her from Cuba to Antarctica.

# CLOSING INTRODUCTORY THOUGHTS
### Keeping up with the changes

Nobody's perfect, but we try. This relocation guide contains thousands of facts and a few are probably wrong, or have become outdated. If you catch an error, let us know. Also drop us a note if you find that a phone number, office location or other bit of information has changed in this ever-changing state. Address your comments to:

*DISCOVERGUIDES*
**P.O. Box 231954**
**Las Vegas, NV 89123-0033**

# PART ONE
# THE STATE

Like a sunny magnate, Arizona lures millions of people across its borders each year. About 18 million tourists come for the state's seductive climate, its rich variety of scenic attractions and its historic and cultural offerings.

While some come to play, many come to stay. According to U.S. Census Bureau figures, the state's population increased by a whopping 40 percent between 1990 and 2000, from 3.66 million to 5.13 million.

Hundreds of thousands of families, soured by January blizzards and stagnating economies back home, have snipped their roots and headed for Arizona. Legions of retirees have chosen to spend their golden years under the state's smiling sun. Additionally, more than a million Snowbirds—long-term seasonal visitors—fly south to winter here each year.

In this section, you'll meet the State of Arizona. You'll learn all about its history, its alluring desert climate (and how to handle it) and its various departments and services. Later chapters discuss schooling, job prospects and the best places in the state for retirees and Snowbirds.

# Arizona

## Chapter One

# WHY ARIZONA?
## MAKING THE DECISION

**A**s Arizona galloped into the new millennium, its population galloped past five million people. In just a single decade, from 1990 to 2000, nearly 1.5 million new residents arrived. They had made a profound decision—to pack their families, their worldly goods and possibly their pets. They chose to relinquish the comfort of familiar terrain, friends and relatives.

Uprooting and relocating a family is not a venture taken lightly. What has prompted so many to undertake such a move? Why Arizona?

We'll sum it up in two sentences, and then spend the rest of this book on elaboration.

**1.** Arizona offers that rare combination of natural attractions, cultural and recreational facilities, essential services and a fairly strong job market.

**2.** It's all wrapped up in an alluring package of warm climate and affordability.

If you and your family are planning to join this statistical surge to Arizona—or if you're retiring and leaving your family behind—this is your book. It's packed with information for job-seekers, retirees and winter Snowbirds. On the pages that follow, we'll tell you everything you need to know about the Grand Canyon State—how and where to find a job, and which communities offer the best climate, cultural opportunities, schools, retirement and medical facilities and affordable housing.

According to the year 2000 census, Arizona had the nation's second highest rate of population gain during the 1990s, exceeded only by Nevada. The census report revealed the same parallel between their largest cities. Las Vegas had the highest percentage population gain of any major city in America and Phoenix was second. And although Nevada out-performed Arizona percentage wise during the last decade, Arizona gained more people.

The state's growth boom started in the 1970s, then it slowed a bit toward the end of the 1980s as the economy flattened. It then surged forward again in the middle 1990s and it continues that surge into this century.

### The hot spots

Arizona's growth is focused in a few select areas, while other regions show very little gain. Maricopa County (Phoenix) gained the most people in the year 2000 census, soaring from 1,812,700 to 2,454,525; that's an increase of 44.8 percent and nearly a million individuals. And growth continues; during the first two years of the new century, Maricopa gained more new residents than any other county in America, even outpacing Los Angeles County, which was second. Pima County (Tucson) went from 666,957 to 843,746 for a 26.5 percent gain and 176,789 new people, according to the year 2000 census. Of Arizona's five million residents, four million live in one of these two areas, giving the state a very lopsided population distribution.

The Phoenix metropolitan area, which local promoters like to call the "Valley of the Sun," is home to three out of five Arizonans and eight of the state's ten largest cities are here. Phoenix itself had 1.3 million residents at the 2000 census, a gain of 34.3 percent. Tucson gained 20.1 percent and its people count rose from 405,371 to 486,699. Remove them and Arizona would be one of America's least populated states!

By percentage, the fastest growing county from 1990 to 2000 was Mohave along the upper Colorado River corridor; it had a 65.8 percent increase. Other hot spots were Yavapai County (Prescott and the Verde Valley), from 107,714 to 167,517 for a gain of 55.5 percent; Pinal (on the I-10 corridor between Phoenix and Tucson), from 116,397 to 179,727 for 54.4 percent; Yuma in the state's southwest corner, from 106,895 to 160,026 for 49.7 percent; and La Paz (in the central Colorado River corridor), from 13,884 to 19,715 for 42.4 percent.

Among the state's ten fastest growing cities by percentage, five are in the Valley of the Sun, although some of these were rather small to begin with. The top five growth champs in the 2000 census were Marana, 519.8 percent (2,187 to 13,566); Oro Valley, 345.3 percent (6,670 to 20,700); Surprise, 333.1 percent (7,122 to 30,848); Gilbert,

276.7 percent (29,122 to 109,697; and San Luis, 263.8 percent (4,212 to 15,322). Surprise and Gilbert are in the Valley of the Sun; Marana and Oro Valley are north of Tucson and San Luis is near the Mexican border in Yuma County.

The slowest growth area is along Arizona's eastern edge. Greenlee County, just below the large Navajo Nation, gained only 6.7 percent and Apache County to the north increased by 12.7. Greenlee is the state's least populated county and it apparently will stay that way, with the smallest gain in percentage and people count. Cochise County in the southeastern corner increased by 20.6 percent. Coconino County in north central Arizona grew by 20.4 percent although that's a bit misleading. The state's largest county, it has vast empty spaces, although it's home to some rather active communities, such as Cottonwood and Sedona, which gained 55.1 and 32 percent respectively. Flagstaff, the county seat, had a 15.3 percent increase. It's Arizona's eleventh largest city.

### They came, they saw, they stayed

Much of Arizona's growth is rooted in tourism, which generates $7.2 billion a year. Folks come to play, and then decide to stay. This is no accident, since the state operates one of America's most aggressive tourist promotion campaigns. Officials realize that visitors and conventioneers require few services and leave behind lots of money.

The state-sponsored *Arizona Highways* magazine has wooed visitors for decades. Its pages brim with color pictures of pristine canyons, handsome Native Americans and cactus wrens looking quite at home in giant saguaros. The slick magazine has projected Arizona's vast sweeps of sunny terrain into millions of American households.

Many communities work to lure outsiders as well—both visitors and residents. Phoenix in particular is unabashedly pro growth. Both the Phoenix and Tucson areas have broadened their employment bases by attracting high-tech industries and promoting white collar and service jobs. Several major corporations have moved their headquarters to the state. Service industries, including tourism, account for 25 percent of Arizona's payroll. Another 20 percent comes from retail trades and 11 percent stems from manufacturing.

Other factors that motivate migration are moderate home prices and a rather conservative state government that tries to keep the lid on taxes. Although both housing prices and taxes are rising, they're still far below those of some other Sunbelt states, notably neighboring California. Home prices in the San Francisco Bay Area and Los Angeles Basin are nearly double those in the Phoenix and Tucson areas. Rents also are considerably cheaper.

*A useful information source* ● Arizona's Department of Commerce and Department of Economic Security collect and eagerly disseminate statistics that track—and thus promote—the state's economic boom. The commerce department issues in-depth community profiles

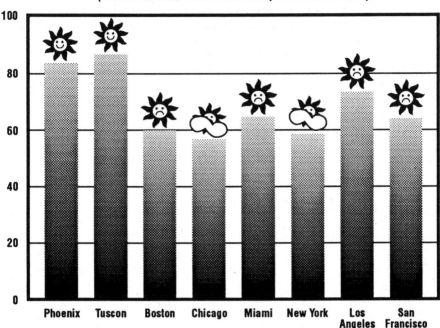

**PERCENTAGE OF SUNNY DAYS**
*(Source : National Oceanic and Atmospheric Administration)*

of more than a hundred cities and 23 Native American communities. Available on the internet, they cover employment, population, climate, history, transportation, communication, utilities, educational facilities, churches, recreational and cultural lures, nearby attractions and lodging. For information, contact:

**Arizona Department of Commerce**
3800 N. Central Ave., Phoenix, AZ 85012
(602) 280-1300
*www.azcommerce.com*

# WEATHER OR NOT

Many families or retirees contemplating a move to Arizona may be concerned about summer temperatures. Certainly, it's a great place for a winter retreat, but can one handle the August heat? Bear in mind that Phoenix set an all-time record of 124 degrees during the summer of 1990.

Sizzling summers don't seem to bother most of the state's residents. Eighty-five percent of them live in desert climes, well below the cooler heights of northern Arizona. With air conditioning and a little common sense, they do just fine.

Heat is not a problem if you keep a cool head. For one thing, Arizona's desert heat is dry. Humidity, not heat alone, causes the greatest discomfort. It slows surface evaporation from your skin, which is nature's cooling device. For instance, at zero humidity, 115 degrees has a "discomfort rating" of only 103. (Only?) The discomfort rating, incidentally, is like a wind chill factor in reverse. If the mercury hits 115 and the humidity is 40 percent, the discomfort factor spirals to 151, which would make survival impossible. Fortunately, that combination never occurs in the Arizona desert.

We often travel about the Southwest in summer and we function quite comfortably. On the other hand, during trips to the soggy tropics, we've wilted at 85 degrees because of the humidity.

## Beating the heat

Follow these steps to keep your cool when the weather's not:

✪ Don't be a mad dog or an Englishman. Plan active outdoor activities in the early morning and evening.

✪ Avoid dehydration by drinking plenty of water. And we mean *plenty*. A gallon a day will keep heatstroke away. If you're hiking—and you'll want to do a lot of that in the Grand Canyon—take all the water you can carry. If there are water sources along a hiking trail, carry a ceramic water filter to replenish your supply. Never drink untreated stream or spring water, even if it does look like Evian.

✪ In desert areas, the ground absorbs and then radiates the sun's rays, so temperatures may remain high until sundown and well beyond. It's best to do your summer hiking in the morning. In the Grand Canyon, we mean *early* in the morning. Trails begin on the rim and descend, meaning that the end of your hike is always uphill. While it may be cool on the rim, the inner canyon has a desert climate. People have died of heatstroke down there.

✪ Avoid sweet drinks or alcohol, which speed up dehydration. Besides, you chubby little rascal, a typical twelve-ounce soft drink contains about 12 teaspoons of sugar!

✪ Don't take salt tablets, despite what they told you in boot camp. Salt causes you to retain water, and you want to perspire. That's what keeps you cool. You should keep plenty of fluid circulating through your system.

✪ Don't exert yourself on a hot day. Your body will lose more fluid than it can replace.

✪ Wear light colored, reflective clothing—preferably cotton or linen. Avoid nylon and polyester, since these fabrics don't "breathe" and this traps body heat against your skin.

✪ If you must work outdoors in the heat, dip your shirt or blouse in water frequently. The garment's evaporation, along with that from your body, will help keep you cool.

## Shielding the sun

Southwestern states such as Arizona have high skin cancer rates. Because of the southern latitude and clear air, more of the sun's damaging ultraviolet rays reach the earth. With the ongoing depletion of our ozone layer, scientists tell us that the skin cancer rate is increasing dangerously. It can develop late in life, even years after you've stopped getting your annual tan. One form—melanoma—can be fatal. Even if you don't get skin cancer, which is nearly 100 percent preventable, constant sun exposure will lead to premature wrinkling.

Some drugs increase the skin's sensitivity to the sun, so check with your pharmacist. Among the suspect items are hormone based drugs including birth control pills, some tranquilizers, diuretics, sulfa drugs and antibiotics such as vibramycin and tetracycline. Even some artificial sweeteners and perfumes are suspect.

### Take these precautions to keep your hide from being fried

✪ Use sunscreen with a high PABA content; it ranges from five to 33 percent (which is a virtual sunblock). Even if you're working on a tan, use sunblock on sensitive areas, such as your lips, nose and—yes—the tops of your ears. If you have a bald pate, remember to protect that—preferably by wearing a hat instead of a sun visor. In case you're curious, PABA stands for para-aminobenzoic acid. (No wonder people use the acronym!) A few individuals are allergic to PABA; if a rash appears, try something else.

✪ Bear in mind that suntan lotion will rinse off when you swim or perspire, so re-lather yourself after swimming or exercising.

✪ Always wear a broad brimmed hat or visor outdoors. It'll shade your eyes and protect them from sun glare and shield your face from sunburn. There's some evidence that sun glare may be a cause of cataracts. The vaqueros knew what they were doing when they created the sombrero.

✪ If you spend a lot of time outdoors, some specialists recommend getting a careful, light tan. Moderately tanned skin will resist sunburn—up to a point. You can still get singed from prolonged exposure. Get your tan very slowly, limiting your initial exposure to a few minutes a day. Do your tanning in the morning or late afternoon when the sun's rays are less direct. Take Rudyard Kipling's advice; avoid the noonday sun.

We prefer to keep moving when we work on tans—hiking, swimming, bike riding and such. If you baste yourself in the sun, you may doze off and get too much exposure. Besides, it's boring. Incidentally, clouds don't block all ultraviolet rays. Also, reflections from sand, pool decks or water can intensify burning. Wet T-shirts may look rather fetching on the right bodies and they do help keep you cool, although they offer little sun protection.

If you do get burned, ease the pain with a dip in the pool or a cool shower, then use one of those over-the-counter anesthetic sprays. Antihistamine will relieve the itch—the same stuff that you take for the sniffles. Keep your skin out of the sun until it's fully healed.

### Avoiding "heat sickness"

Heat exhaustion and its lethal cousin heatstroke are real dangers on hot summer days. Both are brought on by a combination of dehydration and sun.

Signs of heat exhaustion are weariness, muscle cramps and clammy skin. The pulse may slow and you may become unusually irritable. If left untreated, heat exhaustion can lead to deadly heatstroke. The skin becomes dry and hot, the pulse may quicken and you'll experience nausea and possibly a headache. Convulsions, unconsciousness, even death can follow.

At the first sign of heat sickness, get out of the sun and into the shade. Stay quiet and drink water—plenty of water. If you're near a pool, faucet or stream, douse your face and body with water, and soak your clothes to lower your body temperature quickly.

## Driving and surviving the desert

Arizona's deserts occupy thousands of square miles of open spaces; population is thinly scattered. These can be intimidating places if you're stranded. If you're tempted—as we often are—to explore this remote and beautiful world, save the urge for fall or spring, when it's not so darned hot. Winters can be biting cold in higher desert elevations such as southeastern Arizona, creating hypothermia risks if you become stranded.

When you venture into the wilds, let someone know where you're going, and when you intend to return. Keep these pointers in mind if you wander off well-traveled asphalt:

✿ First, foremost and always, take plenty of water. Water to drink, to soak your clothes, to top off a leaky radiator. It's cheap, it's easily portable and it can save your life.

✿ Give your car, SUV or RV a physical checkup before going into the boonies, to ensure that it'll get you back. Take extra engine oil, coolant and an emergency radiator sealant. Include spare parts such as fan belts, a water pump, radiator hoses—and tools to install these things. Take an extra spare tire, along with a tire pump and patching.

✿ Take food with you—stuff that won't spoil. If your vehicle breaks down, you may be out there for a while. Also pack matches, a small shovel, aluminum foil (for signaling), a can opener, a powerful flashlight and a space blanket so you can snooze in the shade of your car. The shiny side of a space blanket also is a good signaling device.

✿ A cellular phone or CB radio can be a lifesaver. Remember that 911 is the emergency number on a cellular and any other phone, and channel 9 is the emergency CB band, monitored by rescue agencies.

✿ Never drive off-road, particularly in an on-road vehicle. Loose, sandy desert soil can trap your car in an instant, even if the ground looks solid. We don't leave established roadways as a matter of principle, because tires are hell on the fragile desert environment.

✿ Even if you keep to the roads, you might get stuck in an area of blowing sand or on a soft shoulder. It could happen when you leave the road to set up camp. Carry a tow chain and tire supports such as strips of carpeting. An inexpensive device called a "come-along"—sort of a hand winch—can get you out of a hole, if you can find something for an anchor.

✿ If you become stranded in the desert, stay in the shade of your car—not in the vehicle itself. If you're far from civilization and not sure of your bearings, don't try to walk out, particularly during the heat of the day. Besides, a vehicle is easier to spot than a lone hiker. Use a mirror, foil or space blanket as a signal device if you see a plane approaching, and build a signal fire. A spare tire will burn, and a douse of oil will make the fire nice and smoky. Start your blaze in a cleared area away from your vehicle. You don't want to launch a wildfire that might compound your predicament.

✿ If you're on a road and you know that you can reach civilization on foot, do your walking at night. Take plenty of water, a flashlight with extra batteries and some food for nibbling.

✿ Bear in mind that heat isn't your only problem in the desert. Flash floods can roar down dry washes and across roadway dips, particularly during spring and summer rain squalls. If you're driving or hiking in the desert and a sudden rainstorm hits, keep to the high ground until it passes. Storms can be unpredictable, so avoid camping in dry washes.

**Chapter Two**

# GETTING TO KNOW YOU

## THE WAY IT IS

---

**A**sking someone to describe Arizona is like asking one to describe an elephant in the dark. It depends on which part you're feeling.

The state fits its well-known desert stereotype. Indeed, two thirds of it is arid. It's the only state in the Union with a national park and national monument named for varieties of cactus—Saguaro and Organ Pipe.

At the same time, it defies this stereotype. Humphreys Peak north of Flagstaff is one of America's highest mountains, at 12,633 feet. A fourth of the state is covered by forest, and Arizona shelters the largest stand of virgin ponderosa pines in the country. And of course it contains the deepest gorge—the Grand Canyon, which is Arizona's grandest stereotype of all.

The state's physical appearance is summed up rather well by Reg Manning, Pulitzer Prize winning cartoonist for Phoenix's *Arizona Republic*. In his whimsical book, *What is Arizona Really Like?*, he says the topography can be taken in three bites, starting from the Four Corners area in the northeast.

The first bite is a remote, often hauntingly beautiful semiarid plateau containing the large Navajo and Hopi reservations, Monument Valley and the Painted Desert. The second semicircle, curving from northwest through east central Arizona, is a greenbelt of ponderosa pines, including the forest-rimmed Grand Canyon. The Mogollon Rim, a great fault extending in a 200-mile arc, marks the edge of this high country.

The final bite—consuming nearly two thirds of the state—is a great sweep of desert and high prairie, reaching from the western edge to the southeast corner. This is the Sunbelt. That term originated in Arizona and now is used to describe just about any place south of a Minnesota blizzard.

Although most of Arizona is desert, it isn't necessarily hot. Much of this land, particularly in the central and northeastern areas, is high desert that's often quite cold in winter. Southeastern Arizona actually is more of a prairie than a desert. Naturally, the northwestern mountain regions get regular snowfall. Even in the southern Sunbelt, evenings can be quite cool, so don't put *all* of your winter clothing into the Salvation Army collection box.

Nearly 85 percent of Arizona's population is focused in this warm belt—mostly in and around Phoenix and Tucson. These two metropolitan centers offer every imaginable service and convenience, and an abundance of cultural and recreational lures.

However, Arizona's greatest charms lie in its open spaces and scenic wonders; in its small towns with their affable wanna-be-cowboy attitudes. We found our Arizona in the high, silent reaches of the San Francisco Peaks and in the hidden depths of the Grand Canyon. We discovered it in the dignity of the Indian nations and the scruffy charm of Mexican border towns; in the solitude of a wilderness cactus garden reached only by a dusty road.

## THE WAY IT WAS

Arizona is one of the youngest states in the union, admitted as the last of the lower 48 in 1912. Yet, river-runners and hikers in the Grand Canyon will see two-billion-year-old Precambrian schist, some of the oldest exposed rock on this third rock from the sun. Native Americans have occupied Arizona's deserts and high plateaus for at least 20,000 years.

Its first residents were nomadic hunters who drifted down from the Great Plains. When droughts drove the mammoths and antelope away, they swapped their spears for plowshares and became—about eleven centuries ago—North America's first farmers. Freed from the constant search for food, they developed complex societies and built large pueblos whose ruins survive today. The state is a treasure-trove of archaeological sites.

Anthropologists call these early people Hohokam, Anasazi, Sinagua and Mogollon. We don't know what they called themselves, for they left no written language. Like most ancient tribes, they probably just referred to their kind as "The People." Through the centuries, they evolved into highly-developed societies, occupying great pueblos of adobe or stone atop mesas or tucked into hidden canyons and precipi-

*Spain was the first outside nation to explore Arizona. Francisco Vasquez de Coronado came looking for golden cities in 1540 and found mostly trouble.*

tous cliffs. They dug irrigation canals and became excellent farmers. Their pottery, weaving and other crafts were among the most advanced of their time.

About eight centuries ago, this highly developed society began coming apart at the seams. The great pueblos were abandoned and left to weather away in the wind and hot sun. Scientists speculate that a persistent drought may have driven them from their corn and bean fields. Some experts blame their downfall on disease, soil depletion or the arrival of more aggressive tribes.

Most people identify Navajos and Apaches with Arizona, yet these were latter-day arrivals, coming from the cold north. They were Athabaskans who drifted down from Canada, starting about six hundred years ago. Warlike hunters, they may have driven off many of the native tribes. Ironically, they adopted some of the original residents' farming and weaving techniques, particularly those who would become Navajos. Scientists have been unable to pinpoint the ultimate fate of the Hohokam, Sinagua or Mogollon. Similarities in culture and crafts suggest that today's Hopi may be Anasazi descendants.

### What's in a name?

Historians have fun feuding over the origin of Arizona's name. There are four Indian versions: Arizuma, an Aztec word for "silver bearing"; *Ali shonak* or *Ari-son*, meaning "small spring" or "young spring," which were names of Pima settlements; and a Tohono O'odham term, *Aleh-zone*, also meaning young spring. Basque settlers insist that Arizona comes from *Aritz ona*, their term for "good oak." This name was given to a silver strike site in 1736. Some unimaginative scholars suggest that "Arizona" is merely a derivation of "arid zone." The name "Arizona" first appeared in print in a 1750s document by one Padre Ortega, a Spanish missionary.

Spaniards were the area's first outside visitors, and they got here by accident. In 1528, a group led by Alvar Núñez Cabeza de Vaca set out to explore Florida's west coast. Part of the group became lost after an Indian attack and they spent more than eight years wandering through what is now Texas, New Mexico, Arizona and northern Mexico. Some accounts say they were befriended and protected by the locals, after De Vaca convinced them that he was a powerful medicine man. When four surviving members of the group finally stumbled across some of their countrymen in western Mexico, they reported Indian legends of fabulously wealthy cities which lay to the north.

Antonio de Mendoza, viceroy of New Spain, knew of an eighth century Moorish legend about seven golden cities, hidden somewhere in the unexplored world. Could these be the same? In 1539, with golden greed glittering in his eyes, he dispatched a party of explorers from Mexico City to find these treasure-laden towns. It was led by Franciscan Father Marcos de Niza. Accompanying the group—probably reluctantly—was a Moorish slave named Estévan, one of the survivors of the De Vaca trek.

### The legend of Cibola

As the Spaniards entered present-day Arizona and New Mexico, native people said the area through which they traveled was called "Cibola." Thus, the legend of the Seven Cities of Cibola was born. Later, the party saw a Zuni pueblo and Father de Niza sent an advance party to investigate, led by Estévan. The Zunis weren't very nice hosts; they killed the visitors.

An intimidated Father de Niza kept his distance. But he drew near enough to see that the pueblos glittered in the sun. He returned home and advised the Viceroy of Mexico that he may have found one of the golden cities. However, the good padre most likely had been fooled by the glitter of mica, embedded in the adobe.

A year later, that great and brutal explorer, 30-year-old Francisco Vásquez de Coronado headed north to continue the search. He found no gold, pillaged a few pueblos and explored as far north as Kansas. After two years, he returned to Mexico City empty-handed. More than a century passed before the curious Spanish again began pestering natives of the Southwest. In the late 1600s, Father Eusebio Francisco Kino and other padres started building missions throughout the Southwest. They succeeded in converting thousands of native people to Christianity—an act most likely encouraged by accompanying soldiers, who set up military presidios to protect the missions.

However, many of the Indians did not yield their land or their free spirits easily. Angered by abusive treatment from the Spanish intruders, they staged several violent revolts. The Hopi emptied their pueblos of Spaniards in a savage rebellion in 1680. Spanish occupation—punctuated by native uprisings—continued into the early 1800s. When Mexico won its independence from Spain in 1821, most of the soldiers were withdrawn from this northern outpost. In the absence of the military, the native folks—primarily Apaches—again went on the warpath, driving frightened settlers to the safety of the walled cities of Tucson and Tubac.

Much of what is now Arizona and New Mexico was ceded to the United States in the 1848 Treaty of Guadalupe Hidalgo, at the end of the Mexican War. Sandwiched between California and Texas, they were lumped together as the New Mexico Territory. However, as far as the original residents were concerned, this was still their land and warfare with the intruders continued. In the late 1800s, more than a dozen U.S. Army forts were built to protect American settlers from raids. Not until Geronimo surrendered in 1886 was the area considered safe for settlement.

## A major force

Today, native people are a major force in the state, culturally and politically. Vast tracts of land were set aside as reservations, which have become self-governing entities. The Navajo and Hopi nations occupy a huge chunk of northeastern Arizona. Combined with other reservations, native lands cover a fourth of the state.

The California gold discovery in 1848 spurred the greatest human migration since the Crusades. Many gold-seekers traveled south through the New Mexico Territory to avoid the precipitous Sierra Nevada range that formed a barrier on California's eastern edge. Part of this southern route dipped into Mexico, so the government decided to make it all-American by negotiating the Gadsden Purchase. In 1854, cash-poor Mexico sold 30,000 square miles of its northern frontier for $10 million. This would become a large chunk of southern Arizona.

Four years later, the government awarded the Butterfield Overland Stage Company a contract to forge a mail a route through this area, from St. Louis to San Francisco. It was needed to link fast-growing California with the rest of the U.S., which at that time ended at the Missouri border.

The New Mexico Territory, settled primarily by Southerners, sided with the South during the Civil War. A Texas militia seized Mesilla, New Mexico, in 1861. The Texans claimed all of the land from the Rio Grande to the Pacific as Confederate territory. But a column of Union-sympathizing Californians soon put an end to that. In 1862, the Confederates were routed in the Battle of Picacho Pass, south of Phoenix. Little more than a skirmish with only eight casualties, it was the Civil War's westernmost engagement. The following year, President Lincoln moved to ensure the area's Union support by signing a bill creating separate Arizona and New Mexico territories.

For the next two decades, the Arizona Territory epitomized the Wild West. Cattle barons battled over water and grazing rights and knocked down sodbusters' pesky fences. Tombstone and its O.K. Corral shootout and Yuma's infamous Territorial Prison became the stuff of which legends—and certainly movies—were made. Then in the 1880s, several minor gold strikes, major copper discoveries and Mormon migrations from Utah brought a more settled brand of citizens to the territory. The railroad arrived late in the century to complete the taming of this last outpost of the Wild West. Then on St. Valentine's Day in 1912, portly President William Howard Taft signed the proclamation making Arizona the last of the 48 contiguous states.

Hampered by lack of water, the new state grew slowly in the first half of this century. Several military air bases were built in its wide open spaces during World War II, and many GIs who trained here returned at war's end. In the Fifties, Arizona's numbers began to swell, aided by air conditioning, the creation of the Snowbird cult, and a court ruling granting the state a larger share of Colorado River water.

And suddenly, Arizona was on a roll. It grew by a whopping 53 percent during the 1970s, second only to Nevada in percentage increase. In the next decade it added another 35 percent, outgained only by Nevada and Alaska. In numbers of people, it is considerably larger than the two combined, with a population now topping five million. Among Western states, only California has more people; the 2000 census revealed that Arizona had passed Washington, which had held second place for decades. Phoenix has blossomed into a major city; it's now the sixth largest in America. As we noted in the previous chapter, three of five Arizonans live in Phoenix and its surrounding Valley of the Sun communities.

As the state entered the new century, Phoenix and several other Arizona communities again were numbered among the nation's fastest growing cities. In percentage population gain, Phoenix was second fastest growing major city in America, behind Las Vegas.

# THINGS ARIZONAN

Several things—cultural, historic or climatic—are distinctly Arizonan, or at least distinctly Southwestern.

**Bola tie** ● This curious form of neckware, with a braided cord drawn through some kind of Western or native American ornament, was born in Arizona and hopefully it will die there.

**Cowboys** ● The American cowboy's roots are mostly Mexican, and the cowboy himself originated in Arizona, New Mexico and west Texas. His standard gear—wide-brimmed hat, lariat, saddle with a horn (used for snubbing the lariat) and chaps—are all of Mexican *vaquero* origin. The rodeo originated in Mexico and the guitar that cowboys like to strum is Spanish. Levi's were contributed by Californian Levi Strauss, although the originals were gray tent canvas; blue denims didn't come along until the late 1800s. We have no idea why all those Southern country singers dress like cowboys and play guitars. Round 'em up and head 'em out to—Nashville?

***Howling coyotes*** ● That coyote, wearing a neckerchief and howling at the moon, is a typical object on Arizona jewelry and ceramics. No one seems to know where he came from.

***Indian fry bread and Navajo tacos*** ● Common among most Arizona tribes, Indian fry bread is something like pizza crust without the pizza. It's used like bread, or it can be turned into a pastry by sprinkling it with cinnamon and sugar. A dish popular with Navajos and many other Arizona tribes and a few hearty whites is the infamous Navajo taco, also called the Indian taco. Neither Navajo nor taco, it's more like a Mexican tostada, with pinto beans, chili, ground beef, grated cheese, chopped onions and shredded lettuce layered over a disk of fry bread. Served in many Arizona restaurants, they're usually quite huge. After a Navajo taco meal, you won't want to eat again for hours—possibly for days.

***Native American casinos*** ● A phenomenon of recent years, Indian casinos are cropping up all over Arizona. They range from a small slot machine parlor above Pipe Springs National Monument on the Arizona Strip to the large, handsome Mazatzal Casino just outside Payson. Since reservations are sovereign territories, native people can establish casinos once work out arrangements with the host states, and there is of course an abundance of native land in Arizona. Most gaming parlors are small by Las Vegas standards, offering primarily slot machines, video poker and keno. Some, however, are quite elaborate. The largest, which rivals some of the big Nevada resorts, is the Avi Hotel and Casino operated by the Fort Mohave Tribe. Although the tribe has land in Arizona and Nevada, the casino itself is in Nevada, challenging the gaming resorts of Laughlin, just to the north.

***Silver and turquoise*** ● The Navajo and Hopi of Arizona and Zuni of New Mexico are noted for their beautiful silver and turquoise jewelry. The Hopi work primarily with silver while the Navajo jewelry often combines silver with turquoise, particularly in the famous "squash blossom" necklace. However, it is not native to their culture, despite their love of adornment. The turquoise-silver concept was introduced to them by none other than Fred Harvey, who had gotten his start by developing Southwest tourism along rail routes in the late 1800s. It was crafted then as it is now—primarily as something to sell to tourists.

***Southwest cuisine*** ● The *nouveau* cuisine movement started about 25 years ago in California, featuring fresh ingredients simply prepared, interestingly spiced and lightly cooked. Chefs in Arizona and New Mexico, where fresh year-around vegetables are abundant, started adding red and white chili, pinto beans and *polenta* to these recipes and *voile!* Southwest cuisine.

**Southwestern architecture** • The look is earthy, squarish and adobe, with salmon and turquoise as the preferred colors. Probably more of New Mexican origin than Arizonan, it was inspired by a combination of Hopi and Zuni dwellings and Frank Lloyd Wright's earthy, geometric architecture. Wright spent his final years at Taliesen West, near Scottsdale.

**Saguaro cactus** • Pronounced *sa-WHA-ro*, this large and thick-limbed plant is often portrayed as a "typical" cactus in illustrations, cartoons and Western souvenirs. Yet its habitat is strictly limited; it grows only in the Sonoran Desert of southern Arizona and northern Mexico. It's also found frequently on bola ties.

## JUST THE FACTS

**Size** • 113,909 square miles; sixth largest state; about 340 miles wide by just under 400 miles deep.

**Population** • The year 2000 census counted 5,130,632 Arizonans; largest city is Phoenix with 1,321,045 residents. Tucson is the second largest city with 486,699. Arizona's population density is about thirty-two per square mile.

**Elevations** • Highest point, Humphreys Peak north of Flagstaff, 12,633 feet; lowest point, Colorado River as it enters Mexico below Yuma, 70 feet.

**Admitted to the Union** • February 14, 1912, as the 48th state; capital—Phoenix.

**Time zone** • Mountain; one hour later than the West Coast, two hours earlier than the East. Except for the Navajo Reservation, Arizona doesn't switch to summer Daylight Saving Time; apparently those warm desert evenings are long enough!

**Area codes** • Arizona has five area codes: (602) for metropolitan Phoenix, (480) for Scottsdale and the eastern side of the Valley of the Sun, (623) for the west side; (520) for Tucson and southwestern Arizona and (928) for the rest of the state.

**Official stuff** • STATE MOTTO—*Didat Deus* (God enriches); STATE SEAL depicts the five "Cs" of copper, cotton, climate, citrus and cattle; STATE BIRD—cactus wren (medium brown with speckled breast, likes to hang around saguaro cactus); STATE FLOWER—saguaro cactus blossom (white with yellow center); STATE TREE—paloverde (desert tree identified by green limbs, which is what *palo verde* means in Spanish); STATE GEM—turquoise.

**State nicknames** • The Grand Canyon State; the Copper State (appropriate, since it produces more than half of America's supply).

**Alcohol** • None may be imported from another state—although there are no border checks. Wine, beer and hard liquor is readily available in liquor stores, supermarkets and other outlets. Minimum drinking age 21 and legal bar hours are 7 a.m. to 1 a.m.

*Hunting and Fishing* ● Out-of-state hunting and fishing licenses are available at most sporting goods stores. Anyone over 14 may get one; fees vary. Contact the Arizona Game & Fish Department; see below. State licenses aren't required on Indian reservations, but each has its own laws and permit fees; check before you go.

*Motorists' laws* ● Safety belts required for drivers and front seat passengers. Children under six or weighing less than 40 pounds must be secured by child restraints in vehicles. Helmets required for motorcyclists under 18. Speed limit is 65 to 75 mph (as posted) on rural freeways and 55 mph on most urban freeways and other highways. Highway patrolmen use radar, and to even the score, radar detectors are permitted.

*Road conditions* ● Call (888) 411-7623.

## SOME USEFUL CONTACTS & INFO SOURCES

The state government website is *www.state.az.us*

**Arizona Department of Commerce**, Economic Research Division, 3800 N. Central Ave., Phoenix, AZ 85012; (602) 280-1300; *www.azcommerce.com*

*Arizona Department of Economic Security*, 1789 W. Jefferson St., Phoenix, AZ 85007; (602) 542-3871; *www.de.state.az.us*

**Arizona Game & Fish Department**, 2222 W. Greenway Rd., Phoenix, AZ 85023; (602) 942-3000.

*Arizona Highways Magazine*, P.O. Box 6018, Phoenix, AZ 85005-6018; (800) 543-5432 or (602) 712-2000; *www.arizonahighways.com*. This splendidly illustrated state-produced magazine can provide prospective new Arizonans with a good insight into the state's natural beauty, communities, visitor lures and history.

**Arizona Office of Tourism,** 2702 N. Third St., Suite 4015, Phoenix, AZ 85004-4608; (888) 520-3434 or (602) 230-7733; *www.arizonaguide.com* or *www.arizonavacationvalues.com*.

**Arizona Public Lands Information Center**, 222 N. Central Ave., Phoenix, AZ 85073; (602) 417-9300; *www.publiclands.org*. An information office and books and maps store jointly operated by the Bureau of Land Management, U.S. Forest Service and Public Lands Interpretive Association.

**Arizona State Parks**, 1300 W. Washington St., Phoenix, AZ 85007; (602) 542-4174.

**Arizona Travel Parks Association**, 3030 N. Third St., Phoenix, AZ 85012; (602) 241-8554.

**Motor Vehicle Division** or the main office at 1801 W. Jefferson (P.O. Box 2100), Phoenix, AZ 85001-2100; (800) 251-5866 (in Arizona) or (602) 712-7011; *www.dot.state.az.us*.

**U.S. Bureau of Land Management,** 222 N. Central Ave., Phoenix, AZ 85073; (602) 417-9200; *www.blm.gov*.

## Chapter Three

# ESSENTIAL ARIZONA

## ALMOST EVERYTHING YOU NEED TO KNOW

---

**A**s you contemplate Arizona in your future, it's a good guess that one of your first concerns will be taxes. By law and impulse, Arizonans try to keep them down. Property tax has a cap of one percent of full value, similar to California's Proposition 13. With their basic pro-growth attitude, officials try to rein in business taxes as well. If you have any taxing questions, contact the **Arizona Department of Revenue,** 1600 W. Monroe St. (P.O. Box 29086, Phoenix, AZ 85038-9089), (800) 352-4090 or (602) 255-3381; or 400 W. Congress, South Building, Tucson, AZ 85701; *www.revenue.state.az.us.*

### Individual income tax

Income received while you reside in Arizona is subject to state income tax, whether or not you're a permanent resident. Tax credits are available for seniors, renters (including mobile home occupants) and low income people. Renters must occupy property in the state for more than six months to qualify for this credit. Other credits are given for installing solar energy equipment or groundwater measuring devices.

State income taxes have been reduced in recent years. The current rates range from 2.8 percent for singles with a taxable income of less than $10,000 a year or for married couples with a taxable income of less than $20,000 to 5 percent for singles making more than $150,000 and married couples earning more than $300,000.

The Arizona Department of Revenue has walk-in offices at 1600 West Monroe and 2902 N. Washington Street in Phoenix and 400 West Congress in Tucson. For information and forms, contact the department at P.O. Box 29002, Phoenix, AZ 85038-9002, or phone (602) 255-3381 or toll-free (800) 352-4090 from other Arizona area codes. For recorded tax information, call (602) 542-1991 or (800) 845-8192. Or go to the web at *www.revenue.state.az.us.*

## Estate (inheritance) tax

Arizona is rather generous with estate taxes, allowing a $675,000 exemption. For estates valued higher, a return must be filed with the Department of Revenue, Estate Tax Division, within nine months of the person's demise.

## Property taxes

Real Estate taxes in Arizona are well below the national urban average. In fact, according to *Money Magazine,* Phoenix is among the lowest among all major American cities, with an average annual residential property tax of under $2,000 for a 2,600-square-foot home.

To help keep taxes down, counties, cities and schools can increase their levies by only two percent a year. Reevaluation of property for taxing purposes is limited to ten percent a year, even if the appraised value is higher. Owner-occupied property is assessed at ten percent of its real value, with a tax rate cap of one percent of the full cash value. Other rates are ten percent for rental property, 16 percent for farm land and vacant property and 25 percent for commercial property.

The state property tax bite is 47 cents per $100 assessed valuation. Above that, tax rates vary widely from one community to the next. They're listed in our community profiles in Part Two.

Like most states, Arizona offers property tax breaks for certain people, including surviving spouses and the disabled.

## Sales tax

Arizona collects a five percent sales tax on most items purchased, except for food and pharmaceuticals. In addition, most cities levy another one or two percent, and they have the option of taxing food and drugs. The state also levies tax from three-eights of a percent to five percent on business sales.

# THINGS AUTOMOTIVE

Since you likely will be driving to Arizona, you'll need to know about drivers' licenses, vehicle registration, insurance requirements and such. For details, ask for a copy of the *Consumer Service Guide and Driver License Manual* available at the nearest office of the **Motor Vehicle Division** (MVD) or the main office at 1801 W. Jefferson (P.O. Box 2100), Phoenix, AZ 85001-2100; (800) 251-5866 (in Arizona), or (602) 712-7011; *www.dot.state.az.us.*

**AUTO INSURANCE** • Arizona drivers are required to carry liability insurance in the amounts of $15,000 medical per person or $30,000 per accident, plus $10,000 property damage. Evidence of insurance must be carried in the vehicle. This can be the policy itself or an insurance company's ID card.

If you can't prove financial responsibility, you're subject to a fine for the first offense and possible suspension of your driving license and vehicle registration. Penalties increase greatly for additional violations. Also, you must notify MVD of any change in liability coverage, such as switching vehicles or changing insurance companies.

**AUTO REGISTRATION** • See "Vehicle registration" below.

**AUTO REPAIR** • The Arizona Automobile Association (AAA) provides a list of approved auto repair establishments. Call (602) 274-1116 for Valley of the Sun AAA offices, (520) 296-7461 or (520) 885-0694 in Tucson, and (928) 776-4222 in Prescott.

**AUTOMOTIVE LEMON LAW** • The state has a "lemon law" that protects new car buyers. It requires the dealer to offer a full refund or replacement vehicle if a defect can't be fixed after four tries within a year; or if the vehicle is in the shop for more than thirty days during that year.

**DISABILITY LICENSE PLATES** • People with physical disabilities that severely inhibit their ability to walk can obtain special vehicle license plates that permit parking in blue spaces designated for the handicapped. They must first obtain a statement from a physician confirming their disability. Able-bodied people who use handicapped parking spaces face stiff fines.

**DRIVER'S LICENSES** • If you become a resident, you must obtain an Arizona driver's license. Seasonal visitors are not considered permanent residents and may use their back-home licenses. Arizona defines a resident as anyone who remains in the state for seven or more consecutive months in one year. Also, you become a resident if you enroll a child in school (but not a student who pays an out-of-state tuition), set up a business or accept employment other than seasonal agricultural work.

For teen drivers, a restricted instruction permit can be obtained at age fifteen years and seven months for a car or motorcycle, and a regular license at age sixteen. Fees for an instruction permit and motorcycle endorsement are $7 each.

Driver's license fees are based on age: 16 to 39—$25; 40 to 44—$20; 45 to 49—$15; and 50 and over—$10. State ID cards are $12; they're free for anyone over 65. You can get a copy of your motor vehicle record for a $3 fee (or $5 for a certified five-year record). A duplicate driver's license or ID card costs $4 and a duplicate instruction permit is $2.

When applying for a driver's license, you must surrender your license from the previous state, and show evidence that you have a clear driving record in that state. For details on fees and requirements, contact the nearest MVD station.

**DRUNK DRIVING LAWS** • Arizona is tough on drunk drivers. You are presumed to be under the influence if you have a blood alcohol level of .08 percent or higher. A law enforcement officer can require that you submit to a blood, breath or urine test if there is "reasonable grounds" to believe you were driving under the influence of alcohol or drugs. You can lose your license for a year if you refuse to submit to a test, even if you are ultimately cleared of the drunk driving charge. Also, under the "reasonable grounds" rule, you can be cited for a DUI even if your BA level is below .08.

The best rule for driving in Arizona is: Stay sober! If you're apprehended on suspicion of driving under the influence of alcohol or drugs and you fail a blood, breath or urine test, you lose your driving privileges on the spot. The penalty for conviction of a first offense is not less than ten consecutive days in jail and a fine of at least $250. Guilty drivers also must undergo alcohol screening, education and treatment. For two or more offenses, drivers are jailed for at least 90 days, fined at least $500 and they lose their license for a year. Penalties for DUI are more severe if your BA is .15 or more, starting with 30 days in jail and a $250 fine for the first offense.

Arizona has a zero tolerance law for any driver under 21; they will lose their license for two years if *any* amount of alcohol, illegal drugs or drugs that impair driving ability is detected in their systems.

State law also prohibits possession of an open container of alcohol in the passenger compartment of a vehicle on a public street or highway. However, this doesn't include passengers in a limousine, bus, taxi or the living area of a motorhome.

**MOTORCYCLE HELMET LAW** • Anyone under age eighteen must wear a safety helmet when riding a motorcycle. Also, all motorcyclists must wear protective eyewear if their cycle is not equipped with a windshield.

**NATIONAL DRIVER REGISTER** • You can run but you cannot hide... Arizona is a member of a nationwide computer system called the National Driver Register, which provides interstate information about problem drivers. Your out-of-state record will be checked when you apply for an Arizona driver's license. If you have an outstanding warrant or unresolved traffic citation in any other state, your application will be denied. If you conceal this information on your application, you'll lose your application fee.

**PERSONALIZED LICENSE PLATES** • They're available for a one-time fee. See "Vehicle registration" below.

**SAFETY BELTS** • Safety restraints are required for front seat passengers in all vehicles. All children less than five years old must be secured in an approved child restraint. The MVD requires that child restraints meet U.S. Department of Transportation standards, and that they "must be used by following the seat manufacturer's and automobile manufacturer's instructions."

Because of the danger of air bag inflation to small children in front seats—and particularly infant seats in which the child faces to the rear—manufacturers strongly recommend that child restraints be placed in a back seat of a vehicle.

**SMOG CHECKS** ● If you register a vehicle in Maricopa or Pima counties (Phoenix or Tucson areas), it must be checked to ensure that it meets emission standards and that emission equipment hasn't been tampered with, removed or bypassed. Also, most 1981 or newer gasoline-powered cars and light trucks registered in the greater Phoenix area must undergo a smog check every two years. To learn the location of the nearest vehicle testing station, call the Arizona Car Care Hot Line at (800) 2-VIP-SITE or (602) 470-4646. Electric and diesel powered vehicles and those with engines under 90 cubic centimeters are exempted.

**SPEED LIMITS** ● The limit is 65 to 75 mph on rural freeways (as posted) and 55 mph on urban expressways and most surface roads (or as posted). Highway patrolmen use radar and, to even the score, radar detectors are permitted.

**"THIRD PARTY" & ON-LINE SERVICES** ● The Motor Vehicle Division has contracted with several private "third party" firms to conduct some of its services and take the workload off its staff. Among services available from these third party providers are driver's licensing, vehicle title change and registration, and vehicle inspection. For the name of the nearest authorized third party provider, call (602) 712-8217 for driver licensing and registration, and (602) 712-8340 for vehicle inspection.

Some MVD services also are available on line, including vehicle registration and renewal, personalized license plate application, vehicle sold notices, duplicate drivers' licenses and address changes. These services, which require a major credit card, are provided by ServiceArizona via MVD's web site at *www.dot.state.az.us.*

Also, registration renewal can be accomplished through an interactive phone system by dialing (888) 713-3031.

**VEHICLE REGISTRATION** ● If you become a resident, you must register your car at a Motor Vehicle Division office. Anyone who remains in Arizona for seven consecutive months in a year, enrolls a child in school, starts a business or accepts employment other than seasonal agricultural work is considered a resident. (See "Driver's license" above.) Vehicle owners must pay a basic registration fee plus an annual Vehicle License Tax (VLT), which is collected in lieu of personal property tax. The VLT varies, depending on the vehicle's value.

Once your vehicle is registered, if you move or change your name, you must notify the Motor Vehicle Division with ten days. Incidentally, license plates are assigned to the vehicle owner, not the vehicle itself.

If a vehicle is sold, the owner must remove the plate and—within 30 days, transfer it to another vehicle, turn it in to MVD or sign a statement that the plate has been destroyed.

# EVERYTHING ELSE YOU NEED TO KNOW
## and now you know where to ask

**ACCOUNTANTS** • To find an accountant, contact the Arizona Society of CPAs at 2120 N. Central Ave., Phoenix, AZ 85004; (602) 252-4144.

**ALCOHOL** • Alcoholic beverage sale hours are 7 a.m. to 1 a.m. Legal age for buying or consuming alcohol is 21. It may not be drunk in a vehicle or in public areas in its original container. Distilled spirits, wine and beer are readily available in liquor stores, supermarkets and other licensed outlets.

**ARCHITECTS** • For a list of AIA members, contact the American Institute of Architects at 1 N. 12th St., Phoenix, AZ 85034; (602) 257-1925.

**ATTORNEYS** • To find a lawyer, contact the Maricopa County Bar Association Lawyers Referral Service at 303 E. Palm Lane, Phoenix, AZ 85004, (602) 257-4200; or the Pima County Lawyer Referral Service at 177 N. Church Ave., Tucson, AZ 85701 (520) 623-4625.

**AUTO CLUB** • The Arizona Automobile Association is the state's AAA affiliate. The main office is at 3144 N. Seventh Ave., Phoenix, AZ 85012; and other Valley of the Sun offices are in **Phoenix** at 4046 E. Greenway Rd., **Mesa** at 262 E. University Dr., **Peoria** at 7380 W. Olive Ave., **Scottsdale** at 701 N. Scottsdale Rd., and Sun City West at 19802 R.H. Johnson Blvd.; all can be reached by calling (602) 274-1116. Other offices are at 3767 Karicio Lane, #1-D, **Prescott**, AZ 86303; and 6950 N. Oracle Road, northern **Tucson**, AZ 85704; and 8204 E. Broadway, in central **Tucson**, AZ 85710. The club's web site is *www.aaa.com*.

**BAD CHECKS** • Writing a bad check in Arizona is bad news, for it's a misdemeanor. Rubber check writers who don't make good within 12 days may be fined and/or jailed, in addition to having to cover the check.

**BICYCLING** • Bicycles are subject to the same basic traffic regulations as motor vehicles, and must travel in the same direction as street traffic. They are required to have brakes (we should hope!), plus a front light and rear reflector if they are ridden at night.

**BOAT REGISTRATION** • Pleasure boats moored or used on public waterways must be registered with the Game and Fish Department, which will issue numbers that must be displayed on the craft. For other specifics and tips about boating safety, get the *Arizona Boating Guide* from the Arizona Game and Fish Department, 2222 W. Greenway Rd., Phoenix, AZ 85023; (602) 942-3000.

**CAMPGROUNDS** ● For a directory of campgrounds in the state, contact the Arizona Office of Tourism, 2702 N. Third St., Suite 4015, Phoenix, AZ 85004-4608; (888) 520-3434 or (602) 230-7733; *www.arizonaguide.com* or *www.arizonavacationvalues.com.*

**COMMUNITY PROFILES** ● Sketches of more than a hundred Arizona cities and towns are available on line from the Arizona Department of Commerce, 3800 N. Central Ave., Phoenix, AZ 85017; (602) 280-1300; *www.azcommerce.com.*

**CONSUMER PROTECTION** ● These agencies offer consumer protection services:

**Arizona Board of Osteopathic Examiners,** 9535 E. Doubletree Ranch Rd., Scottsdale, AZ 85258; (480) 657-7703.

**Arizona Department of Real Estate,** Office of the Commissioner, Consumer Representative, 2910 N. 44th St., Phoenix, AZ 85018; (602) 468-1414.

**Better Business Bureau,** phone (602) 264-1721 or check your local phone directory.

**Board of Medical Examiners,** (480) 551-2700.

**Consumer Products Safety Department** (U.S.), (800) 638-2772; *www.cpsc.gov.*

**Registrar of Contractors,** 800 W. Washington St., Phoenix, AZ 85007, (602) 542-1525; or 416 W. Congress, Tucson, AZ 85701; (520) 628-6345.

**Securities Division,** Arizona Corporation Commission, 1200 W. Washington St., Suite 201, Phoenix, AZ 85007; (602) 542-3076.

**State Department of Insurance,** 2910 N. 44th St., Suite 210, Phoenix, AZ 85018-7256; (602) 912-8444.

**Superintendent of Banks,** 3225 N. Central Ave., Suite 815, Phoenix, AZ 85012; (602) 255-4421.

**CONTRACTORS** ● They're listed with the Registrar of Contractors in Phoenix and Tucson; see above.

**COUNTY GOVERNMENT** ● Arizona has fifteen counties, each run by a three-member board of supervisors. Elected county officials—all serving four-year terms—are supervisors, county attorney, treasurer, superintendent of schools, recorder, assessor, sheriff and clerk of the superior court.

**CROSS-COUNTRY SKIING** ● See "Winter sports" below.

**DAY CARE** ● Anyone who cares for more than four children (not related to them) must be licensed by the Department of Health Services. For the publication *Guidelines for Choosing a Day Care Center,* contact the Arizona Department of Health Services, (602) 674-4220 in Phoenix; (520) 628-6540 in Tucson and (928) 774-2707 in Flagstaff. These offices also can tell you if complaints have been lodged against a particular day care center.

These agencies offer assistance in finding child care: **Association for Supportive Child Care,** 2510 S. Rural Rd., Tempe, AZ 85282, (602) 829-0500; and the **Tucson Child and Family Resources,** 1030 N. Alvernon Way, Tucson, AZ 85711, (520) 881-8940.

**The Family Service Agency** offers assistance in finding child care facilities, as well as providing counseling for family problems, unplanned pregnancies and adoption services. The main office is at 1530 E. Flower St., Phoenix, AZ 85014; (602) 264-9891. Other offices are in Phoenix at 914 W. Hatcher Rd., (602) 749-1584 and 3101 Peoria Ave., (602) 863-1862; and in Mesa at 943 S. Gilbert Rd., (480) 545-9626; *www.fsaphoenix.org.*

*DENTISTS* • Misery with a molar? To find a dentist, contact the Arizona Dental Association, 4131 N. 36th St., Phoenix, AZ 85018; (602) 957-4777 or (602) 957-4864.

*DIVORCE* • Misery with a mate? Arizona is a no-fault divorce state and a community property state. In ruling on alimony, courts will consider contribution made by one spouse to the other's earning ability, loss of potential earning power by spending years as a homemaker and other factors. The community property law simply means that property acquired by either marital partner during the marriage is considered to be the equal property of both.

*DOCTORS* • To find a medical doctor, contact the Arizona Medical Association at 810 W. Bethany Home Rd., Phoenix, AZ 85013, (602) 347-6900; or the Arizona Osteopathic Medical Association at 5150 N. 16th St., Phoenix, AZ 85016, (602) 266-6699. Two county medical societies also provide names of local physicians: the Maricopa County Medical Society, 326 E. Coronado Rd., Phoenix, AZ 85004, (602) 252-2015; and the Pima County Medical Society, 5199 E. Farness Dr., Tucson, AZ 85712; (520) 795-7985.

*DRUG USE* • Arizona gets mean about substance abuse. Possession of a "usable" amount of marijuana will earn you a hefty fine, plus jail time or community service. If you're found with more of the stuff, or if you're arrested with a little weed near a school grounds, the penalties get worse. Laws are really tough for heroine, crack and cocaine possession.

*ELECTIONS* • The state primary is held in September of even-numbered years, followed by the general election in November. You must pick a major party to vote in the primary, but not in the general election. The state doesn't conduct a Presidential primary. Precinct committeemen, who are elected to two-year terms, pick the state's party candidates.

Arizona's elected officials are the governor, secretary of state, attorney general and superintendent of public instruction, who all serve four-year terms; and the state mine inspector, who serves two years. Office holders are subject to recall elections if enough voters sign petitions. Voters also can place statewide initiatives and referendums on the ballot, with sufficient petition signatures. (Also see "Legislature" and "Political parties" below.)

**GOLFING** ● For a list of more than 150 golf courses in the state, contact the Arizona Golf Association at 7226 N. 16th St., Phoenix, AZ 85020; (602) 944-3035.

**GUN CONTROL** ● With its Old West attitude, Arizona allows someone to buy a handgun or rifle and pack it in view. However, you can't own an automatic weapon or sawed-off shotgun. Also, you can't possess any weapon if you have a felony record or a history of mental illness. A legally owned weapon can't be concealed. (You can, however, carry your Swiss army knife in your pocket.) For specifics on firearm laws, contact the Law Library of Arizona, 1501 W. Washington St., Phoenix, AZ 85007; (602) 542-5297.

**HEALTH CARE** ● Contact the Health Services Department at 1740 W. Adams St., Phoenix, AZ 85007; (602) 542-1000. For information on senior care, contact the Governor's Advisory Council on Aging, 1717 W. Jefferson St., Phoenix, AZ 85007; (602) 542-4710.

**HOUSING** ● The best source for housing information are chambers of commerce and real estate offices, since no single agency compiles data on prices and availability. (Pricing information is included in many of the community listings in Part Two.) If you want to build your own home and need a contractor, contact the Registrar of Contractors, 800 W. Washington ST., Phoenix, AZ 85007, (602) 542-1525; or 416 W. Congress, Tucson, AZ 85701; (520) 628-6345.

**HUNTING AND FISHING** ● Hunting and fishing licenses are required for anyone fourteen and older, and are available from most sporting goods stores. Fishing license fees are $18 for residents and $51.50 for nonresidents, or $37.50 for a four month and $26 for a five-day nonresident permit. Trout stamps are $10.50 for residents and $49.50 for out-of-staters. Combined hunting-fishing licenses is $44 for residents and $177.50 for nonresidents. For specifics on limits and such, get a copy of fishing and hunting regulations at sporting goods stores or contact the Arizona Game and Fish Department, 2222 W. Greenway Rd., Phoenix, AZ 85023; (602) 942-3000; *www.azgfd.com.* Fishing and hunting licenses may be purchased on line; and the web site also has fishing reports, updated weekly.

State licenses aren't required for hunting and fishing on Indian reservations, although most have their own regulations and fees. (See "Other Indian nations" in Chapter Seventeen.)

**IDENTIFICATION CARDS** ● ID cards for non-drivers, handy for use in proving your age and identification, can be obtained for a $5 fee from any office of the Motor Vehicle Division.

**IMMIGRATION** ● For matters concerning immigration and naturalization, call the U.S. Immigration and Naturalization Service at (800) 375-5283; *www.ins.usdoj.gov.*

# CACTUS LEAGUE: THE BOYS OF SPRING

Shouts of "play ball!" have echoed from southern Arizona every March since 1947 as the boys of summer become the boys of spring for Cactus League baseball action. The Valley of the Sun is the focal point for spring training, hosting seven major league teams; another three play in Tucson.

Fans like the informality and vigor of Cactus League baseball, and the intimacy of the small stadiums. It's baseball played with enthusiasm, gusto and mistakes; the way we played as kids on sandlots. Fans like the ticket prices, too—under $15 for the best seats in the stands.

Many people come to Arizona specifically to watch these exhibition games, particularly "Snowbirds"—retired fall-through-spring visitors. A survey during the 1990s showed that three-fourths of spring training ticket-buyers were from out of state.

Tickets for Cactus League games are available a few days in advance, and often on the day of the game at the respective ballparks. Dillard's sells tickets for several Cactus League teams; call (480) 503-5555. For others, dial the numbers listed below. Most games start at 1:05. **For information:** *www.baseballarizona.com.*

## Who plays where: Valley of the Sun

*Anaheim Angels* play at Tempe Diablo Stadium at 2200 W. Alameda Dr., Tempe; (602) 438-9300; *www.angelsbaseball.com*).

*Chicago Cubs* play at HoHoKam Park at 1235 N. Center St., Mesa; (480) 964-4467; *www.cubspringtraining.com.*

*Milwaukee Brewers* play at Maryvale Baseball Park, 3600 N. 51st Ave., Phoenix; (623) 245-5500; *www.milwaukeebrewers.com.*

*Oakland A's* play at Phoenix Municipal Stadium, 5999 E. Van Buren St., Phoenix; (602) 392-0217; *www.oaklandathletics.com.*

*San Diego Padres* play at the Peoria Sports Complex, 16101 N. 83rd Ave., Peoria; (623) 878-4337; *www.padres.com.*

*San Francisco Giants* play at Scottsdale Stadium, 7408 Osborn Rd., Scottsdale; (480) 990-7972; *www.sfgiants.com.*

*Seattle Mariners* also play at the Peoria Sports Complex; (623) 878-4337; *www.mariners.com.*

## Tucson

*Arizona Diamondbacks* play at Tucson Electric Park, 2500 E. Ajo Way; (520) 434-1111; *www.azdiamondbacks.com.*

*Chicago White Sox* also play at Tucson Electric Park; (520) 434-1111; *www.whitesox.com.*

*Colorado Rockies* play at the Qwest Sports Complex at Hi Corbett Field, 3400 Camino Campestre; (520) 327-9467; *www.coloradorockies.com.*

**INCORPORATING A BUSINESS** • See "Starting a business" in Chapter Five.

**INSURANCE** • As in other states, insurance rates vary from city to city. Auto insurance rates are highest in busy Phoenix, somewhat lower in Tucson and lower still in smaller towns and rural areas. The Department of Insurance will send you a survey of companies selling automobile and homeowners insurance in the state. It also maintains records of complaints against insurance carriers. To get a copy of the survey, send a self-addressed stamped business-size envelope to: State Department of Insurance, 2910 N. 44th St., Suite 210, Phoenix, AZ 85018-7256; (602) 912-8444. (Also see "Auto insurance" above.)

**LEGISLATURE** • Arizona is sliced into thirty legislative districts, and each sends one representative and one senator to the capital in Phoenix. Members of both houses serve two-year terms. The legislature convenes in early January and usually stays in session about four months. Phone numbers are (602) 542-4900 for the Arizona Senate and (602) 542-3032 for the House of Representatives.

**LIQUOR** • See "Alcohol" above.

**LOTTERY** • The Arizona Lottery sells chances at $1 each and conducts computer drawings on Wednesdays and Saturdays. The jackpot often tops a million dollars; grand prize winners are paid over a 20-year period. About two-thirds of the money collected goes to prizes and the rest is used for programs such as public transportation, street maintenance and senior vans. If you get lucky, call (480) 921-4400 for the redemption center at (480) 829-7425 for a recording of the winning numbers.

**MAJOR LEAGUE SPORTS** • Tickets for the **Phoenix Suns** of the National Basketball Association are available by calling (800) 462-2849 or (602) 379-SUNS; they play at the America West Arena at 201 E. Jefferson St. The **Arizona Cardinals** of the National Football League play at Arizona State University's Sun Devil Stadium, although a new facility is under construction; for ticket information, call (602) 379-0102. The **Arizona Diamondbacks** National League baseball team plays at Bank One Ballpark at Jefferson and Fourth Streets in Phoenix; call (888) 777-4664 or (602) 514-8400 for tickets. The **Phoenix Coyotes** of the National Hockey League (formerly the Winnipeg Jets) play at America West Arena; call (480) 563-7825 for ticket information.

**MAPS** • State highway maps are available for a dollar from the **Arizona Office of Tourism**, 2702 N. Third St., Suite 4015, Phoenix, AZ 85004-4608; (888) 520-3434 or (602) 230-7733; *www.arizonaguide.com*. They're also available at many chambers of commerce in the state and at visitor information centers in Phoenix and Tucson.

The **Arizona Automobile Association** also has state maps, plus maps of several communities, available to AAA members only. The main office is at 3144 N. Seventh Ave., Phoenix, AZ 85013; (602)

274-1116. There also are offices in Mesa, Peoria, Prescott, Scottsdale, Sun City West and Tucson; *www.aaa.com.*

National Forest maps and Bureau of Land Management maps are sold at forest service offices and some BLM visitor centers in the state, and at the **Arizona Public Lands Information Center**, 222 N. Central Ave., Phoenix, AZ 85073; (602) 417-9300; *fs.fed.us* or *www.publiclands.org.* Topographical maps can be purchased from the **U.S. Geological Survey,** Denver Federal Building 41, Denver, CO 80225; *www.usgs.gov.*

**MARRIAGE LICENSES** ● Although it isn't noted as a marriage mill, Arizona makes it easy to take the plunge. A license can be secured from any justice court for modest fee and there's no waiting period or blood test requirement. Anyone from eighteen to twenty-two years old must provide proof of age (a birth certificate or driver's license), and those sixteen and seventeen need parental consent. Those under sixteen need the court's consent, given only in special circumstances.

**MEXICO** ● See "Exploring south of the border," Chapter Eighteen.

**MOBILE HOME PARKS** ● Towns and cities with RV parks that cater to long-term winter visitors are listed in Chapter Seven.

**NO SMOKING AREAS** ● Most cities restrict smoking to certain areas and many require restaurants to designate no smoking sections. Many employers, either voluntarily or by local ordinance, provide no smoking areas in the workplace.

**ORGAN DONORS** ● You can indicate on your state driver's license if you want to donate organs or other usable body parts in case of death. The program has a nice name—the Anatomical Gift Act.

**PASSPORTS** ● No, you don't need a passport to enter Arizona, although you'll need one to go overseas from there. Call (900) 225-5674 for information on obtaining a passport or check the web at *http//travel.state.gov.*

**POLITICAL PARTIES** ● Despite its conservative reputation, Arizona has more registered Democrats than Republicans. To become involved—should you wish—contact the Democratic Party at 3105 N. 24th St., Phoenix, AZ 85016, (602) 956-1947; or the Arizona Republican Party at 3501 N. 24th St., Phoenix, AZ 85016-6607; (602) 957-7770. The state has the usual splinter parties, plus a rather active Libertarian Party; (602) 248-8425.

**PRIVATE SCHOOLS** ● Contact the Arizona Private School Association at 202 E. McDowell Rd., Phoenix, AZ 85004; (602) 254-5199.

**PROFESSIONAL ORGANIZATIONS** ● See Chapter Five.

**PUBLICATIONS** ● Copies of Arizona laws and other state publications may be obtained from the Publications Office, Secretary of State, 1700 W. Washington St., Phoenix, AZ 85007; (602) 542-4086. If you don't know what to ask for, the office will send you a list.

**RAINFALL** • See individual community listings in Part Two.

**RENTING** • If you're a winter visitor looking for rentals, local chambers of commerce can be helpful, or check the Yellow Pages under "Rentals."

Regulations governing rentals are set down in the Arizona Residential Landlord and Tenant Act, and a copy is available from the Secretary of State's office. Among its provisions are these:

• Final month's rent and deposits can't exceed one and a half times the monthly rent.

• A rental agreement must state which deposits are refundable and which are not.

• Either the tenant or landlord must give thirty days notice prior to the next rental due date before terminating a tenancy agreement.

• Tenants must be told within two weeks of their departure from a rental of the disposition of all deposits. In other words, deposits must be returned or reasons must be given for their forfeiture.

• Landlords are required to provide trash removal containers, and to keep the property in compliance with building codes that affect health and safety.

• If a landlord neglects or refuses to make repairs affecting health and safety—or repairs called for in the rental agreement—the tenant has several options. They include terminating the rental agreement, seeking temporary quarters and billing the landlord, or having the work done by a licensed contractor and deducting the cost from the rent. Generally, after receiving written notice from the tenant, the landlord has fourteen days to make repairs.

• Landlords can't add surcharges to utility bills; they may collect only the actual amount of the bill from the tenant.

• Landlords must give two days notice of intention to enter a tenant's unit, but they can enter immediately in case of an emergency.

**RETIREMENT COMMUNITIES** • Dozens of retirement communities are located throughout the Arizona sunbelt, and we discuss them in greater detail in Chapter Six. Retirement communities can require that one member of a household—not necessarily the head of household—be a particular age or older. The right to set age limitations is covered by law, spelled out in Arizona Revised Statutes 9-46201 A11.

**RV PARKS** • Many towns and cities with RV parks that cater to long-term winter visitors are listed in Chapter Seven.

**SCHOOLS** • For information on the state's public schools, contact the Arizona Department of Education, 1535 W. Jefferson St., Phoenix, AZ 85007; (602) 542-5393. The department publishes a directory of all schools in the state, and results of periodic student testing. For details on the state's education system, see Chapter Four.

**SENIOR COMMUNITIES** • See "Retirement communities" above.

**SENIOR SERVICES AND HEALTH CARE** • See "Senior service agencies" listed in Chapter Six.

**SMALL BUSINESSES** • See Chapter Five under "Starting a business."

**SMALL CLAIMS** • Residents can file for small debt collection in Small Claims Court for a modest fee. Lawyers aren't required or permitted in Small Claims Court unless both sides agree to legal representation. Although a judgment may be granted, courts do not assist in collecting. The ruling only confirms the legitimacy of the debt. Contact the Small Claims Division of local courts for specifics.

**SKIING** • See "Winter sports" below.

**SOCIAL SECURITY OFFICES** • For Social Security assistance, call (800) 772-1213; *www.ssa.gov*. Offices are located in these Arizona communities: 501 N. Marshall St., **Casa Grande**; 397 Malpais Lane, **Flagstaff**; 5907 W. Kings Ave., **Glendale**; 1801 S. Extension, **Mesa**; Chaparral Plaza Suite 192, **Miami**; 7227 N. 16th St., **Phoenix**; 3200 N. Hayden Rd., and 1122 N. Seventh St., Suite 100, both in **Scottsdale**; and 4601 E. Broadway and 2716 S. Sixth Ave., both in **Tucson**

**SPEED LIMITS** • See "Things automotive" above.

**TELEPHONE SERVICE** • Arizona has five area codes: (602) for metropolitan Phoenix, (480) for Scottsdale and the eastern side of the Valley of the Sun, (623) for the west side; (520) for Tucson and southwestern Arizona and (928) for the rest of the state. Most of Arizona is served by Qwest. To order phone directories, call (800) 422-8793; *www.qwestdex.com*.

**TIME ZONES** • All of Arizona is in the Mountain time zone and it doesn't go on Daylight Saving Time in the summer. Why not? Because those desert summer evenings are already long enough, thank you. The Navajo Reservation, however, does observe Daylight Saving Time.

**TRADE ORGANIZATIONS** • See Chapter Five.

**VETERANS' ASSISTANCE** • The Veterans Administration regional center is at 3225 N. Central Ave., Phoenix, AZ 85012; (800) 827-1000; *www.va.gov*. The Carl Hayden VA Medical Center is at 650 E. Indian School Rd., Phoenix, AZ 85012; (602) 277-5551; *www.phoenix.med.va.gov*. Call for the location of other VA medical centers or clinics. A Veteran Counseling and Guidance Center is at 77 E. Weldon Ave., Suite 100, Phoenix, AZ 85012; (602) 640-2981.

**VISITOR INFORMATION** • For a copy of the *Arizona Travel Planner*, contact the Arizona Office of Tourism, 2702 N. Third St., Suite 4015, Phoenix, AZ 85004-4608; (888) 520-3434 or (602) 230-7733; *www.arizonaguide.com*. State welcome centers are located in Flagstaff, Kearny, Painted Cliffs, Phoenix, Scottsdale, Sedona/Oak Creek Canyon, Tempe and Verde Valley.

**VOTING** • Arizona makes it easy to vote. You can register at any city clerk or county recorder's office, Department of Elections office, driver's license examining station, justice of the peace, political party headquarters or with any deputy registrar. The state embraces all federal voting requirements: You must be an eighteen-year-old American citizen who hasn't been convicted of treason or other felony, and you must be sane and not under mental guardianship. The state residency requirement is fifty days. (Also see "Political parties" above.)

Absentee ballots are available to anyone who lives more than fifteen miles from the polls, or will be absent from their precinct on election day, or is sixty-five or older, or has a vision or physical defect.

**WAGES** • See Chapter Five for details on wage ranges for various occupations.

**WEATHER** • See "Weather or not" in Chapter One. High and low seasonal temperatures are listed for communities in chapters eight through eleven.

**WILLS AND THE RIGHT TO DIE** • If you're eighteen or older, you can make out a will, which must be witnessed by two parties who aren't beneficiaries of the will. However, if it's hand-written, witnesses aren't required. Out-of-state wills are recognized, although you should check with an attorney to confirm that your will's provisions conform to Arizona law. Generally, jointly-held property should be placed in joint tenancy, so the surviving partner inherits it.

Arizona is a "right to die" state, which means that you can establish a living will that sets forth procedures for dealing with a terminal illness. Based on a 1987 court ruling, patients can refuse treatment if they are terminally ill. If patients are medically or mentally unable to make that decision and no living will has been made, courts can appoint a guardian to act on their behalf.

**WINTER SPORTS** • Arizona offers these downhill ski areas: **Arizona Snowbowl** above Flagstaff, (800) 842-7293 or (928) 779-1951; **Mount Lemmon Ski Valley** above Tucson, (520) 576-1321 or (520) 576-1400; the small **Williams Ski Area** above Williams, (928) 635-9330; and the **Sunrise Ski Area**, an Apache-owned year-around resort on the White Mountain reservation, (928) 737-7669 for the ski area and (800) 55-HOTEL or (928) 735-7676 for the lodge.

Groomed cross-country trails are available at the **Flagstaff Nordic Center** at the Arizona Snowbowl, (928) 779-1951; **Mormon Lake Ski Center** near Flagstaff, (928) 354-2240; **Montezuma Nordic Ski Center,** also near Flagstaff, (928) 354-2221; and the **Williams Ski Area,** (928) 635-9330.

## Chapter Four

# SCHOOL DAYS
## ARIZONA'S EDUCATION PICTURE

**I**f you're moving a family to Arizona, you'll be concerned about the quality of education in your future hometown. You'll be pleased to know that—overall—Arizona rates at or above the national average in most student test scores. It ranks among the highest states in the nation in per capita student expenditures, and the student-teacher classroom ratio also is better than the national average.

The state requires that all elementary and high school students be tested annually for their scholastic proficiency in reading, language and math. Elementary students take the Iowa Test of Basic Skills, while high school kids take either the Stanford Achievement Test (freshmen) or Stanford Test of Academic Skills (sophomores through seniors).

In annual tests, nearly all school districts in Arizona score higher than the national norm. Statewide, most grades (one through 12) score higher than the U.S. average in language skills. Most intermediate and high school grades also top national scores in reading. In math, most Arizona students score at or near the national average. Significantly, reading, language and math test scores for virtually all grades have shown improvement in recent years.

To encourage continued student proficiency, outstanding elementary and secondary schools are honored in an annual School Recognition Program. It's sponsored by the Arizona Educational Foundation and Department of Education. For more information on public schools and specific school districts, contact the **Arizona Department of**

**Education** at 1535 W. Jefferson St., Phoenix. AZ 85007; (602) 542-5393. For GED test information, call (602) 542- 5802 and for the Academic Achievement department, call (602) 542- 3824. The Arizona Department of Education's web site is *www.ade.state.az.us*. For "school report cards" on the scholastic standing of various schools, go to *www.ade.state.az.us/schools/schools/districts.htm*.

## School attendance

Arizona's school attendance laws are pretty much the same as in other states. Parents or guardians of any child between eight and sixteen must ensure that the kid attends classes. Youngsters can leave school before age sixteen only if they have finished the tenth grade or are employed in a vocational or work training program.

The following immunization shots are required for school-age children: measles, mumps, rubella, diphtheria, tetanus and polio. Proof of immunization must be provided by parents or guardians within fifteen days after a child starts classes.

## Private schooling

For a list of accredited private schools, contact the **Arizona Private School Association**, 202 E. McDowell Rd., Phoenix, AZ 85004; (602) 254-5199.

Children can be taught at home if someone in the household has passed the Arizona Teacher Proficiency Examination within six months of the beginning of instruction. The child still must take state-required achievement tests. For specifics on home teaching, contact the Department of Education at (602) 542-5393.

# Some of the top public schools

Generally speaking, schools in the Phoenix and Tucson suburbs are among the state's leaders, based on results of annual student achievement tests. As a rule, suburban kids outscored their city center and rural peers. According to recent test results, these were among Arizona's top-rated public schools. (This is not a precise analysis, but a general comparison of scores. And of course, testing result often change from year to year, so this is only a rough guide.)

## Elementary (grades one through eight)

### Cochise County

**St. David Unified District**—St. David School.

### Coconino County

**Flagstaff Unified District**—Knoles Elementary School.

### Maricopa County (Phoenix area)

**Mesa Unified District**—Alma School, Field School, Franklin School, Washington School, MacArthur School, Jordan School, Sirrine

School, Ishikawa School, Kino Junior High, Poston Junior High, Rhodes Junior High, Taylor Junior High and Hendrix Junior High.

**Peoria Unified District**—Oakwood School, Kachina School, Heritage School, Pioneer School, Desert Palms School, Sahuaro School, Skyview Elementary School and Desert Valley School.

**Scottsdale Unified District**—Cochise School, Kiva School, Hopi School, Cherokee School, Anasazi School, Laguna School, Sequoya School, Zuni School, Mohave Middle School, Ingleside Middle School and Cocopah Middle School.

**Paradise Valley Unified District**—Mercury Mine School, Liberty School, Sandpiper School, Desert Springs School and Desert Shadows Middle School.

**Chandler Unified District**—Goodman Elementary School.

**Washington Elementary District**—Lookout Mountain School, Richard E. Miller School and Desert Foothills Middle School.

**Alhambra Elementary District**—Alhambra Traditional School.

### *Pima County (Tucson area)*

**Tucson Unified District**—Fruchthendler School, Whitmore School, Gale School, Lineweaver School and Wrightstown School.

**Tanque Verde Unified District**—Tanque Verde School.

**Catalina Foothills Unified District**—Sunrise Drive School, Manzanita School, Canyon View School and Orange Grove Junior High.

**Sonoita Elementary District**—Elgin Elementary School.

## Secondary schools (grades nine through 12)
### *Coconino County*
**Flagstaff Unified District**—Coconino High School.
### *Maricopa County*
**Mesa Unified District**—Mountain View High School and Dobson High School.

**Scottsdale Unified District**—Arcadia High School, Saguaro High School and Chaparral High School.

**Tempe Union High School District**—Corona del Sol High School and Evening High School.
### *Pima County*
**Tucson Unified District**—University High School and Sabino High School.

# COLLEGES & UNIVERSITIES

Arizona boasts some of America's leading institutes of higher education. They include the three-campus University of Arizona and America's only accredited four-year aeronautical university.

Since joining the Pacific Ten, Tucson's University of Arizona and Arizona State University in Tempe have earned national attention for their athletic teams, particularly in football and basketball. For instance, UA won the national collegiate basketball title in 1997. However, such achievements are mostly for fun and television coverage. More importantly, they rank scholastically among America's leading state universities, and the Northern Arizona campus at Flagstaff is regarded as one of the country's finer small universities.

The state also supports a network of nineteen community colleges. These two-year schools provide broad-based science and liberal arts courses for high school graduates who've not yet decided on a major, or who need to tidy up their grades prior to four-year school admission. Equally important, they are "terminal education facilities," providing vocational studies and training to prepare young students for the job market, and to give adults needed training to switch careers.

In the listings that follow, tuition, fees and room and board figures are per school year, unless indicated otherwise. These are for general guidance only and are subject to change—invariably upward.

## The state universities

**University of Arizona** • *P.O. Box 210040, Tucson, AZ 85721-0040; (520) 621-3237; www.arizona.edu.* ☐ Founded in 1885, Arizona's oldest university offers a broad base of undergraduate and graduate programs. Its colleges include agriculture, architecture, arts and science, business and public administration, education, engineering and mines, law, medicine, nursing and pharmacy. Special programs include anthropology, astronomy, classical archaeology, management information studies and arid land studies. Admission requirement: Must be in the top 25 percent of high school graduation class. Tuition: $2,088 for residents and $9,040 for nonresidents. On-campus housing available, including family units; room and board $7,754. About 30,000 students.

**Arizona State University** • *P.O. Box 870112, Tempe, AZ 85287-0112; (480) 965-9011; www.asu.edu.* ☐ The state's largest university, ASU offers programs in a variety of fields. It specializes in architecture and environmental design (the campus theater was designed by Frank Lloyd Wright), engineering and applied sciences, accounting, graphic design, journalism and telecommunications, plus fine arts programs such as dance, theater, art and music. Admission requirements: Must be in the top 25 percent of high school graduation class. Tuition and fees: $2,180 for residents and $9,340 for nonresidents. On-campus housing available; room and board averages $5,010 per year. About 36,000 full-time students.

**Northern Arizona University** • *P.O. Box 4084, Flagstaff, AZ 86001; (928) 523-9011; www.nau.edu.* ☐ Several years ago, NAU was rated by *Money Magazine* as one of the ten top university values in the country, based on its quality of education for a relatively low tuition. Its nine colleges offer programs in arts and sciences, business, education, forestry, health professions, the hospitality industry, engineering, social and behavioral sciences and creative and communications arts. Admission requirement: 3.0 grade point average. Tuition: $1,293 per semester for residents and $5,558 for nonresidents. On-campus housing; room and board about $2,578. About 14,000 students.

# Other colleges & universities

**Chaparral College** • *4585 E. Speedway, #204, Tucson, AZ 85712; (520) 327-6866.* ☐ This small school offers two-year courses with associate degrees in accounting, business administration, administrative assistant, criminal justice and legal assistant, plus a four-year course with a bachelor's degree in business administration. Admission requirements: high school graduate or GED equivalency; 2.0 grade average. Fees vary with the programs. No housing on campus; about 400 students.

**DeVry University-Phoenix Campus** • *2149 W. Dunlap Ave., Phoenix, AZ 85021; (602) 870-9201; www.devry-phx.edu.* ☐ This technical university offers courses in electronics engineering technology, computer information systems and computer engineering technology and telecommunications management, plus associate degrees in electronics technology. Admission requirement: high school diploma or GED equivalent. Tuition: $4,445 per semester for residents and nonresidents. No on-campus housing; about 2,700 students.

**Embry Riddle Aeronautical University** • *3200 Willow Creek Rd., Prescott, AZ 86301; (800) 888-3728 or (928) 708-3728; www. pr.erau.edu.* ☐ America's only university-level aeronautical school, Embry Riddle offers majors in aviation technology, aerospace engineering, aerospace science, aviation administration and related fields. The school has its own fleet of training planes at nearby Ernest A. Love Field and can qualify its students in single and multiple engine craft. Total yearly cost about $27,850; campus housing available. About 1,500 students.

**Grand Canyon University** • *P.O. Box 11097 (3300 W. Camelback Rd.), Phoenix, AZ 85061; (800) 800-9776 or (602) 589-2855.* ☐ A private Christian liberal arts school, it offers degrees from eight colleges—business, Christian studies, communications and fine arts, continuing studies, education, liberal arts, science and allied health, and nursing. Graduate programs are available in business and education. Tuition and fees: $8,040. On-campus housing available; room and board $3,400. About 2,100 students.

**ITT Technical Institute** • *4837 E. McDowell Rd., Phoenix, AZ 85008; (602) 252-2331. Second campus at 1840 E. Benson Highway, Tucson, AZ 85714; (520) 294-2944.* ☐ This technical school offers one- year courses in computer science, electronics and computer engineering, drafting and computer-aided design. Admission requirements: high school graduate or GED equivalency. Tuition varies, based on study courses. No on-campus housing, although roommate assistance is available. About 315 students. Job placement assistance offered during school and after graduation.

**Prescott College** • *301 Grove Ave., Prescott, AZ 86301; (928) 778-2090; www.prescott.edu.* ☐ A small liberal arts school, it emphasizes experimental learning programs and field studies. Majors are environmental studies, integrative studies, humanities, arts and letters and adventure education. The school also has undergraduate, masters and teacher certification programs. Admission requirements: individual analysis, essay and review of transcripts. Tuitions range from $6,990 to $10,448, depending on the program. No on-campus housing; about 1,100 students.

**Southwestern College** • *2625 E. Cactus Rd., Phoenix, AZ 85032; (800) 247-2697 or (602) 992-6101; www.southwesterncollege.edu.* ☐ A Conservative Baptist school, it focuses on biblical studies, elementary education, pastoral studies, theology and related subjects. Admission requirements: high school diploma or equivalent, plus a written essay. Tuition and fees: $8,270. On-campus housing; room and board about $3,570.

**University of Phoenix** • *4615 E. Elwood St., Phoenix, AZ 85040; (800) 800-7000 or (602) 921-5332; www.uophx.edu.* ☐ This highly regarded proprietary upper level institution offers undergraduate and graduate courses in business administration, management, information systems and nursing. Extension courses are available in 34 cities throughout the West and Southeast, or via the internet. Admission requirements: 2.5 GPA and at least two years of degree-related work experience. Tuition varies by program. No on-campus housing.

**Western International University** • *9215 N. Black Canyon Hwy., Phoenix, AZ 85021; (602) 943-2311; www.wintu.edu.* ☐ This small university offers graduate and undergraduate business oriented programs to employed professionals who want to further their education. Fields of study include marketing, international business management, accounting, finance and management. Admission requirement: 3.0 for masters programs and 2.75 for bachelor studies. Tuition: $260 per unit for bachelor programs and $285 for masters programs. No on-campus housing; about 2,500 students.

## Two-year community colleges

Arizona's community college program is open to anyone eighteen years or older who "demonstrates evidence of potential success" by taking college classes. For some courses of study, there are additional requirements, such as a high school diploma, GED equivalency or college transfer credits. For more information, contact the Arizona Community College Board at 3225 N. Central Ave., Phoenix, AZ 85012; (602) 255-4037.

**Arizona Western College** • *P.O. Box 929, Yuma, AZ 85364-0929; (928) 317-6000; www.awc.cc.az.us.* □ Part of the state community college system, it offers associate of arts degrees in a variety of liberal arts and science subjects, plus vocational and continuing education programs. Open enrollment. Tuition and fees: about $500 for residents and $4,000 for nonresidents. No on-campus housing; 6,200 students.

**Central Arizona College** • *8470 N. Overfield Rd., Coolidge, AZ 85228; (520) 436-4260; www.centralaz.edu.* □ A member of the Arizona Community College system, it offers university transfer and associate degree programs in fifty-two areas of study. Admission requirements: open enrollment except for nursing program, which has prerequisites. Tuition and fees: $402 for 24 credits per semester for residents and $5,008 for nonresidents. On-campus housing available; room and board $1,910 per semester. About 14,000 students.

**Cochise College** • *4190 W. Highway 80, Douglas, AZ 85607; (800) 966-7943 or (520) 364-7943; www.cochise.edu.* □ AA degrees available in a variety of subjects. Specialties include pilot training, aviation maintenance, computer sciences and nursing, plus vocational and continuing education programs. Admission requirement: high school diploma or GED equivalency. Tuition: $33 per semester unit for residents, $173 for out-of-state students. Dorms and family apartments available; room and board $1,648 per semester. About 5,000 students.

**Dené College (Navajo Community College)** • *P.O. Box 126, Tsaile, AZ 86556; (928) 724-6600; www.crystal.ncc.cc.nm.us.* □ This is a federally supported college on the Navajo Reservation, offering a variety of lower division liberal arts programs, including Native American studies. Admission requirements: high school diploma or equivalent. Tuition and fees: $2,020 per semester. On-campus housing and room and board available. About 1,800 students; 96 percent are Native American.

**Eastern Arizona College** • *600 Church St., Thatcher, AZ 85552-0769; (928) 428-8233; www.eac.edu.* □ This community college offers AA degrees in several subjects, plus occupational and continuing education programs. Open admission. Tuition: $394 per semester of twelve units or more for residents, $2,454 for nonresidents. On-campus housing: $630 for fall semester and $420 for spring semester, plus $960 to $1,080 for meals. About 2,200 students.

**GateWay Community College** • *108 N. 40th St., Phoenix, AZ 85034; (602) 392-5000; www.gwc.maricopa.edu.* □ A unit of the Maricopa County Community College District, GateWay offers transfer degrees as well as many occupational programs, including nursing, computers, heating/ventilation, physical therapy, respiratory therapy, medical radiography and automotive repair. Open admission; requirements for some courses of study. Tuition: $46 per credit unit for Maricopa County residents; higher for non-residents. No on-campus housing; about 8,000 students.

**Glendale Community College** • *6000 W. Olive Ave., Glendale, AZ 85302; (623) 435-3000; www.gc.maricopa.edu.* ☐ This large community college offers the usual variety of lower division academic programs, plus occupational courses in automotive technology, administration of justice, business, emergency medical technology, computer-aided design, semiconductor manufacturing and other fields. It's noted for its high tech programs. Open admission. Tuition: about $2,100 for Maricopa County and $4,500 for nonresidents. No on-campus housing; 12,000 students.

**Lamson College** • *1626 N. Scottsdale Rd., Tempe, AZ 85281; (480) 898-7000; www.lamsoncollege.com.* ☐ This community college offers several lower division academic courses, plus trade and technical programs. Open enrollment, although some courses require a high school diploma or equivalent. Tuition varies; about $34 per semester unit for Maricopa County residents, higher for out of area and out of state students.

**Mesa Community College** • *1833 W. Southern Ave., Mesa, AZ 85202; (480) 461-6000; www.mc.maricopa.edu.* ☐ This school offers a variety of lower division programs, plus trade and technical courses. It's the primary transfer institution for Arizona State University. Open enrollment. Tuition: $40 per credit unit for Maricopa County residents and $65 to $177 for out of county and out of state students. No on-campus housing, although the Office of Student Activities provides a free housing directory and roommate service. About 22,000 students.

**Mohave Community College** • *1971 Jagerson Ave., Kingman, AZ 86401; (928) 757-0847; www.mohave.cc.az.us.* ☐ Mohave offers two-year degrees and certificates in a variety of programs as well as personal interest courses. The college serves residents of Mohave County with campuses in Kingman, Bullhead City and Lake Havasu City, plus the North Mohave Center in Colorado City. All four are linked via a microwave system that enables teaching of classes simultaneously. Tuition and fees: about $900 for district residents and $3,800 for nonresidents. Approximately 10,000 students on the four campuses.

**Northland Pioneer College** • *Admission information: (928) 536-6257; www.npc.edu.* ☐ This community college serves about 12,000 students throughout Navajo and Apache counties with campuses in Winslow, Holbrook, Snowflake/Taylor and Show Low. Education centers are in Heber, Polocca, Kayenta, St. Johns, Springerville/Eagar and Whiteriver. The college offers five degree programs: Associate of Arts, Associate of Business, Associate of Science, Associate of Applied Science and Associate of General Studies. Course are available in more than 30 vocational areas, including business, computer science, building and industrial trades, and medical-health related fields. NPC's cultural anthropology course takes advantage of nearby native sites for field studies. Tuitions vary and are among the lowest in the state. Residence halls are available on Holbrook's Painted Desert campus.

**Phoenix College** • *1202 W. Thomas Rd., Phoenix, AZ 85013; (602) 264-2492; www.phoenixcollege.edu.* □ A campus of the Maricopa Community College system, it offers a variety of lower division academic courses, plus trade, technical and continuing education programs. Open admission. Tuition and fees: $43 per semester unit for residents, $68 for out of county and $180 for out of state residents. No on-campus housing. About 12,000 students.

**Pima Community College** • *4905 E. Broadway Blvd., Tucson, AZ 85709-1120; (800) 860-7462 or (520) 206-4500; www.pima.edu.* □ One of Arizona's largest community colleges, Pima offers certificates and two-year degrees in sixty-three program areas, including academic studies transferable to universities, trade, technical, continuing education and corporate and community education. Specialties include aviation technology, dental lab and assistant programs, landscaping, legal assistant, nursing, radiological and emergency medical technology and respiratory care. Pima has the only EPA-approved environmental training center in the Southwest. Open admission. Tuition: $878 for residents and $5,225 for nonresidents. No on-campus housing. About 30,000 full time and part time students.

**Rio Salado Community College** • *2323 E. 14th St., Tempe, AZ 85281; (480) 517-8000; www.rio.maricopa.edu.* □ Part of the Maricopa Community College district, it offers assorted lower division programs, continuing education and technical courses. Open admission. Tuition: $46 per credit unit for county residents and $180 for out of county and out of state students. About 20,000 students.

**Scottsdale Community College** • *900 E. Chaparral Rd., Scottsdale, AZ 85256; (480) 423-6000; www.sc.maricopa,edu.* □ Part of the Maricopa Community College District, it offers a variety of liberal arts, technical and continuing education programs. Open admission; tuition and fees: $43 per credit unit for county residents, $180 for out of state students. No on-campus housing; 11,500 students.

**South Mountain Community College** • *7050 S. 24th St., Phoenix, AZ 85040; (602) 243-8000; www.smc.maricopa.edu.* □ A Maricopa Community College District school, it offers AA programs in business administration, commerce, management and computer information systems. Open admission. Tuition and fees: $1,024 for county residents and $5,014 for non-residents. No on-campus housing available; about 3,000 students.

**Yavapai College** • *1100 E. Sheldon St., Prescott, AZ 86301; (800) 922-6787 or (928) 445-7300; www.yavapai.cc.az.us.* □ This small community college offers several science and liberal arts programs, with transfers targeted to the three Arizona state universities. It's noted for its national championship soccer team. Tuition and fees: $700 for residents and $5,600 for non-residents. On-campus housing available; room and board $2,460. About 7,000 students. Second campus in Clarksdale and extension programs throughout Yavapai County.

**Chapter Five**

# THE JOB-SEEKERS
## ARIZONA'S EMPLOYMENT BASE

**A**rizona's economic growth galloped briskly into the new millennium, as the state increased its population by more than 30 percent from 1990 to 2000. Hundreds of thousands of new jobs were created, particularly in manufacturing, technology, construction, real estate, retail and the service industries. The economy slowed along with the rest of the nation in 2001 and 2002, although modest growth continued and future projections are optimistic.

However, a growing or stable economy doesn't necessarily mean that good jobs are easy to find. Landing that well-paying position still requires a lot of effort. This chapter has a triple focus. It covers the Arizona employment picture, offers suggestions for starting a business, and then it covers the steps needed to land that ideal job.

## Wages & the cost of living

Overall wages are lower in Arizona than the national average, although that gap is closing. By the turn of the century, wages were only fractionally lower than the national average and they were actually higher in the retail trades by nearly a thousand dollars a year.

A bright side of the wage coin is that the cost of living is lower here than in many other states, so your paycheck will go further. Figures released by the Arizona Department of Economic Security recently revealed that the composite cost of living index was 99 in the Phoenix metro area, 98.8 in Tucson and 102.5 in Flagstaff, compared with

147.7 in Los Angeles, 120.8 in San Diego, 110 in Denver and 107 in Portland, Oregon. And if you're tempted to flee to Arizona from an Eastern city, the survey provides added incentive: New York's index was 241, Boston's was 132.5 and Washington's was 114.7.

That same study showed that housing is a relative bargain in Arizona. The housing cost index was 100.9 in Phoenix metro, 108.1 in Tucson and 113.5 in Flagstaff, compared with 241.5 in Los Angeles, 142.6 in San Diego, 123.4 in Denver, 485.3 in New York, 171.2 in Boston and 129 in the nation's capital.

### Average annual wages of major industries

|  | Arizona | U.S. |
|---|---|---|
| Mining | 51,452 | 54,653 |
| Construction | 30,859 | 34,798 |
| Manufacturing | 44,198 | 41,918 |
| Transportation/utilities/communications | 37,831 | 41,729 |
| Wholesale trade | 42,664 | 44,144 |
| Retail trade | 18,418 | 17,592 |
| Finance/insurance/real estate | 38,597 | 50,865 |
| Services | 28.135 | 31,491 |

### Hourly wages of the most common jobs

| Type of job | Total employed | Hourly wages |
|---|---|---|
| Cashier | 52,547 | 7.82 |
| Retail salesperson | 52,102 | 9.99 |
| Office clerks, general | 44,989 | 9.49 |
| Managers & executives | 41,811 | 31.19 |
| Exec. & med. secretaries | 37,098 | 11.30 |
| Waiters & waitresses | 36,080 | 5.78 |
| Marketing supervisors | 34,954 | 17.11 |
| Janitors & cleaners | 30,837 | 7.60 |
| Registered nurses | 28,392 | 19.84 |
| Office admistrators | 27,810 | 15.86 |
| Bookkeepers & accountants | 27,747 | 11.23 |
| Fast food workers | 27,189 | 6.21 |
| Receptionists & info clerks | 26,507 | 8.81 |

# Twin plant manufacturing

One curious aspect of the Arizona job market is the so-called "twin plant" or "offshore" manufacturing program. Working in concert with the Mexican government, several American firms have set up manufacturing plants near the Arizona-Mexico border to draw from Mexico's cheap labor pool. Often, plants are located on both sides of the border; thus, the twin plant reference.

This helps the U.S. compete with cheap overseas labor and it boosts Mexico's economy. However, it offers little for Arizona job hunters, other than a few management positions. Among twin-plant communities are San Luis below Yuma, Naco south of Bisbee, the twin cities of Nogales south of Tucson and Douglas-Agua Prieta in southeastern Arizona. Because of low wages and intense competition from hard-working Mexicans, we don't recommend job hunting along the border.

## Right to work

Arizona is a "right to work" state, which means that mandatory union membership is prohibited. Thus, there are no closed shops. Right to work laws create mixed blessings: They tend to attract business but they suppress wages in fields that are generally unionized elsewhere. Predictably, union membership in Arizona is low—seven percent of the work force, compared with a national rate of 17 percent.

## Employee rights

On the other side of the coin, Arizona is pro-labor when it comes to employee rights. If you switch jobs, the law requires that you receive copies of all communication between your present and prospective employer.

Blacklisting to prevent someone from getting a job is forbidden. Employers can exchange only specific information on job performance, qualifications, past experience, education and training.

# WHERE THE JOBS ARE

Direct contact is the best way to get work, and we discuss it toward the end of this chapter, under "Finding that job." Employment agencies, and trade and professional organizations are useful tools as well.

The Arizona Department of Economic Security has a variety of publications to aid your job search, including the *Arizona Job Seekers Guide, Arizona Employer Wage Survey, Arizona Workforce, Arizona High Tech Directory* and *Arizona Industrial Directory*. There are fees for some, while others are free and/or can be downloaded from the department's web site. For these and other publications, contact the **Arizona Department of Economic Security**, (800) 321-0381 within Arizona, (800) 827-4966 outside the state and (602) 542-3871 in the Valley of the Sun; *www.de.state.az.gov/links/economic/webpage/*.

A good starting point for job-hunting is the **Arizona Job Service**, which has offices throughout the state. Some are "One-Stop Career Centers," that offer job counseling as well as listings of available openings. It's part of the Arizona Department of Economic Security and can be accessed by the same web site. Like other employment offices, it offers lists of local job openings, and it provide counseling to job-seekers; the general information number is (602) 252-7771.

## Job service offices

**Bisbee** • 209 Bisbee Road, Bisbee, AZ 85603-1122; (520) 432-5703.

**Bullhead City** • 813 Hancock Rd., Bullhead City, AZ 86442-5078; (928) 763-4154.

**Casa Grande** • 401 N. Marshall St., Casa Grande, AZ 85222-5244; (520) 426-3529.

**Coolidge** • 1155 N. Arizona Blvd., Coolidge, AZ 85228-3023; (520) 723-5351.

**Cottonwood** • 1645 E. Cottonwood St., Suite E, Cottonwood, AZ 86326-4500; (928) 634-3337.

**Douglas** • 1140 F Ave., Douglas, AZ 85607-1919; (520) 364-4446.

**Flagstaff** • 397 Malpais Lane, Suite 9, Flagstaff, AZ 86001-6281; (928) 779-4557.

**Glendale** • 6666 W. Peoria Ave., Suite 101, Glendale, AZ 85302-7014; (623) 486-9891.

**Globe** • 605 S. Seventh St., Globe, AZ 85501-1405; (928) 425-3101.

**Kingman** • 301 Pine St., Kingman, AZ 86401-5627; (928) 753-4333.

**Lake Havasu City** • 232 London Bridge Rd., Lake Havasu City, AZ 86403-4647; (928) 680-6004.

**Mesa** • 225 E. Main St., Suite 110, Mesa, AZ 85201-7433; (480) 962-7678.

**Nogales** • 480 N. Grand Ave., Nogales, AZ 85621-2734; (520) 287-4635.

**Payson** • 122 E. Highway 260, Suite 110, Payson, AZ 84441-4925; (928) 472-9339.

**Phoenix** • four offices:

4635 S. Central Ave., Phoenix, AZ 85040-2148; (602) 276-5587.

9801 N. Seventh St., Phoenix, AZ 85020-1701; (602) 861-0208.

3406 N. 51st Ave., Phoenix, AZ 85031-3002; (602) 247-3304.

438 W. Adams St., Phoenix, AZ 85003-1607; (602) 252-7771.

**Prescott** • 234 N. Grove Ave., Prescott, AZ 86302-2912; (928) 445-5100.

**Safford** • 1938 W. Thatcher Blvd., Safford, AZ 85546-3318; (928) 428-2911.

**Show Low** • 40 S. 11th St., Show Low, AZ 85901-6001; (928) 537-2948.

**Sierra Vista** • 2981 E. Tacoma Ave., Sierra Vista, AZ 85635-1353; (520) 459-3206.

**Tuba City** • P.O. Box 1140, Tuba City, AZ 86045-1140; (928) 283-5201.

**Tucson** • three offices:

316 W. Fort Lowell Rd., Tucson, AZ 85703-3816; (520) 293-1919.

5441 E. 22nd St., Tucson, AZ 85701-5405; (520) 584-8226.

195 W. Irvington Rd., Tucson, AZ 85714-3050; (520) 741-7188.

**Willcox** • 265 S. Curtis Ave., Willcox, AZ 85643-2115; (520) 384-3583.

**Window Rock** • 54-B Hwy. 264 (P.O. Box 1570), Window Rock, AZ 85615-1570; (928) 871-4131.

**Winslow** • 319 E. Third St., Winslow, AZ 86047-3901; (928) 289-4644.

**Yuma** • 201 S. Third Ave., Yuma, AZ 85634-2254; (928) 783-1221.

## The internet & other job-hunting aids

Several web sites offer job-finding help, such as *www.monster.com,* which lists openings by state and allows you to post your resume. Two helpful Arizona sites are *www.jobsearch.org* for Arizona's Job Bank and *www.de.state.az.us/oscc/* for the Arizona Job Service's "One-Stop Career Centers."

For other job-seeking and resume-posting sites, go to search engines such as *yahoo* or *google* and enter key words like "job search" or "employment."

An excellent job-hunting source is the Yellow Pages of the local phone directory, since it lists businesses and firms by type, as well as employment agencies and resume services. **Qwest** provides phone service for most Arizona communities and you can order local directories by calling (800) 422-8793; *www.qwestdex.com.*

As for *where* the jobs are, most are in the greater Phoenix area and Tucson. As we noted earlier, four out of five Arizonans live in these two metropolitan centers. Both areas are growing rapidly and opening up new employment opportunities. The Valley of the Sun is the core of Arizona's economy, providing homes and jobs for 60 percent of the state's population. Several major corporations are based here, including Greyhound, America West Airlines, Ramada Inns, U-Haul and Circle K Corporation. If you're seeking a large and diversified employment base, the Valley of the Sun is your best bet.

Other areas that have relatively low unemployment rates and thus offer fairly good job potential are Prescott, Flagstaff, Pinal County between Phoenix and Tucson, and Kingman and Lake Havasu City in Mohave County. Highest unemployment rates and worst job prospects are in the counties of Yuma, Santa Cruz, Navajo, Apache and Greenlee.

## Phoenix

A useful job source for greater Phoenix is *The Book of Lists*, published annually by the *The Business Journal*. Although it doesn't provide specific job listings, it publishes names, phone numbers and addresses of the area's largest firms. Listings include the type of work they do, what products they create and names of company principals. Other useful lists in the book include leading radio and TV stations, scheduled airline service, car rental agencies, hotels and resorts, colleges and even women-owned firms. For pricing and shipping information, contact *The Business Journal*, 3030 N. Central Ave., Phoenix, AZ 85012; (602) 230-8400.

For more information on the Valley of the Sun employment situation, try these contacts:

**City of Phoenix**, Community and Economic Development, 200 W. Washington St., 20th Floor, Phoenix, AZ 85003-1611; (602) 262-5040; *www.ci.phoenix.az.us.*

**Phoenix Economic Growth Group**, 400 N. Fifth St., Room 1625, Phoenix, AZ 85004; (602) FOR-PHNX or (602) 253-9747.

**Greater Phoenix Economic Council**, Two N. Central Ave., Suite 210, Phoenix, AZ 85004; (602) 256-7700; *www.gpec.org.*

**Greater Phoenix Chamber of Commerce**, 201 N. Central, Suite 2700, Phoenix, AZ 85073; (602) 254-5521; *www.phoenixchamber.com.*

## Tucson

Arizona's number two city, Tucson obviously offers its second largest job market. Major employers include the University of Arizona, Davis-Monthan Air Force Base and high tech firms such as Raytheon Systems.

To learn more about the city's economic and employment situation, contact:

**Tucson Metropolitan Chamber of Commerce**, 465 W. St. Mary's Rd., Tucson, AZ 85702; (520) 792-1212; *tucsonchamber.org.*

**Greater Tucson Economic Council**, 33 Stone, Suite 800, Tucson, AZ 85701; (520) 882-6079; *www.futurewest.com.*

**City of Tucson Economic Development Department**, P.O. Box 27210, Tucson, AZ 85726-7210; (520) 791-5093; *www.ci.tucson.az.us/oed.*

## Other job markets

Job availability diminishes as you travel farther from the two metropolitan areas. However, some smaller communities still offer fairly good prospects—particularly in tourism and the service sector. If you want to avoid urban congestion, you might try some of the fast growing towns on the edge of the Valley of the Sun. What follows is a list of communities that offer average to better-than-average employment possibilities. You'll find more detail on these communities in Part Two. And again, you will note that most of these cities and towns are in the Valley of the Sun.

***Avondale*** • This is the largest of several small communities on the western rim of the Valley of the Sun, with about 40,500 residents. It occupies an area originally settled by the Goodyear Tire and Rubber Company in 1916. With major developments at nearby Phoenix-Goodyear Airport and firms such as Rubbermaid and Lockheed-Martin in the area, it offers rather good prospects. *For information: City of Avondale, 525 N. Central, Avondale, AZ 85223, (623) 932-6183, www.avondale.org; and Southwest Valley Chamber of Commerce, 289 N. Litchfield Rd., Goodyear, AZ 85338; (623) 932-2260; www.southwestvalleychamber.org.*

**Buckeye** • A small town of about 7,000, Buckeye is 30 miles west of Phoenix. The growing community is actively promoting light industry and there are several large manufacturing plants, plus new growth at the nearby Phoenix-Goodyear Airport. Its labor force jumped about 40 percent in the past ten years. *For information: Buckeye Valley Chamber of Commerce, 508 E. Monroe Ave., Buckeye, AZ 85326; (623) 386-2727, www.buckeyevalleychamber.org; and Town of Buckeye Planning & Economic Development, 100 N. Apache Rd., Buckeye, AZ 85326; (623) 386-4691.*

**Bullhead City** • Primarily a Snowbird community, Bullhead City sits across the Colorado River from Laughlin, Nevada, a fast-growing gaming center whose casinos and other services employ more than 14,000 people. And that's where most of the jobs are. Bullhead is a rather unlovely town, strung along the banks of the river, but it *is* growing, with a population topping 34,000. *For information: Bullhead Area Chamber of Commerce, 1251 Highway 95, Bullhead City, AZ 86429, (928) 754-4121; and Bullhead City Economic Development Authority, 1255 Marina Blvd., Bullhead City, AZ 86422-5733; (928) 763-9400, www.bullheadcity.com.*

**Casa Grande** • Midway between Tucson and Phoenix, this small city actively seeks light industry, and it has seen a 30 percent gain in its labor force in the past decade. Its population increased 33 percent from 1990 to 2000, now topping 25,000. *For information: City of Casa Grande Planning & Development Department, 510 E. Florence Blvd., Casa Grande, AZ 85222, (520) 421-8637, www.ci.casagrande.az.us; Greater Casa Grande Chamber of Commerce, 575 N. Marshall St., Casa Grande, AZ 85222-5244, (800) 916-1515 or (520) 836-2125, www.casagrandechamber.org; and Greater Casa Grande Valley Economic Development Foundation, 201 E. Third St., Casa Grande, AZ 85222, (520) 836-6868.*

**Chandler** • A growing city southeast of Phoenix, with a population topping 176,000, Chandler offers a broad-based job market. Space age firms such as Intel Corporation, Motorola, Microchip Technology and Space Data Corporation offer potential high tech jobs. Manufacturing accounts for one out of four jobs—one of the highest rates in the state. *For information: Chandler Chamber of Commerce, 25 S. Arizona Place, Suite 201, Chandler, AZ 85225, (480) 963-4571; and City of Chandler Economic Development Division, 215 E. Buffalo St., Chandler, AZ 85225, (480) 782-3030, www.chandleraz.org.*

**Flagstaff** • One of our favorite Arizona cities, this is a vibrant, growing community 70 miles south of the Grand Canyon and rimmed by ponderosa forests. It has experienced a 30 percent job growth in the past decade. Tourism, science, high tech manufacturing and education are leading industries in this town of 53,000. *For information: City of Flagstaff, 211 W. Aspen St., Flagstaff, AZ 86001; (928) 774-5281;*

*www.flagstaff.az.us; and Greater Flagstaff Economic Council, 1300 S. Milton Rd., S-125, Flagstaff, AZ 86001-6354; (928) 779-7658.*

**Gilbert** ● Half an hour southeast of Phoenix, this bedroom community was the fastest growing city in America in the decade of the eighties. It topped 109,000 in the 2000 census, with a single-decade gain of 277 percent. Most jobs are in manufacturing and a rapidly expanding retail base. It generally has one of Arizona's lowest unemployment rates. *For information: Gilbert Chamber of Commerce, P.O. Box 527, Gilbert, AZ 85299-0527, (480) 892-0056, www.gilbertaz.com; and Economic Development Department, Town of Gilbert, 1025 S. Gilbert Rd., Gilbert, AZ 85296, (480) 545-6865, www.gilbertaz.com.*

**Glendale** ● Northwest of Phoenix, Glendale is another fast growing city, with a population approaching 220,000. It has job opportunities in aerospace, communications, precision metal work, chemicals, electronics and warehousing. Nearby Luke Air Force Base offers potential civil service jobs. *For information: Glendale Chamber of Commerce, P.O. Box 249, Glendale, AZ 85311; (800) ID-SUNNY or (623) 937-4754 or Glendale Office of Tourism, 5800 W. Glenn Dr., Suite 140, Glendale, AZ 85301; (623) 930-4500; www.glendaleaz.com and www.ci.glendale.az.us.*

**Goodyear** ● Half an hour west of Phoenix, this small but growing community of about 23,000 has diversified from its role as a company town for the Goodyear aircraft facility. It has lured firms such as McKesson, McLane Sunwest, Rubbermaid, Southwest Specialty Foods and the Lockheed-Martin complex at Phoenix-Goodyear Airport. Its population has doubled in the past decade, with job availability increasing by more than 65 percent. For more information: City of Goodyear, 190 N. Litchfield Rd., Goodyear, AZ 85338, (623) 932-3025, www.ci.goodyear.az.us; Southwest Valley Chamber of Commerce, 289 N. Litchfield Rd., Goodyear, AZ 85338; (623) 932-2260; *www.southwestvalleychamber.org.*

**Kingman** ● It's a smaller version of Flagstaff, although in a lower desert altitude, and with a population of over 20,000. Its labor force has increased by nearly 30 percent in the past ten years. "Kingman has been very successful in job creation in manufacturing and distribution businesses, because of its key location (on I-80 near the California border) and its transportation infrastructure," according to a spokesman. *For information: Kingman 2005 Inc., 7000 Flightline Dr., Kingman, AZ 86401, (928) 757-2005; Kingman Area Chamber of Commerce, P.O. Box 1150, Kingman, AZ (928) 753-6253; and Economic & Tourism Development Commission, City of Kingman, 310 N. Fourth St., Kingman, AZ 86401; (928) 753-8130, www.ci.kingman.az.us.*

**Litchfield Park** ● With a population of about 4,000, this is a planned community sixteen miles west of Phoenix. Like neighboring Goodyear, it offers a growing base of light manufacturing and service jobs. Its employment base increased nearly 35 percent in the past ten

THE JOB-SEEKERS — 59

years. *For information:* City of Litchfield Park, 214 W. Wigwam Blvd., Litchfield Park, AZ 85340, (623) 935-5033, www.litchfieldpark.org; Southwest Valley Chamber of Commerce, 289 N. Litchfield Rd., Goodyear, AZ 85338; (623) 932-2260; www.southwestvalleychamber.org.

**Mesa** • East of Tempe and Phoenix, Mesa is a thriving community with a low unemployment rate and a broad economic base. It's Arizona's third largest city after Phoenix and Tucson, with a population nearing 400,000. Among major employers are Boeing Aircraft, General Motors Desert Proving Grounds, TRW Safety Systems and Motorola. *For information:* Mesa Chamber of Commerce, P.O. Box 5820 (120 N. Center St.), Mesa, AZ 85211-5820, (800) 283-6372 or (480) 827-4700, www.mesachamber.com; City of Mesa Economic Development, 100 N. Center, Mesa, AZ 85201; (800) 290-6372 or (480) 644-2398; and City of Mesa Planning Department, 55 N. Center St., Mesa AZ 85201; (480) 644-2185; www.ci.mesa.az.us.

**Peoria** • Just northwest of Glendale, Peoria is another growing Phoenix suburb. With a population topping 108,000, it offers employment potential in light manufacturing, the services industry and retailing. Nearly one job in four is in manufacturing. Also, one can commute to civil service work at Luke Air Force Base. *For information:* Peoria Chamber of Commerce, P.O. Box 70, Peoria, AZ 85380, (623) 979-3601, www.peopriachamber.com; City of Peoria, 8401 W. Monroe St., Peoria, AZ 85345, (623) 773-7300, www.peoriaaz.com; and Peoria Economic Development Group, Inc., 10601 N. 83rd Dr., Peoria, AZ 85345, (623) 486-2011.

**Prescott** • Handsomely situated in the pines of central Arizona, Prescott offers a mix of history (as the first territorial capital), culture and steady economic growth. The job base in this attractive town of 35,000 has increased more than 35 percent in the past ten years. Its economic mix includes mining, ranching, light manufacturing and education—with two small colleges and an aeronautical university. *For information:* Prescott Chamber of Commerce, P.O. Box 1147 (117 W. Goodwin St.), Prescott, AZ 86302, (928) 445-2000; and City of Prescott, P.O. Box 2059 (201 S. Cortez St.) Prescott, AZ 86302, (928) 445-3500, www.cityofprescott.net.

**Sierra Vista** • This is an Arizona surprise—a significant population center in the otherwise sparsely populated southeast. Located southeast of Tucson, with a population of approaching 40,000, it offers a mild climate and a relatively large employment base. Nearby Fort Huachuca Army base has nearly 12,000 military and civilian personnel. Sierra Vista itself is working to attract more light industry. It offers the best job potential in southeastern Arizona, and the work force has increased about ten percent in the past ten years. *For information:* Greater Sierra Vista Chamber of Commerce, 21 E. Wilcox Dr., Sierra Vista, AZ 85635; (800) 288-3861 or (520) 458-6940; www.sierravis-

*tachamber.org; Sierra Vista Economic Development Foundation, P.O. Box 2380, Sierra Vista, AZ 85636-2380, (520) 458-6948; and City of Sierra Vista, 1011 N. Coronado Dr., Sierra Vista, AZ 85635, (520) 458-3315, www.ci.sierra-vista.az.us.*

**Tempe ●** With a people count of nearly 160,000, Tempe is home to Arizona State University, the largest school in the state and one of the town's largest employers. Manufacturing provides about one in five Tempe jobs, with 200 companies producing electronics, clothing, processed foods, prefabricated housing and machine products. Tempe is considered the high tech capitol of Arizona, with 20 percent of the state's companies located within its borders. *For information: Tempe Chamber of Commerce, P.O. Box 28500, Tempe, AZ 85285-8500, (480) 967-7891; and City of Tempe Economic Development, 31 E. Fifth St., Tempe, AZ 85281, (480) 350-8036, www.tempe.gov.*

# WHAT THE JOBS ARE

Arizona's total non-farm labor force topped 2.25 million at last count, with the service industry providing nearly a third of the jobs. (That category includes lodging, business services and health services.) Wholesale and retail trades are second with 23.8 percent, with retail accounting for three-fourths of the jobs in this category. Federal, state and local governments are Arizona's third largest employer with 17.5 percent of the workforce. The balance of jobs go to manufacturing, 8.68 percent; construction, 6.7 percent; finance, insurance and real estate, 6.6 percent, transportation, communications and public utilities 4.7 percent; and mining, with a paltry .3 percent.

Although overall employment numbers look good, it's best to come to Arizona with a skill. Other than mining, there is very little heavy industry, so most of the unskilled jobs are in the service sector and agriculture. Mexican "guest workers" and resident Mexican nationals take most of the farm labor jobs.

The tourist industry absorbs a lot of folks—desk clerks, maids, culinary workers, waiters, tour guides and such. As in the rest of the world, however, most of these jobs pay little more than minimum wage. And much of the work is seasonal, with fall through spring as the peak tourist season in the sunbelt and summer in the north.

# THE MOST-NEEDED JOB SKILLS

According to the Arizona Department of Economic Security, these occupations offer the best employment potential, with annual growth rates of four percent or more. The list starts with those in highest demand:

| | |
|---|---|
| Computers support specialists | Telemarketing & direct sales |
| Computer engineers | Loan counselors & officers |
| Systems analysts | Adjustment clerks |
| Bill & account collectors | Mechanics & assistants |

Farm workers
Computer programmers
Sales agents
Engineers & systems managers
Counter clerks
Hand packers & packagers
Human & labor relations
Landscapers & groundskeepers
Office supervisors & managers
Accountants & auditors

Management support workers
Top managers and execs
Electricians
Assemblers & fabricators
Maintenance & repair,
  general utility
Cashiers
Para-professionals &
  technical workers
Unskilled laborers

## STARTING A BUSINESS

Perhaps you're interested in creating jobs instead of getting one. With its pro-growth attitude, Arizona is very supportive of individuals and corporations wanting to go into business.

If you want to set up shop, several publications are available, either in hard copy or on line:

*The Small Business Book* outlines steps for starting, developing and maintaining a business in the state. It's free, available from the Arizona Department of Commerce Business Assistance Center, 3800 N. Central Ave., Phoenix, AZ 85012; (602) 280-1480; *www.azcommerce.com.*

*Small Business Package* is a selection of pamphlets concerning Arizona business taxes and tax regulations. It's free from the Arizona Department of Revenue, Community Outreach Education, 1600 W. Monroe St., Phoenix., AZ 85007-2650; (602) 542-3062; *www.revenue.state.az.us.*

*Smart Start Your Arizona Business* is a detailed 300-page guide to planning, starting and running a business in Arizona. It's available for a fee from the Phoenix Chamber of Commerce, 201 N. Central Ave., 27th floor, Phoenix, AZ 85073; (602) 254-5521; *www.phoenixchamber.com.*

For information on business licenses and taxes, contact the **Arizona Department of Revenue,** 1600 W. Monroe St., Phoenix, AZ 85007; (602) 255-1112.

If you want to incorporate, contact the office of the **Secretary of State,** 1700 W. Washington St., Phoenix, AZ 85007, (602) 542-4285; or 400 W. Congress St., Suite 504, Tucson, AZ 85701, (520) 628-6583. For specific requirements on incorporation, check with the **Arizona Corporation Commission,** 1200 & 1300 W. Washington St., Phoenix, AZ 85007, (602) 542-3076.

A particularly useful organization for new businesses is the **Arizona Small Business Association,** 4130 E. Van Buren St., Phoenix, AZ 85008; (602) 265-4563. It's a nonprofit group set up to assist small business owners. Among its services are legislative representation, group medical and dental plans, a credit union and a group legal and accounting referral plan.

## Types of businesses

What business to start? Restaurants are the most common new businesses in the state, although they also have the highest failure rate. In a growing state, there's obviously room for new construction and contracting firms, housing developers, mortgage companies and real estate firms. Surveys show that these are among the businesses most in demand:

| | |
|---|---|
| Accounting firms | Insurance agencies |
| Attorneys | Investment firms |
| Auto dealers (new and used) | Laundries and dry cleaners |
| Beauty parlors | Management consulting firms |
| Clothing stores | Mortgage companies |
| Computer stores | Physicians |
| Furniture stores | Printers and copy shops |
| General contractors | Real estate companies |
| Housing developers | |

# LICENSED OCCUPATIONS

Many professions require licensing or certification in Arizona. Some may have reciprocity with other states; check this out before starting your job hunt. Two state agencies that post state licensing requirements and procedures on the internet are the **Arizona Department of Revenue** (*www.revenue.state.az.us/license/subject.htm*) and the **State of Arizona Overseeing Boards** (www.state.az.us/licensing/html)

These are the agencies that oversee state regulated occupations:

*Accounting* • Arizona State Board of Accountancy, 3877 N. Seventh St., Suite 109, Phoenix, AZ 85014; (602) 255-3648.

*Architect* • Arizona State Board of Technical Registration, 1951 W. Camelback Rd., Suite 406, Phoenix, AZ 85015; (602) 255-4053.

*Assayer* • Arizona State Board of Technical Registration, 1951 W. Camelback Rd., Suite 406, Phoenix, AZ 85015; (602) 255-4053.

*Attorney* • Executive Director, State Bar of Arizona, 111 W. Monroe St., Phoenix, AZ 85003; (602) 252-4804.

*Auctioneer* • License and Registration Section, Department of Revenue, 1600 W. Monroe St., Phoenix, AZ 85007; (602) 542-4576.

*Aviation* • (commercial pilots, flight instructors, crop-dusters, aviation mechanics, etc.) Federal Aviation Administration, Flight Standards Office, 15041 N. Airport Dr., Scottsdale, AZ 85260; (480) 419-0111.

*Bail bondsman* • Department of Insurance, 2910 N. 44th St., Suite 210, Phoenix, AZ 85018; (602) 912-8470.

*Boxer or wrestler* • Arizona State Boxing Commission, 1400 W. Washington St., Phoenix, AZ 85007; (602) 542-1417.

*Barber* • Arizona Board of Barbers, 1400 W. Washington St., Phoenix, AZ 85007; (602) 542-4498.

**Behavioral health** • Board of Behavioral Health Examiners, 1400 W. Washington St., Suite 350, Phoenix, AZ 85007; (602) 542-1882.

**Chauffeur** • Motor Vehicle Division, Department of Transportation, 1801 W. Jefferson St., Phoenix, AZ 85007; (602) 255-0072.

**Chiropractor** • Board of Chiropractic Examiners, 5060 N. 19th Ave., Room 416, Phoenix, AZ 85015; (602) 255-1444.

**Collection agent** • State Banking Department, 2910 N. 44th St., Suite 310, Phoenix, AZ 85018; (602) 255-4421.

**Contractor** • Registrar of Contractors, 800 W. Washington St., Phoenix, AZ 85007, (602) 542-1525.

**Cosmetologist** • (including manicurist and hairdresser) Board of Cosmetology, 1721 E. Broadway, Tempe, AZ 85282; (408) 784-4539.

**Dentist and dental hygienist** • Board of Dental Examiners, 5060 N. 19th Ave., Suite 406, Phoenix, AZ 85015; (602) 242-1492.

**Driving instructor** *(private)* • Motor Vehicle Division, Department of Transportation, 1801 W. Jefferson St., Phoenix, AZ 85007; (602) 255-0072.

**Driving instructor** *(high school)* • Teachers Certification Office, State Board of Education, 1535 W. Jefferson St., Room 126, Phoenix, AZ 85007; (602) 542-4367.

**Emergency medical technician** • Emergency Medical Services, Arizona Department of Health Services, 1647 E. Morten St., Suite 110, Phoenix, AZ 85020; (602) 861-0708.

**Engineer** • Arizona State Board of Technical Registration, 1951 W. Camelback Rd., Suite 406, Phoenix, AZ 85015; (602) 255-4053.

**Escrow agent and mortgage broker** • Department of Insurance, 2910 N. 44th St., Suite 210, Phoenix, AZ 85018; (602) 912-8470.

**Funeral director and embalmer** • Board of Funeral Directors and Embalmers, 1645 W. Jefferson St., Phoenix, AZ 85007; (602) 542-3095.

**Geologist** • Arizona State Board of Technical Registration, 1951 W. Camelback Rd., Suite 406, Phoenix, AZ 85015; (602) 255-4053.

**Home inspector** • Arizona State Board of Technical Registration, 1951 W. Camelback Rd., Suite 406, Phoenix, AZ 85015; (602) 255-4053.

**Homeopathic medicine practitioner** • Board of Homeopathic Medical Examiners, 1400 W. Washington St., Phoenix, AZ 85007; (602) 542-3095.

**Insurance agent** • (also broker and adjustor) Department of Insurance, 2910 N. 44th St., Suite 210, Phoenix, AZ 85018; (602) 912-8470.

**Midwife** • Office of Maternal and Child Health, Arizona Department of Health Services, 1647 E. Morten St., Suite 110, Phoenix, AZ 85020; (602) 542-1000.

**Landscape architect** • Arizona State Board of Technical Registration, 1951 W. Camelback Rd., Suite 406, Phoenix, AZ 85015; (602) 255-4053.

**Naturopath** • Naturopathic Physicians Board of Medical Examiners, 1400 W. Washington St., Phoenix, AZ 85007; (602) 542-8242.

**Notary public** • Secretary of State, 1700 W. Washington St., Phoenix, AZ 85007; (602) 255-4285.

**Nurse** • Arizona State Board of Nursing, 1651 E. Morten Ave., Phoenix, AZ 85020; (602) 331-8111.

**Nursing care administrator** • Board of Administrators, Nursing Care Institution, 1400 W. Washington St., Phoenix, AZ 85007; (602) 542-3095.

**Occupational therapist** • Occupational Therapy Examiners Board, 1400 W. Washington St., Phoenix, AZ 85007; (602) 589-8352.

**Optician** • (including opthamologist and optometrist) Board of Dispensing Opticians, 1400 W. Washington St., Phoenix, AZ 85007; (602) 542-3095.

**Osteopath** • Arizona Board of Osteopathic Examiners, 9535 E. Doubletree Ranch Rd., Scottsdale, AZ 85258; (480) 657-7703.

**Pawnbroker** • License and Registration Division, Department of Revenue, 1600 W. Monroe St., Phoenix, AZ 85007; (602) 542-4576.

**Pest control** *(agricultural)* • Arizona Department of Agriculture, 1688 W. Adams St., Phoenix, AZ 85007; (602) 542-4373.

**Pest control** *(structural)* • Structural Pest Control Commission, 9545 E. Doubletree Ranch Rd., Scottsdale AZ 85258-5514; (602) 255-3664.

**Pharmacist** • State Board of Pharmacy, 4425 W. Olive Ave., Glendale, AZ 85302; (623) 463-2727.

**Physician and surgeon** • State Board of Medical Examiners, 9545 E. Doubletree Ranch Rd., Scottsdale, AZ 85258; mailing address P.O. Box 6299, Scottsdale, AZ 85261; (480) 551-2700; *www.azdocinfo.com.*

**Physical therapist** • State Board of Physical Therapy, 1400 W. Washington St., Suite 230, Phoenix, AZ 85007; (602) 542-3095.

**Physicians assistant** • State Board of Medical Examiners, 9545 E. Doubletree Ranch Rd., Scottsdale, AZ 85258; mailing address P.O. Box 6299, Scottsdale, AZ 85261; (480) 551-2700; *www.azdocinfo.com.*

**Podiatrist** • Board of Podiatry Examiners, 1400 W. Washington St., Suite 230, Phoenix, AZ 85007; (602) 542-3095.

**Private investigator and polygraph examiner** • Department of Public Safety, 2102 W. Encanto Blvd., Phoenix, AZ 85009; (602) 223-2361.

**Psychologist** • Board of Psychologist Examiners, 1400 W. Washington St., Suite 235, Phoenix, AZ 85007; (602) 542-8162.

**Racetrack worker** • Arizona Department of Racing, 3877 N. Seventh St., Phoenix, AZ 85014; (602) 277-1704.

**Radiology worker** • Medical Radiologic Technology Board of Examiners, 4814 S. 40th St., Phoenix, AZ 85040; (602) 255-4845.

**Real estate broker and agent** • Department of Real Estate, 2910 N. 44th St., Phoenix, AZ 85018; (602) 468-1414.

***Respiratory therapist*** • Arizona Board of Respiratory Care Examiners, 1400 W. Washington St., Phoenix, AZ 85007; (602) 542-5995.

***Sanitation worker*** • Arizona Department of Environmental Quality, 3033 N. Central Ave., Phoenix, AZ 85012; (602) 257-2300.

***Securities dealer*** • Securities Division, Arizona Corporation Commission, 1300 W. Washington St., Third Floor, Phoenix, AZ 85007, (602) 542-4242.

***Security guard*** • Department of Public Safety, 2102 W. Encanto Blvd., Phoenix, AZ 85009; (602) 223-2361.

***Surveyor and assayer*** • Arizona Board of Technical Registration, 1951 W. Camelback Rd., #406, Phoenix, AZ 85015; (602) 225-4053.

***Teacher*** *(community college)* • Community College Board, 2020 N. Central Avenue, Phoenix, AZ 85004; (602) 255-5582.

***Teacher*** *(elementary and high school)* • Teachers Certification Office, State Board of Education, 1535 W. Jefferson St., Room 126, Phoenix, AZ 85007; (602) 542-4367.

***Travel agent*** • Department of Insurance, 2910 N. 44th St., Suite 210, Phoenix, AZ 85018; (602) 912-8470.

***Veterinarian and veterinary technician*** • Veterinary Medical Examining Board, 1400 W. Washington St., Phoenix, AZ 85007; (602) 542-3095.

***Weighmaster*** • State Department of Weights and Measures, 9535 E. Doubletree Ranch Rd., Scottsdale, AZ 85258; (480) 255-5211.

***Well driller*** • Department of Water Resources, 500 N. Third St., Phoenix, AZ 85004; (602) 417-2400.

# TRADE & PROFESSIONAL ORGANIZATIONS

For union locals, check the Yellow Pages of various communities under "labor organizations."

***Accounting*** • Arizona Society of Certified Public Accountants, 2120 N. Central Ave., Phoenix, AZ 85004; (602) 252-4144.

Arizona Society of Practicing Accountants, 1646 S. Villas Lane, Chandler, AZ 85248; (480) 782-8872.

***Advertising, public relations & marketing*** • American Marketing Association, 1051 E. Camelback Rd., Phoenix, AZ 85014; (602) 265-1161.

Public Relations Society of America, 200 W. Washington St., Phoenix, AZ 85003; (602) 258-7772.

***Architects*** • American Institute of Architects, 1 N. 12th St., Phoenix, AZ 85034; (602) 252-4200.

***Banking and finance*** • American Institute of Banking, 201 N. Central Ave., Phoenix, AZ 85004; (602) 258-1200.

Arizona Bankers Association, 2001 N. Third St., Phoenix, AZ 85005; (602) 222-5717.

Arizona Credit Union League, Inc., 3611 N. Black Canyon Hwy., Phoenix, AZ 85015; (602) 264-6701.

Arizona Mortgage Lenders Association, 15770 N. Greenway Hayden Loop, Scottsdale, AZ 85260; (480) 348-7488.

**Construction trades** • Arizona Concrete Contractors Association, 916 W. Adams St., Phoenix, AZ 85007; (602) 631-4083.

Arizona Contractors Association, 5701 N. Black Canyon Hwy., Phoenix, AZ 85015; (602) 246-8627.

Arizona Masonry Contractors Association, 1610 W. Encanto Blvd., Phoenix, AZ 85007; (602) 262-0510.

Arizona Roofing Contractors Association, 5033 N. 19th Ave., Phoenix, AZ 85015; (602) 335-0133.

Arizona Subcontractors Association, 3030 N. Third St., Phoenix, AZ 85012; (602) 241-8566.

Associated General Contractors of America, 1825 W. Adams St., Phoenix, AZ 85007, (602) 274-8222.

District Council of Carpenters, 1401 N. 29th Ave., Phoenix, AZ 85009; (602) 272-2700.

Home Builders Association of Central Arizona, 3200 E. Camelback Rd., AZ 85018; (602) 274-6545.

National Electrical Contractors Association, 4315 N. 12th St., Phoenix, AZ 85014; (602) 263-0111.

**Cosmetology** • American Association of Cosmetology, 15825 N. 71st St., Scottsdale, AZ 85254; (480) 281-0431.

**Education** • Arizona Association of School Business Officials, 2100 N. Central Ave., Phoenix, AZ 85004; (602) 253-5576.

Arizona Community College Association, 2411 W. 14th St., Tempe, AZ 85281; (480) 731-8116.

Arizona Education Association, 100 W. Clarendon Ave., Phoenix, AZ 85013; (602) 264-1774.

Arizona Private School Association, 202 E. McDowell Rd., Phoenix, AZ 85004; (602) 254-5199.

Arizona School Administrators, 2526 W. Osborn Rd., Phoenix, AZ 85017; (602) 252-0361.

Arizona School Board Association, 2100 N. Central Ave., Phoenix, AZ 85004; (602) 254-1100.

Arizona State Professional Educators, 1424 E. Stapely Dr., Mesa, AZ 85204; (480) 503-2737.

**Engineering** • Arizona Consulting Engineers Association, 1309 E. Echo Lane, Phoenix, AZ 85020; (602) 995-2187.

Arizona Society of Professional Engineers, 1309 E. Echo Lane, Phoenix, AZ 85020; (602) 995-2187.

Structural Engineers Association of Arizona, 17149 E. Kensington Place, Fountain Hills, AZ 82628; (480) 816-4797.

**Farming & ranching** • Arizona Cattlemen's Association, 1401 N. 21 St., Phoenix, AZ 85003; (602) 267-1129.

Arizona Cotton Growers Association, 4139 E. Broadway Rd., Phoenix, AZ 85040; (602) 437-1344.

**Financial services** ● American Society of Appraisers, 3134 E. Camelback Rd., Phoenix, AZ 85016; (602) 265-5001.

Society of Financial Service Professionals, (480) 991-5151.

**Flight attendants** ● Association of Flight Attendants, 505 S. 48th St., Tempe, AZ 85281; (480) 966-1231.

**Guides and outfitters** ● Arizona Guide Association, (480) 425-9001.

**Health care** ● Arizona Association of Chiropractic, 5060 N. 19th Ave., Phoenix, AZ 85015; (602) 246-0664.

Arizona Association of Midwives, Phoenix; (602) 942-0900.

Arizona Dental Association, 4131 N. 36th St., Phoenix, AZ 85018; (602) 957-4777.

Arizona Health Care Association, 5020 N. H Place, Suite A, Phoenix, AZ 85014; (602) 265-5331.

Arizona Hospital and Healthcare Association, 2901 N. Central Ave., Phoenix, AZ 85012; (602) 445-4300.

Arizona Medical Association, 810 W. Bethany Home Rd., Phoenix, AZ 85013; (602) 870-0053.

Arizona Naturopathic Medical Association, Phoenix; (602) 237-7353.

Arizona Nurses Association, 1815 E. Southern Ave., Tempe, AZ 85282; (480) 831-0404.

Arizona Optometric Association, 3625 N. 16th St., Suite 119, Phoenix, AZ 85016; (602) 279-0055.

Arizona Osteopathic Medical Association, 5150 N. 16th St., Phoenix, AZ 85015; (602) 266-6699.

Arizona Pharmacy Association, 1845 E. Southern Ave., Tempe, AZ 85282; (480) 838-3385.

Arizona Physical Therapy Association, Phoenix, (602) 912-5310.

Arizona Psychological Association, 6210 E. Thomas Rd., Phoenix, AZ 85251; (602) 675-9477.

Arizona Public Health Association, 4001 N. Third St., Phoenix, AZ 850121 (602) 631-6562.

Arizona Society of Anesthesiologists, 810 W. Bethany Home Rd., Phoenix, AZ 85013; (602) 347-6900.

Arizona Society of Medical Assistants, Phoenix; (602) 843-1959.

Arizona Society of Pathologists, 810 Bethany Home Rd., Phoenix, AZ 85013; (602) 347-6900.

Arizona State Dental Hygienists Association, Phoenix; (602) 254-7210.

Arizona State Physicians' Association, 3002 N. Central Ave., Phoenix, AZ 85012; (602) 265-2524.

Arizona State Society of Radiological Technologists, P.O. Box 3013, Scottsdale, AZ 85271; (480) 946-3092.

National Association of Independent Nurses, 3901 S. Farmer Ave., Tempe, AZ 856282; (480) 557-9020.

***Home care*** • Arizona Association for Home Care, 2334 S. McClintock Dr., Tempe, AZ 85282; (480) 967-2624.

***Hotels and motels*** • Arizona Hotel and Motel Association, 1240 E. Missouri Ave., Phoenix, AZ 85014; (602) 604-0729.

***Insurance*** • Arizona Association of Health Underwriters, 7225 W. Oakland St., Chandler, AZ 855226; (480) 4010.

Arizona Association of Insurance Agents & Brokers, Inc., 2828 N. 36th St., Phoenix, AZ 85008; (602) 468-1392.

Arizona Association of Life Underwriters, 11655 N. 109th St., Scottsdale, AZ 85259; (480) 661-6393.

***Interior design*** • American Institute of Interior Design, 16855 E. Parkview Ave., Fountain Hills, AZ 85269; (480) 946-9601.

American Society of Interior Designers, Phoenix; (602) 569-8916.

***Jewelers*** • Arizona Jewelers Association, Phoenix; (602) 254-3328.

***Legal services*** • Arizona Court Reporters Association, 7225 W. Oakland St., Chandler, AZ 85226; (480) 496-4010.

State Bar of Arizona, 111 W. Monroe St., Phoenix, AZ 85003; (602) 252-4804.

***Media*** • Arizona Book Publishers Association, Phoenix; (602) 274-6264.

Arizona Broadcasters Association, 2302 N. Third St., Phoenix, AZ 85004; (602) 252-4833.

Arizona Newspapers Association, 1001 N. Central Ave., Phoenix AZ 85004; (602) 261-7655.

National Academy of TV Arts & Sciences, 1131 W. Citrus Grove, Avondale, AZ 85323; (623) 872-8302.

***Real estate and property management*** • Arizona Association of Realtors, 255 E. Osborn Rd., Phoenix, AZ 85012; (602) 248-7787.

Building Owners and Managers Association, 4745 N. Seventh St., Phoenix, AZ 85014; (602) 200-3898.

Phoenix Association of Realtors, 5033 N. 19th Ave., Phoenix, AZ 85015; (602) 246-1012.

Tucson Association of Realtors, 1622 N. Swan Rd., Tucson, AZ 85712; (520) 327-4218.

***Restaurants*** • Arizona Restaurant Association, 2400 N. Central Ave., Phoenix, AZ 85004; (602) 307-9134.

***Retail and wholesale*** • Arizona Retailers Association, 224 W. Second St., Mesa, AZ 85201; (480) 833-0009.

National Association of Purchasing Management, 2055 E. Centennial Circle, Tempe, AZ 8585284; (480) 752-6276.

National Association of Sales Professionals, (480) 951-4311.

***Senior care*** • Arizona Association of Homes for the Aging, 3839 N. Third St., Phoenix, AZ 85012; (602) 230-0026.

***Small businesses*** • Arizona Small Business Association, 4130 E. Van Buren St., Phoenix, AZ 85008; (602) 265-4563.

National Association of the Self Employed, 4600 S. Mill Ave., Tempe, AZ 85282; (480) 839-8404.

**Social workers** • National Association of Social Workers, 1050 E. Southern Ave., Tempe, AZ 865282; (480) 968-4595.

**Solar energy** • Arizona Solar Energy Industries Association, 2034 N. 13th St., Phoenix, AZ 85006; (602) 253-8180.

**Travel Agents** • American Society of Travel Agents, 7001 E. Main St., Scottsdale, AZ 85251; (480) 947-8614.

**Trucking** • Arizona Motor Transport Association, 2111 W. McDowell Rd., Phoenix, AZ 85009; (602) 252-7559.

**Veterinarians** • Arizona Veterinary Medical Association, 5502 N. 19th Ave., Phoenix, AZ 85015; (602) 242-7936.

**Women's professional groups** • American Association of University Women, 8139 E. Via del Sol Dr., Scottsdale, AZ 85255; (480) 585-6003.

National Association of Women Business Owners, 7225 W. Oakland St., Chandler, AZ 85226; (480) 496-5755.

National Association of Women in Construction, 5060 N. 19th Ave., Phoenix, AZ 85015; (602) 841-7900.

# HOW TO LAND THAT JOB

The day after I graduated from a small rural high school in Idaho, I hit the road, seeking fortune, if not fame. With only a high school diploma and no specific skills, I found neither. However, I did find out how to get a job. After wandering around the western states for several months, I took shelter at the home of a favorite uncle in southern Oregon. I was broke and needed work.

Uncle Clark took me to a pear packing shed and asked the foreman if he could use a hard-working, skinny 17-year-old kid. Unfortunately, all the jobs were taken. My uncle then pointed to a stack of pallets.

"I'm gonna sit this kid over there," he told the foreman. "Sooner or later, one of your crew will get mad and quit, or he'll get lazy and you'll fire him. And when that happens, here's his replacement."

I was put to work shortly after lunch.

My point is simple. To find a job, go where the jobs are. Direct contact with a prospective employer is the best way to get work, whether you're looking for something glamorous, highly skilled or mundane. I realize that my pear packing plant experience is a bit simplistic. You'll want to be more professional than that—developing a list of prospective companies, finding out who to contact, and then making appointments to see them.

Even with today's emphasis on college degrees and vocational skills, prospective employers still admire job-seekers with drive and spunk. It suggests that they'll be enterprising and hard working once they're hired. If two people are equally qualified for a position, the one who makes a good personal appearance—and shows a bit of grit—usually gains the edge.

## The key is timing

Also, there's the advantage of timing. If you wait until a job opening is posted on the internet or placed in the want-ads, several people will have applied by the time you send in your resume. However, if you canvas the industry with resumes, and then follow up with phone calls and personal visits, you just might wind up in the right place at the right time.

That's how it worked after I'd gone from pear packing to a stint in the Marine Corps to newspaper reporting. When I decided I was ready to advance to a better job, I'd write to every newspaper in the area where I was interested in working. I'd include a resume and cover letter saying that I'd be in the area in a few days. Then I'd follow up with a phone call, asking if I could make an appointment—at a time convenient for the editor, of course.

A couple of times, I got a job almost before an editor knew he had an opening.

According to a job-finding book called *The Phoenix Job Bank,* job-seekers who use direct contact are twice as successful as those who rely on the want-ads, the internet or an employment agency.

That isn't to suggest that you should ignore those other sources. The best approach is to employ all of them. Incidentally, the Sunday edition of a newspaper generally has the most help wanted ads. Also, some trade and professional organizations offer employment services for their members.

## Finding prospective employers

But how do you determine which employers to contact? Several resources are available to you. Trade and professional groups and unions may have lists of affiliated companies. The internet is becoming a major job-hunting source; see above on page 55.

Also, the *Phoenix Job Bank,* the book we mentioned above, is particularly useful. To get a copy, check the nearest bookstore, or contact Adams Media Corp., 260 Center St., Holbrook, MA 02343; (800) 872-5627; *www.careercity.com.*

Also useful is Phoenix *Business Journal's* **Book of Lists,** which lists many of the city's largest firms. For pricing and shipping information, contact *The Business Journal,* 3030 N. Central Ave., Phoenix, AZ 85012; (602) 230-8400.

And as we mentioned above, try the good old Yellow Pages. To order phone directories, call (800) 422-8793; *www.qwestdex.com.*

You'll find addresses but not all ZIP codes in the phone books, so pick up a copy of the *U.S. Postal Service Zip Code Directory* for complete mailing addresses. They're available for a modest fee from any post office. The directory comes in two volumes and Arizona cities are listed in Volume One.

### The news source

Other possible sources are the business pages of local newspapers. You may encounter stories about businesses that are expanding, have a product breakthrough or are opening branches—all strong indicators of potential jobs. Further, companies on a major hiring binge may place a display ad in the business section instead of using the classified section.

Generally, you can find daily newspapers of major cities in the reference department of the library. The state's major dailies are the *Arizona Republic* in Phoenix, (602) 444-1000, *www.azcentral.com*; the *Tucson Citizen* and *Arizona Daily Star* in Tucson, both (800) 695-4492 or (520) 573-4511, *www.tucson-newspapers.com*; and the *Arizona Daily Sun* in Flagstaff, (520) 774-4545. Phoenix Newspapers, Inc., publishers of the *Arizona Republic,* also issues the weekly *Arizona Business Journal.* Territorial Newspapers in Tucson publishes *Inside Tucson Business,* (520) 294-1200; *www.azbiz.com.*

Other city newspapers are listed in the communities section of Part Two, chapters eight through eleven.

Once you've compiled a list of prospective employers, narrow it down to the firms that interest you, and those most likely to be hiring. Next, find out who to contact. A simple phone call to the company personnel department should work. Never send a job query without addressing it to a specific person. If you do, it'll likely end up in the wastebasket with the rest of the junk mail.

# COVER LETTERS AND RESUMES

Now, armed with a list of companies and a contact at each, prepare your cover letter and resume. Both should be brief, yet complete, convincing and to the point. Don't give a busy personnel manager or foreman too much to read. And don't use corporate doublespeak, redundancy and verbosity. Write about yourself confidently without sounding pompous. Don't brag; let the facts of your background make your case. And avoid clichés like the plague.

Neat appearing resumes can be produced at a copy shop, although the cover letter should be personalized. This doesn't mean that each individual letter must be painfully pecked out by hand on your trusty L.C. Smith typewriter. If you have access to a computer with a word processing program, you can use the automatic mail merging feature that allows you to personalize a mass-produced letter.

If you don't own a computer with word processing software or if you're a hack typist, some copy shops will provide personalized multiple mailing service. Also, many firms specialize in preparing and producing resumes and cover letters.

Above all else, neatness counts. From the look of your cover letter to the style of your tie and the shine on your shoes when you appear for an interview, you will be judged by appearance. When you go in for an interview, you go in as a stranger. Your prospective employer can evaluate you only by the facts you present and the way you present yourself.

A well organized presentation and neat personal appearance suggest a competent, organized individual. In reality of course, this isn't always true. In the writing business, it tends to be the exception. Some of the best, most creative and ambitious writers and photographers I've known usually came to work looking as if they'd just fallen out of bed. (Some probably had.) Still, the reality is that first impressions are extremely important. Get the job and prove your worth before revealing your penchant for grooming yourself like a Neanderthal.

## Writing a cover letter

Experts disagree on the style and content of cover letters and resumes. In reality, there is no best style, since the personalities of the recipients differ. Some personnel managers get off on symphonic prose that oozes buzz words and corporate jargon. Others are no-nonsense types who want you to present your case directly and precisely. One point upon which they all agree: Say positive things about the company; leave the impression that you *want* to work for such an outstanding firm!

I've found that a simple, to-the-point style works best. Save the details and adjectives for the job interview.

Here's a final tip: In your letter, write as if you know the territory. It suggests that you've done your homework; that you've studied up on your future hometown. Use words and phrases familiar to locals, such as "Valley of the Sun" instead of "Phoenix and vicinity." However, don't overdo it. Only guidebook authors are supposed to say "the glorious Grand Canyon state."

## Writing a resume

Like cover letters, resumes can have a variety of styles, as long as they're simple and to the point. If the job you seek is skill-intensive, the resume should emphasize your qualifications and work experience. If you're seeking management opportunities, a chronological resume would be the most effective, showing how you've worked up through the ranks. If you're just starting out, the resume should stress your educational accomplishments, preparedness for the particular kind of work and your career goals. On any resume, toss in a little "Mister Good Citizen" community service stuff.

Although some resume writers disagree, I prefer to give a reason for leaving each job—a positive reason, obviously. On the pages that follow are a sample cover letter, and the kind of resume I'd write if I were applying for work at *DISCOVERGUIDES,* and my wife and I didn't already own the company.

# SAMPLE COVER LETTER

Robin R. Righteous
1494 Confidence Lane
North Chicago, IL 60064
Phone (708) 123-4567

January 14, 2004

Scrooge McTaxbite, Personnel Manager
Moneygrub and Nickelsqueeze, Inc.
1010 Taxshelter Way
Phoenix, AZ 85007

Dear Mr. McTaxbite:

After several years as an accountant with a major Chicago firm, I have decided to move my family to the Valley of the Sun. My research tells me that Moneygrub and Nickelsqueeze is one of Arizona's more aggressive and successful accounting firms. And that's the kind of company I'm seeking.

You will note in my enclosed resume that I have considerable experience in tax accounting, payroll, slush fund concealment and money laundering. These are skills that can be useful in your operation. I thrive in a competitive work environment and I'm seeking the kind of challenge offered by an aggressive company in a growing state such as Arizona.

I'm coming to your area in early March. Can we set up an appointment to discuss job possibilities? You can contact me at the above phone number and address.

Thank you for your attention.

*Robin R. Righteous*
Robin R. Righteous

# SAMPLE RESUME

Don W. Martin
1649 Dust Devil Drive
Las Vegas, NV 89123
(702) 123-4567
E-mail: donmartin@discoverguides.com

## _PROFESSIONAL EXPERIENCE_

**April 1988 to present:** Founder and co-owner (with my wife) of Pine Cone Press, later re-named _DISCOVERGUIDES_. Using the motto of "Remarkably useful guidebooks," we research, write and publish regional travel guides. We currently have more than twenty on the market, with total sales exceeding 300,000. Primary subjects are travel and wine appreciation, plus relocation guides for Arizona and Nevada. I do much of the research and writing, and work with my wife in planning, editing, designing and producing the books.

**March 1979 to March 1988:** Associate editor of _Motorland_, the travel magazine of the California State Automobile Association. I was responsible for much of the editorial operation, working with staff writers and editorial assistants in planning, writing and editing copy. Also researched and wrote travel stories, along with articles on traffic safety, anti-smog programs and other auto-related technical subjects. Left to start my own publishing company.

**March 1978 to February 1979:** Managing editor of the Petaluma (California) _Argus-Courier_, a small daily newspaper north of San Francisco. Directed a news, sports, society and photo staff of eight. I was responsible for the planning and layout of the newspaper, and I wrote some copy. Left to accept travel magazine job.

**June 1963 to February 1977:** Staff member of the Oxnard _Press-Courier_, a mid-sized daily newspaper in southern California. Began as a copy editor on the city desk, then spent four years as editor of the Sunday feature magazine and daily entertainment page. Left to accept the challenge of newspaper management.

**May 1960 to May 1963:** Various editorial posts on the Oceanside _Blade-Tribune_, a small daily newspaper in southern California. Began as a police beat reporter, then was promoted to assistant sports editor, then copy editor and editorial page editor. Left to accept a post on a larger newspaper.

**Other employment: 1950 to 1960:** Began my career as a printer's devil for the weekly Wilder (Idaho) _Herald_ at age sixteen, while still in high school; also was editor of the high school newspaper. Served in the Marine Corps Public Information Service as an editor of several base newspapers and as a correspondent in Korea, Japan and Taiwan.

**Related experience:** I have sold dozens of freelance articles and photos to newspapers and magazines.

## PROFESSIONAL SKILLS

Familiar with Word Perfect, WordStar and Ventura 7 desktop publishing. Comfortable with computers and can surf the Internet with ease. Proficient with professional-level 35mm cameras.

## EDUCATION

Wilder (Idaho) High School, graduated in 1951.
Naval Journalists' School, Great Lakes, Ill., graduated in 1956.
Have taken several college courses in English, journalism, political science and history.

## AWARDS AND COMMUNITY SERVICE

Winner of a Lowell Thomas Travel Journalism Gold Medal for "Best Guidebook of the Year" in 2000.
Member of the Society of American Travel Writers.
Four photo layouts prepared by myself and my photographer at the Oxnard *Press-Courier* won California Press Photographers Association awards.
Was awarded the Ventura County (California) Diane Seeley Award for promoting the performing arts.
Served as founding president of the Ventura County Theater Council and as a board member of the Ventura County Forum of the Arts.
Former member of the Petaluma (California) Kiwanis Club and Daly City (California) Junior Chamber of Commerce.
Won two Department of Defense awards and one Marine Corps Journalism Award for excellence in editing military newspapers.

## PERSONAL INFORMATION

In excellent health and a non-smoker. Married to Betty Woo Martin, co-owner of *DISCOVERGUIDES* and former pharmacist and real estate broker. No children at home and free to travel.
Born April 22, 1934, in Grants Pass, Oregon.
Listed in Marquis' *Who's Who in the World, Who's Who in America* and *Who's Who in the West*.
Listed in *Gale's Contemporary Authors*.

## REFERENCES

Personal and professional references available on request.

## Chapter Six

# THE RETIREES
## A PLACE UNDER ARIZONA'S SUN

**W**e recently saw a television commercial in which an older man was enjoying activities with his grandson. At one point, the youngster—maybe five or six—looks at him quizzically and asks: "Grandpa, don't you ever work?"

Oddly, we can't remember what the commercial was selling, although it reflects a growing trend in America. Contrary to some stereotypes, most retired folks aren't spending their golden years in a home for the aged, or sitting in a creaking rocking chair on the front porch.

Many of them are upbeat, active people who have saved their money and perhaps paid off their homes. They look forward to some of the best years of their lives. If you're reading this chapter, perhaps you're one of these active seniors.

Our average life expectancy is approaching 70 for men and 75 for women. And for people who have achieved age 60, it's considerably higher—into the 80s. More than 30 million Americans are now retired and that number is increasing dramatically as the Baby Boomers, children born between 1946 and 1966, reach retirement age. Statistics reveal that one third of all living Americans were born during that period. Further, many people are retiring at a younger age, adding more numbers to these growing ranks. (However, this trend may reverse as the qualifying age for drawing Social Security benefits is advanced to help save that heavily impacted system.)

With the current emphasis on physical fitness and the decrease in heart attack rates, many older people today are healthier than their parents. This despite the growing popularity of junky fast foods and the fact that more than half of all American adults are overweight! Many of those, of course, don't make it to retirement age.

We are creating a new socio-economic order—a legion of people who retire earlier and live longer. Some spend as many years in retirement as they did raising their families. A recent survey indicated that more than 70 percent of retirees feel that they are secure economically. This security leads to disposable income and mobility. And that leads us into this chapter of *Arizona in Your Future*.

Today's seniors are less inclined to keep the old family roost after the last kid has flown the coop and the dog has died. Further, the kids tend to scatter more, leaving their home towns in search of greener pastures and greener paychecks, so parents don't feel the need to maintain a family base.

Since the brood has left and old Fido is in the Pet Sematary, why put up with another frigid February or urban traffic jam? Why worry about high crime rates and higher taxes? Why deal with all that gardening and house cleaning? Many of today's retirees want to get out and do things. They don't want to trudge through snow to reach indoor tennis courts or swimming pools, or be chased off the golf course by a chilling rain. So why not go someplace that's warm, safe, secure and affordable?

Like Arizona, for instance.

Arizona attracts more migrating seniors than any other state except Florida and California. It's ahead of Texas, Nevada and New Mexico, the other leading sunbelt states, and if current trends continue, it may pass crowded and over-taxed California.

## Shedding the Midwest

Where are these folks drawn from? Although migration figures aren't broken down by age, most sunbelt newcomers are from the Midwest. Within that area, Illinois loses more citizens to Arizona than any other state—more than 10,000 a year. Ohio is a distant second, with about half as many migrants going south, and an equal number comes from Michigan. Surprisingly, California sends more emigrants to Arizona than any other state, although they aren't necessarily retirees. Job opportunities and lower housing prices lure many working families. Other leading sources of migrants are Colorado, New York, Wisconsin, Minnesota, Iowa and Indiana.

Like most states, Arizona permits apartment, condo and subdivision owners to designate a minimum age for residents. This, of course, defines the "retirement complex." They range from full-care apartments and assisted living facilities to condos and planned developments with golf courses, swimming pools, tennis courts and other active-life amenities.

Mobile home parks are popular with year-around retirees, as well as wintertime Snowbirds. In fact, nearly one in ten Arizona residents lives in mobile housing—one of the highest ratios in the Nation. Adults-only parks are particularly numerous along the Colorado River corridor and in and about Phoenix and Tucson.

If you're considering the purchase of a home or condo in a retirement community, remember that the age requirement limits your market and thus may inhibit the unit's resale value. Further, although it can be willed to your children when you pass on, they can't occupy it unless they meet that age requirement, and some retirement complexes limit renters. Except in a few highly desirable communities, retirement units tend to bring less on the resale market than comparable family homes.

And if you're considering a mobile home, bear in mind that they *depreciate* while "stick built" houses almost always increase in value.

On the other hand, since you probably plan to spend all of your remaining years in your retirement home, condo or double-wide, why worry about resale value? Let your heirs worry about it!

The Phoenix Yellow Pages contains several pages of listings for "Retirement & Life Care Communities & Homes." Tucson's phone book has a a fair sized section as well. Both also have extensive adult mobile home park listings.

## WHAT KIND OF RETIREMENT?

Once you've made the decision to move to Arizona, you need to determine which retirement facilities best suit your needs. Basically, they fit into five categories. In the first two, one usually has the option of purchasing, leasing or renting, while the final three are usually on a month-to-month basis, with the cost of care and perhaps meals included. Some advanced care units can be purchased, however.

*Independent living* • As the name suggests, this is retirement in a conventional family community. Some seniors, particularly active ones, prefer this. They like the mix of young and old, which is more akin to the city or town they left behind. Arizona offers a host of planned all-age communities with the same amenities as retirement villages—golf, tennis, swimming and scheduled activities. Some of these colonies have both senior and family sections, with separate-but-equal facilities for each age group.

*Planned adult community* • Like any planned complex, the adult village offers a variety of activities, plus the advantage of facilities geared to older people. Ease of mobility is taken into account in room layouts. And you don't need to worry about a teenage rap party next door. Planned adult dwellings range from detached homes and townhouses to condos and apartments.

*Independent retirement complex* • These facilities, usually offered on a lease plan, are for fully ambulatory people who don't want the bother of housekeeping. They usually offer maid service, planned activities and outings. Meals may be included, or they can be an option offered at a central dining area. One might compare it to living in a hotel, or perhaps a motel with a kitchenette. These complexes are usually set up as townhouses, condos or apartments.

*Assisted living facility* • These offer a higher level of care than the independent complex. Full housekeeping and meal service generally are provided, and aides are on hand to help with mobility problems and perhaps monitor medications. However, they generally don't have on-site nursing care. Most are apartments or condos. Group outings are offered for those unable to drive or prefer not to.

*Life care facility* • These complexes are best for those with impaired mobility or a debilitating illness. Also, some still-ambulatory seniors prefer to turn all of their day-to-day decisions and responsibilities over to someone else. Facilities range from apartments to furnished rooms.

On-site medical care is part of the program at a life care facility, and all housekeeping and meals are furnished. Full time nursing care is available for those in need. The most comprehensive level of life care facilities are nursing homes and—despite their rather misleading names—convalescent hospitals.

## Senior service agencies

Several agencies in Arizona offer advice, assistance and information for seniors. If you're interested in extended health care, the **Office of Long Term Health Care** of the Arizona Department of Health Services will send you *A Guide to Selecting Long Term Health Care Services for the Elderly and Disabled* and a directory to assisted living facilities in Arizona. Contact either of these offices, which are part of the Health Department Service's Assurance and Licensure department:

*Phoenix area* • 1647 E. Morten St., Suite 110, Phoenix, AZ 85020; (602) 674-9705.

*Tucson area* • 400 W. Congress St., Suite 116, Tucson, AZ 85701; (520) 628-6965.

For a directory of nursing homes and related services, contact the **Arizona Nursing Association,** 1817 N. Third St., Suite 200, Phoenix, AZ 85004; (602) 258-8996. Another useful organization is the **Governor's Advisory Council on Aging**, 1717 W. Jefferson St., Phoenix, AZ 85007; (602) 542-4710.

Offices of Arizona's **Agency on Aging** provide a variety of services for people 60 and over. They function as activity and information centers for seniors, and they even offer delivery services for those who can't get about. They also publish guides to local senior living facilities. Offices are in these communities:

**Phoenix area** • 1366 E. Thomas Rd., Suite 108, Phoenix, AZ 85014; (602) 264-HELP; *www.aaaphx.org.*

**Northwestern Arizona** • P.O. Box 57, Flagstaff, AZ 86002; (928) 774-1895.

**Southwestern Arizona** • 100 Maple Ave., Yuma, AZ 85364; (928) 782-1886.

**Central Arizona** • P.O. Box 1129 (512) E. Butte St.), Florence, AZ 85232; (520) 868-4166.

**Tucson area** • 2955 E. Broadway, Tucson, AZ 85716; (520) 795-5800.

**Southeastern Arizona** • 118 Arizona St., Bisbee, AZ 85603; (520) 432-5301.

# RETIREMENT COMMUNITIES

Planned retirement communities were invented in Arizona, although the well known Sun City wasn't the first. A place appropriately called Youngtown is the nation's—and probably the world's—oldest retirement village. Located just west of Phoenix, it was created in 1954 by the Youngtown Land and Development Company. It still thrives today as a busy little city of about 3,000 residents.

Del E. Webb started Sun City, next door to Youngtown, in 1960. It has become America's largest retirement community, with a population around 45,000. A satellite, Sun City West, was started in 1978. It now has more than 25,000 residents and a third and smaller complex, Sun City Grand, is the newest in this area. A fourth Del Web retirement facility, Sun City Vistoso, is just north of Tucson in the small town of Catalina. Sun City communities also are located in several other states.

We offer below a list of some of Arizona's major planned retirement villages. A letter or phone call to each will earn you a quick packet of information.

**Fountain of the Sun** • 8001 E. Broadway, Mesa, AZ 85208; (480) 984-1434.

**Leisure World** • 908 S. Power Rd., Mesa, AZ 85026; (480) 832-7451 or (480) 832-0003.

**SaddleBrooke Country Club** • 64518 E. Saddlebrooke Blvd., Tucson, AZ 85737; (520) 825-3048.

**Sun City** • Visitor Center, 99th Avenue and Bell Road, Sun City, AZ 85351, (623) 977-5000, *www.suncity.com*; and Northwest Valley Chamber of Commerce, 12425 W. Bell Rd., C-305, Surprise, AZ 85374, (623) 583-0692.

**Sun City Grand** • R.H. Johnson Blvd. (off Grand Avenue), Surprise, AZ 85374; (800) 528-2604 or (623) 546-7200; *www.suncity.com/grand.*

# WHERE THE SENIORS LIVE (by percentage)

Source: Population Statistics Unit, Arizona Department of Economic Security

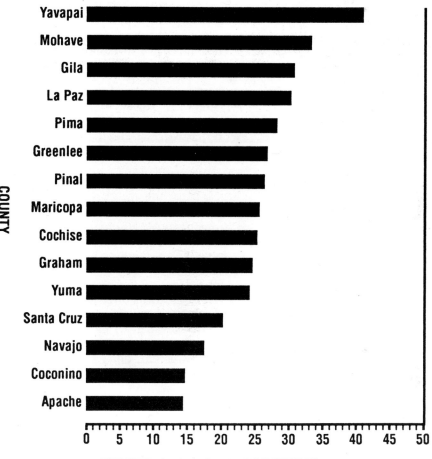

PERCENTAGE OF POPULATION OVER 50

Yavapai County, which contains Prescott and south Sedona, has Arizona's highest ratio of residents over fifty--more than 40 percent. They aren't all retired, of course, but the county is very popular with retirees. Mohave County on the Colorado River Corridor is second in senior ratio.

*Sun City Vistoso* • 13990 N. Desert Butte Dr., Sun City Vistoso, Catalina, AZ 85738; (520) 825-3711; *www.suncity.com/vistoso.*

*Sun City West* • Visitors Center, 13823 W. Camino del Sol, Sun City, AZ 85375; (623) 214-8629; *www.suncity.com/west.*

*SunBird Resort Community* • 6250 S. Sunbird Blvd., Chandler, AZ 85249; (480) 802-4901.

**Westbrook Village** • Westbrook Village Association, 19281 N. Westbrook Parkway, Peoria, AZ 85382; (623) 561-1178.

# RETIREMENT AREAS

Maricopa (Phoenix) and Pima (Tucson) counties are home to most of Arizona's retirees. Not all of these folks live in planned retirement villages like Sun City, of course. Smaller senior complexes are scattered throughout the Valley of the Sun and greater Tucson.

About one in four Maricopa and Pima County residents is over fifty, and incoming Baby Boomers are bound to elevate that figure. However, several other counties have more seniors per capita. Yavapai County, whose main city is Prescott, has Arizona's highest ratio of folks over fifty—41 percent. Mohave County along the Colorado River is second with 33 percent.

The Colorado River corridor ranks third behind Phoenix and Tucson in the total number of retirees. Most are in the communities of Yuma, Parker, Lake Havasu City and Bullhead City. The river towns offer two big advantages—access to water sports and housing that's less expensive than in the Phoenix and Tucson areas. They have disadvantages, as well. For one thing, it can get hotter than the hinges of Hades along *Rio Colorado* in summer. Phoenix and Tucson, at higher elevations, are cooler—which doesn't mean *cool* in July and August, since it's often over 110 degrees. Also, the river towns offer little in the way of cultural lures—unless you count the London Bridge at Lake Havasu City, or the casino shows at Laughlin, Nevada, across the river from Bullhead City.

If you're considering an Arizona retirement, don't restrict yourself to the sunbelt. Places such as Flagstaff, Sedona and Prescott to the north and Sierra Vista in the southeast also have retirement facilities. Small mountain towns northeast of Phoenix like Payson, Pinetop and Show Low offer a mix of retirement and recreational opportunities.

## Nippy but not harsh

Most of these places are more than 4,000 feet high, so some get winter snow—particularly Flagstaff—although the weather is never harsh. Compared with Toronto, Buffalo or Chicago, winters are downright mild. Annual snowfall in Prescott, for instance, is 24 inches. Sierra Vista's is a mere ten inches and the average January low temperature is 35 to 40 degrees.

Some retirees are drawn to these higher elevation towns because they miss the four season back home. In Prescott, Payson, Flagstaff and Sedona, you even get piney woods and fall color.

If we were considering going to Arizona as retirees, we'd pick one of the places listed below. We don't suggest heavily urbanized Phoenix, since there's no reason for a retiree to become entangled in crowds or commuter traffic. However, if you don't mind a little congestion and want to be close to downtown Phoenix with its many cultural and shopping lures, you might consider suburban towns such as Mesa, Tempe (with Arizona State University at your doorstep), Glendale or Peoria.

# CENTRAL ARIZONA

Folks who want to be near the business, economic and social hub of Arizona should set their sights on the Valley of the Sun. Although the basin is beginning to resemble Los Angeles with its sprawl, you still can find your own personal cactus patch on the fringes and escape the congestion.

Phoenix is served by a growing network of freeways and the heart of the city is easily reached during off-commute hours. Scottsdale and Paradise Valley were once difficult to reach because of the Phoenix suburban sprawl, although a new cross-town freeway has penetrated that northeastern edge of the Valley of the Sun. And even during the morning rush, delays are nothing compared with those you'll encounter in large Eastern and Midwestern cities or the Los Angeles and San Francisco Bay areas.

If you'd like to get a bit further out and still be within dinner range, we'd recommend places such as Apache Junction on the eastern edge of the valley, Sun City to the west or Arizona City and Florence to the south. The latter two are near the busy north-south Interstate 10 corridor, providing easy access to both Phoenix and Tucson.

**Apache Junction** • This city of about 33,000 is set against the rough backdrop of the Superstition Mountains, southeast of Phoenix. It offers several mobile home parks and a few planned developments. It's within a short drive of Phoenix, yet well beyond its urban congestion. We particularly like its topography. The terrain is high desert and, for outdoor lovers, the forested hills and reservoirs of the scenic Salt River Canyon are a short drive away. *For information: Apache Junction Chamber of Commerce, P.O. Box 1747, Apache Junction, AZ 85217; (480) 982-3141; www.apachejunctioncoc.com.*

**Arizona City** • The agricultural setting isn't particularly stimulating, although the weather's nice and so is the location—midway between Phoenix and Tucson. This planned community of 2,700 was established in 1960, and it offers amenities such as a fake lake, golf course and community center. *For information: Arizona City Chamber of Commerce, P.O. Box 5, Arizona City, AZ 85223; (520) 466-5141; www.arizonacitychamber.org.*

**Carefree and Cave Creek** • Take your pick of these two small towns, located in the rugged desert northeast of Scottsdale. Carefree, with about 3,000 residents, is a somewhat upscale planned community. Larger Cave creek, with nearly 4,000 folks, is on the rustic side, preserving remnants of an old mining town. They both offer good locations—close to Phoenix and Scottsdale, yet on the uncluttered outer edge of the Valley of the Sun. *For information: Carefree/Cave Creek Chamber of Commerce, 7207 E. Carefree Dr. (P.O. Box 734), Carefree,*

AZ 85337; (480) 488-3381; www.carefree-cavecreek.com.; www.care-free-cavecreek.com.

**Florence** • You don't hear much about it, although Florence is a fine place for retirement, with an historic Western style downtown and some modern subdivisions around the edges. Located in Pinal County midway between Phoenix and Tucson, it has a rather mild climate and a population of 17,500. It's in an agricultural valley, so you won't find any desert or mountain scenery. *For information: Greater Florence Chamber of Commerce, P.O. Box 929, Florence, AZ 85232-0929; (520) 868-9433; www.florenceaz.org; Pinal County Development Board & Visitors Center, P.O. Box 967 (135 N. Pinal St.), Florence, AZ 85232; (888) 469-0175 or (520) 868-4331.*

**Fountain Hills** • This planned community is on the northeastern rim of the Valley of the Sun, with a population of about 21,000. Established in 1970 by the creators of Lake Havasu City, it's a modern town set in attractive high desert terrain. It offers a mix of planned subdivisions and shopping centers. There's no London Bridge, although it does have the world's highest fountain, squirting from a park-rimmed lake as the town's centerpiece. *For information: Fountain Hills Chamber of Commerce, P.O. Box 17598, Fountain Hills, AZ 85269; (480) 837-1654; www.fhchamberofcommerce.org.*

**Paradise Valley** • If you can afford it, Paradise Valley is a retirement paradise, desert style. Just beyond the reach of Phoenix and Scottsdale's congestion, it's a community of elegant homes set in a ruggedly handsome desert and surrounded by equally rugged mountains. Most lodgings are individual homes; there are few planned retirement complexes. It's a stable, slow growing community with a population of about 14,000. Expect summers to be hot here, although if you can afford Paradise Valley, you can afford to keep the air conditioner running. *For information: North Phoenix Chamber of Commerce, 2737 E. Greenwood Rd., Suite 10, Phoenix, AZ 85012; (602) 482-3344.*

**Scottsdale** • Upscale, expensive and expansive, this community of 210,000 sits against dramatic Camelback Peak in the high desert on the edge of Phoenix. Although pricey, it's homes are less expensive than those in next-door Paradise Valley. Scottsdale has become rather urbanized and has lost much of its early Western charm, although the rustic flavor of Old Scottsdale has been preserved. The town offers some of Arizona's finest planned developments, upscale shopping centers and luxury resorts. *For information: Scottsdale Chamber of Commerce, 7343 Scottsdale Mall, Scottsdale, AZ 85251-4498, (480) 945-8481.*

**Sun City, Sun City West & Sun City Grand** • Large Sun City offers a complete assortment of leisure amenities. Lodgings range from detached homes and townhouses to condos. Sun City West is smaller and a bit more modern while Sun City Grand is the newest of this retirement community trio on the Valley of the Sun's western edge. With a combined population of more than 80,000, they provide shopping and other commercial facilities. *For information: Sun City Visitors Center, 99th Avenue and Bell Road, Sun City, AZ 85351, (623) 977-5000, www.suncity.com; Sun City Grand, R.H. Johnson Blvd. (just off Grand Avenue), Surprise, AZ 85374, (623) 546-7200, www.suncity. com/grand; Sun City West Visitors Center, 13823 W. Camino del Sol, Sun City, AZ 85375, (623) 214-8629, www.suncity.com/west; Northwest Valley Chamber of Commerce, 12425 W. Bell Rd., C-305, Surprise, AZ 85374, (623) 583-0692, www.northwestvalley.com.*

**Wickenburg** • This town among rough desert hills just loves to play cowboy. Western shops line its historic streets, half a dozen dude ranches are nearby and real cowboys herd dogies in the surrounding desert. It's 50 miles northwest of Phoenix and well beyond that suburban scatter. Indeed, it feels like another place in another time—"out Wickenburg way." There are few planned retirement facilities in this peaceful town of 5,500 folks. However, if you love a taste of the Old West, this is your place. *For information: Wickenburg Chamber of Commerce, 216 N. Frontier St., Wickenburg, AZ 85390; (928) 684-5479; www.wickkenbergchamber.com; and Town of Wickenburg, 155 N. Tegner St., Suite A, Wickenburg, AZ 85390; (928) 684-5451; www. ci.wickenburg.az.us.*

**Youngtown** • This is where it all began, in America's first planned retirement town. It has the requisite senior leisure facilities—a clubhouse, fake lake, tennis and six golf courses. Another eighteen courses are within five miles. No longer isolated in the desert, Youngtown is now rimmed by Sun City, Peoria and El Mirage. Although it preceded Sun City as a retirement community, it's much smaller, with a population of about 3,200. *For information: Town of Youngtown, 12030 Clubhouse Square, Youngtown, AZ 85363, (623) 933-8286; and Northwest Valley Chamber of Commerce, 12425 W. Bell Rd., C-305, Surprise, AZ 85374, (623) 583-0692; www.northwestvalley.com.*

## NORTH CENTRAL ARIZONA

If you want pine trees and four seasons in your retirement picture, pick one of these north central Arizona towns. Some, such as Flagstaff and Prescott, are more than a mile high. They offer occasional winter snows but severe storms are rare. The Sedona-Oak Creek Canyon-Verde Valley areas are noted for their fall color, so transplanted New Englanders will feel right at home.

**Cottonwood** • Although it's a rather ordinary looking town without fancy subdivisions, this town of 10,000 people offers a fine location, just below beautiful Oak Creek Canyon and Sedona. A relatively mild climate, proximity to a variety of tourist attractions and low housing costs have lured many retirees. One of four residents is over 65. *For information: Cottonwood Chamber of Commerce, 1010 S. Main St., Cottonwood, AZ 86326, (928) 634-7593; www.ci.cottonwood.az.us.*

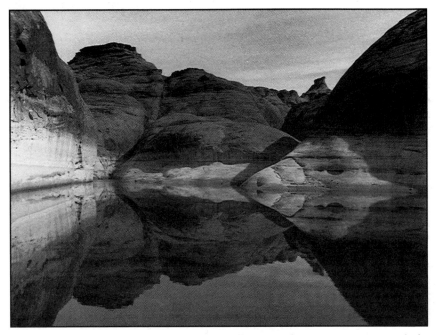

*Weekend sailors who retire to Page will enjoy the water sports and the beauty of Glen Canyon National Recreation Area. Here, a narrow side canyon casts a perfect reflection of itself in Lake Powell.*

**Flagstaff** ● One of our favorite Arizona communities, Flagstaff has a balance of cultural offerings, educational facilities and an appealing location. It sits at the base of the towering San Francisco Peaks, about 70 miles southeast of the Grand Canyon. With a population nearing 60,000, it offers all the services and amenities a retiree would need, plus the cultural lures of Northern Arizona University. It can get cold in winter, however. Not Chicago cold, although the average January low is 15 degrees, and it gets about 84 inches of winter snowfall. *For information: Flagstaff Chamber of Commerce, 101 W. Route 66, Flagstaff, AZ 86001, (928) 774-4505, www.flagstaffchamber.com; and City of Flagstaff, 211 W. Aspen St., Flagstaff, AZ 86001, (928) 774-5281, www.flagstaff.az.us.*

**Lake Montezuma area** ● Lake What? Lake Montezuma, Rimrock and McGuireville are little known outside Arizona. They are three planned villages in the higher reaches of the Verde Valley, with terrain ranging from prairie to forest. These hamlets, with a combined population of about 2,600, are popular with retirees who like the surrounding national forest and don't mind chilly weather in winter. Snowfall is rare. *For information: Camp Verde Chamber of Commerce, P.O. Box 3520, Camp Verde, AZ 86322; (928) 567-9294; www.cvaz.org.*

**Page and Lake Powell** ● If you're a weekend sailor and want to float your boat, Page may be your retirement answer. This desert town of 7,000 people is located adjacent to Lake Powell, which offers unlimited water sports opportunities. Not handsome but prim, neat and well-planned with underground utilities, Page began life as the former construction town for Glen Canyon Dam. A few subdivisions are being developed on its desert outskirts. Although it's not considered a major retirement community, it's "retirement friendly," says the local chamber. *For information: Page/Lake Powell Chamber of Commerce, P.O. Box 727, Page, AZ 86040; (928) 645-2741; www.ci.page.az.us.*

**Payson** • This woodsy town of 14,200 sits a mile high, 78 miles northeast of Phoenix. The Chamber of Commerce says it offers a mix of "Swiss alpine, Old West and contemporary ambiance," which is something of an exaggeration, since the heart of town is mostly an unplanned commercial strip. However, is in an attractive alpine setting and it's a popular senior community; 60 percent of its residents are retired and it sponsors several senior programs. You'll get the four seasons although winters are mild, with perhaps two feet of total snowfall. *For information: Rim Country Regional Chamber of Commerce, P.O. Box 1380, Payson, AZ 85547; (928) 474- 4515; www.rimcountrychamber.com.*

**Pine and Strawberry** • Essentially vacation and retirement towns, these villages with a combined population of 2,500 are in the east-central Arizona woods north of Payson. Many Valley of the Sun residents spend weekends here to escape desert heat; some maintain second homes among the pines. The area is more than a mile up, so winters are chilly although not harsh. Figure on a couple of feet of total snowfall. *For information: Rim Country Regional Chamber of Commerce; see "Payson" above.*

**Prescott** • Like Flagstaff, Prescott offers a mix of culture, education and scenery, located in the west central Arizona pines. This small city of 36,000 residents has extensive senior programs and good medical facilities; one in four residents is retired. This is four seasons country, getting splashes of fall color and about two feet of winter snow. The ambiance and attitude are Old West, although the town has a sturdy and attractive red brick New England look. Incidentally, it's pronounced "PRESS-kit," partner. *For information: Prescott Chamber of Commerce, P.O. Box 1147, Prescott, AZ 86302-1147; (928) 445-2000; www.cityofprescott.net.*

**Sedona** • If we could afford the tariff, we'd be tempted to retire in Sedona and watch those glorious sunups and sundowns against the red rock peaks of Oak Creek Canyon. One of the most dramatically located towns in America, this community of about 10,000 is a haven for tourists, artists, well-heeled retirees and an occasional music festival. Shops, galleries and boutiques abound. Several planned communities extend south; some are tucked into their own awesome red rock niches. At 4,300 feet, Sedona offers mild year-around climate and glorious fall color. *For information: Sedona/Oak Creek Canyon Cham-*

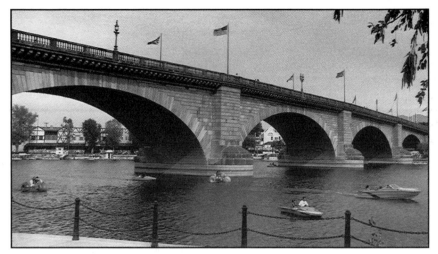

*The transplanted London Bridge lures both tourists and retirees to the planned community of Lake Havasu City.*

ber of Commerce, P.O. Box 478, Sedona, AZ 86339; (928) 204-1123; www.city.sedona.net.

**Verde Village** • This planned complex, next door to Cottonwood, has about 10,200 residents and two-thirds of them are retired. It's in an agricultural valley, between the imposing setting of Oak Creek Canyon and the pine forests of the Prescott area. ***For information:*** *Cottonwood/Verde Valley Chamber of Commerce, 1010 S. Main St., Cottonwood, AZ 86326; (928) 634-7593; www.chamber.verdevalley.com.*

## COLORADO RIVER CORRIDOR

Prepare for extreme summer heat if you choose the Colorado River corridor as your retirement refuge. This area is noted mostly as a Snowbird haven, although many people crank up their air conditioners and stay the year-around. The Colorado River has so many dams that it's now a virtual chain of lakes, so cooling water sports are always available.

**Bullhead City** • Sprawled over 43 square miles along the river corridor, Bullhead is an unlovely city, although it offers great winter climate. Further, if you like one-armed bandits and green felt games, the Nevada gaming center of Laughlin is just across the pond. Summers get very hot here, sometimes topping the national charts. With a growing population approaching 35,000, Bullhead has many mobile home parks and a few planned residential communities. ***For information:*** *Bullhead Area Chamber of Commerce, 1251 Highway 95, Bullhead City, AZ 86429; (928) 754-4121; www.bullheadcity.com.*

**Lake Havasu City** • This bustling community of 42,000 was started by developer Robert P. McCulloch in the 1960s; he had the

London Bridge hauled over here (in pieces, of course) as a focal point. Reassembling England's historic stone bridge in the desert got him the headlines he wanted and his planned community grew quickly. It offers a good mix of retirement villages, all-age subdivisions and mobile home parks. The lake provides water sports and a gimmick English village has been built around the bridge. The only negative: the countryside ain't very pretty. *For information: Lake Havasu Tourism Bureau, 314 London Bridge Dr., Lake Havasu City, AZ 86403; (800) 242-8278 or (928) 855-4115; www.ci.lake-havasu-city.az.us.*

**Yuma** ● If you like living far from the rest of civilization while still enjoying most of its amenities, consider Yuma. With a population approaching 80,000, it's the largest Arizona city outside the Phoenix and Tucson population centers. It offers all the basic essentials and an abundance of water recreation on the adjacent Colorado River. Yuma is rich in history, as the site of Yuma Crossing on the first trail to California. That area is now Yuma Crossing State Historic Park; it and the nearby Yuma Territorial Prison are popular visitor attractions. In 2000, historic downtown Yuma and its riverfront were designated as Yuma Crossing National Heritage Area and many preservation projects are underway. That early trail to California is now Interstate 8, so access to this remote mini-metropolis is easy. Like the other Colorado River corridor towns, Yuma's biggest disadvantage for year-around retirement is summer heat. *For information: Yuma County Chamber of Commerce, 377 S. Main St. Suite 203, Yuma, AZ 85364; (928) 782-2567; www.yumachamber.org.*

## SOUTHERN ARIZONA

The Tucson-to-Nogales corridor is rapidly gaining favor with all-year retirees. Averaging more than a thousand feet higher than Phoenix, the region's towns aren't quite as hot in summer. Another choice is southeastern Arizona, the state's undiscovered corner. Far from the urban and suburban mainstream, it offers a mix of high desert, prairie country and mountains. Winters are relatively mild and the area's largest community, Sierra Vista, is said to have the most temperate year-around climate in America.

**Bisbee** ● This old copper mining town of fewer than 5,000 people isn't well known as a retirement haven. However, we like its funky look and sense of history, and the year-around climate is quite mild. Summer highs are in the upper eighties and winter lows are in the middle thirties; there's virtually no snowfall. Bisbee is about six miles from the Mexican border—a plus for lovers of things Latino. *For information: Bisbee Chamber of Commerce, P.O. Box BA (31 Subway St.), Bisbee, AZ 85603; (866) 2-BISBEE or (520) 432-5421; www.bisbeearizona.com.*

**Catalina** ● Twelve miles north of Tucson, Catalina is home to a pair of major retirement communities, Sun City Vistoso and Saddle-Brooke, which house many of its 6,000 residents. Established in the

1950s, the town is situated in the foothills of the Catalina Mountains, giving it a pleasing backdrop. Although it's in the desert, the elevation is 3,000 feet, so summers are relatively mild—five to ten degrees cooler than Tucson. *For information: Catalina Village Council, P.O. Box 8674, Catalina, AZ 85738; (520) 887-0608.*

**Green Valley** ● Like Sun City, this town of 27,000 was planned as a retirement community, so it offers extensive senior facilities, plus golf, tennis, swimming and such. We like its location midway between Tucson and the Mexican border at Nogales. The terrain is rolling desert, not really attractive, although the climate's great in winter. However, temperatures routinely top 100 degrees in summer. *For information: Green Valley Chamber of Commerce, P.O. Box 566, Green Valley, AZ 85622; (520) 625-7575; www.greenvalleyazchamber.com.*

**Sierra Vista** ● Looking more like a suburb than a city, Sierra Vista is an orderly sprawl of subdivisions and shopping centers southeast of Tucson. The elevation is 4,623 feet, creating a very temperate year-around climate. While not really handsome, this community of nearly 40,000 is clean, well planned and easy to navigate, and it has several modern housing developments. Historic Fort Huachuca, a still-active Army post, is just to the south. *For information: Greater Sierra Vista Chamber of Commerce, 21 E. Wilcox Dr., Sierra Vista, AZ 85635; (800) 288-3861 or (520) 458- 6940; www.sierravistachamber.org.*

**Tubac** ● If you like history and artistic funk with your retirement, check out this weathered little town 40 miles south of Tucson and 23 miles north of Nogales. With a population of about 2,000—two-thirds retirees—Tubac offers several galleries and boutiques and a very laid-back lifestyle. Tubac State Historic Park and Tumacacori Mission National Monument are in the neighborhood. *For information: Tubac Chamber of Commerce, P.O. Box 1866, Tubac, AZ 85646; (520) 398-2704; www.tubacaz.com.*

**Tucson** ● Since we didn't recommend bustling and sprawling Phoenix as a retirement town, why Tucson? Because it's less than half the size, not quite as sprawling and less congested. While the greater Valley of the Sun has more than three million residents, Tucson has only about half a million. (Only?) Further, it's higher and slightly cooler than Phoenix in summer, and it's in a dramatic setting, surrounded by craggy desert mountains. Finally, it offers cultural and historic lures and it is home to the University of Arizona. *For information: Metropolitan Tucson Convention & Visitors Bureau, 110 S. Church Ave., Suite 9100, Tucson, AZ 85701; (800) 638-8350 or (520) 624-1817; www.visittucson.org.*

## Chapter Seven

# THE SNOWBIRDS
## FEATHERING YOUR WINTER NEST

**W**hile hundreds of thousands of retirees snip their roots and nestle here permanently, an even larger number of seniors head for Arizona each year only to enjoy its winter sunshine.

They embrace the best of both worlds—heading south before the snow flies, and then returning home in the spring to keep their ties with family and friends. It's no wonder that they've earned the nickname Snowbirds. Arizona ranks second to Florida and ahead of California, Texas and Nevada as America's leading Snowbird retreat. It draws more than a million winter visitors each year.

An Arizona State University survey of winter visitors in the Valley of the Sun indicated that the largest number arrives in November and departs in April. Chambers of commerce in other areas report a similar pattern. The ASU survey revealed some surprising statistics. Despite the typical Snowbird's image as an RV enthusiast, at least half of Arizona's winter visitors check into apartments or condos, and many own winter homes here. Of those who do occupy RV or mobile home parks, 70 percent leave their rigs in Arizona the year-around. Only 30 percent tow a trailer or drive an RV to the state. So it's evident that most of these visitors, like other migrating birds, like to return to the same nest year after year.

And Snowbirds definitely are migrants. While the state lures tens of thousands of permanent retirees each year, 95 percent of winter visitors responding to the ASU survey said they planned to return home in the spring. The average length of a winter stay is between four and five months. Two-thirds of those questioned had been doing the Snowbird bit for five or more years.

Where do most of the Snowbirds roost? Along the Colorado River corridor and in the greater Phoenix area. Some *Rio Colorado* towns see their populations increase many-fold each winter. The Phoenix Convention and Visitors Bureau estimates that as many as 200,000 Snowbirds flock into the Valley of the Sun.

Where do they come from? Nearly 20 percent are from Canada, despite the fact that its total population is only one tenth that of the U.S. Most American Snowbirds come from the chilly Midwest, but not from Michigan, although that state sends the largest number of permanent retirees to Arizona. In fact, Michigan doesn't even finish in the top ten in the survey. After Canada, Minnesota sends the most winter visitors, with 13 percent of the total; Iowa and Washington are tied in second place with 11 percent. North Dakota is next with seven percent, an amazing figure, since it has a total population of less than 700,000. Others in the top ten are Colorado, six percent; Illinois, four percent; and California, Oregon and Wisconsin, each with three percent.

Winter visitors don't just come for suntans and golf. Three out of four of Arizona's Cactus League Baseball ticket buyers are from another state—although not all are long-term winter visitors. Two-thirds of these fans say they head south *specifically* for spring hardball. (See Cactus League box in Chapter Three, page 36.)

For those interested in finding winter apartments and condos, Tucson, Phoenix and a few other cities list short-term lodgings in their accommodations guides.

Most Arizona RV parks offer special rates for long-term visitors. Many of these parks are elaborate resorts with swimming pools, golf courses, marinas, recreation centers, social programs, group outings and other amenities.

### A chill in the air?

Incidentally, whether you plan to winter in Arizona for two weeks or six months, remember to bring your sweater—perhaps even a jacket. Compared with Bismark, North Dakota, and Edmonton, Alberta, much of Arizona is a balmy winter paradise. However, nighttime temperatures sometimes dip to freezing in the Phoenix and Tucson areas. Days generally are in the 60s, often climbing into the 70s. Tucson is more than a thousand feet higher than Phoenix and therefore slightly cooler the year around.

If you require toastier winter nights, the Colorado River corridor is warmer than the higher desert interior. Bullhead City, for instance, boasts an average low of just 37 degrees and a high of 80 in January. Yuma, Parker and Bullhead often report the nation's highest temperatures, both in winter and summer.

Although higher elevation places such as Flagstaff, Sedona, Prescott and the mountain regions northeast of Phoenix attract many year-around retirees, few Snowbirds choose to fly to these areas. Therefore, our list of recommended roosts is focused on cactus country. Colorado River towns offer a plenitude of RV and mobile home parks, while their selection of condo and apartment rentals is rather limited. So if you want a solid roof over your winter roost, you'll find a much better selection in the Valley of the Sun and Tucson.

## THE BEST SNOWBIRD ROOSTS

Our list ranges from cosmopolitan Phoenix to dusty Quartzsite, and it includes some sun-country places you may not be aware of. Some of our selections also are suggested as retirement towns in the previous chapter, so expect to trip over some repetition.

To learn more about these cities, towns and villages, move along to Part Two of this book. We discuss population growth, advantages and disadvantages, summer-winter climate and many other essentials.

## CENTRAL ARIZONA

Central Arizona is the state's business, social and population hub. You can winter in the busy Valley of the Sun or set up your rig on the fringes to stay away from the crowds. If we had a choice, we'd probably pick our first listing—Apache Junction; Carefree and Cave Creek would be close seconds.

**Apache Junction** • Forty miles southeast of Phoenix in the Superstition Mountain foothills, Apache Junction is popular with winter visitors as well as permanent retirees. With more than a hundred RV parks and resorts, this town of 33,000 people more than doubles its population with winter visitors. We like its setting in a handsomely rugged desert. It's close to Salt River Canyon, pine- clad mountains are nearby and Phoenix is less than an hour's drive. *For information:* Apache Junction Chamber of Commerce, P.O. Box 1747, Apache Junction, AZ 85217; (480) 982- 3141; www.apachejunctioncoc.com.

**Carefree & Cave Creek** • These hamlets with a combined population of about 7,000 are 25 miles north of Phoenix. Cave Creek is a deliberately rustic Western style town; the planned community of Carefree is more contemporary. The only disadvantage for Snowbirds is that the area has a limited number of RV parks and winter apartments. However, some are a-building. If you want a Carefree (sorry about that) or Cave Creek winter escape, you'd better book early. *For information:* Carefree/Cave Creek Chamber of Commerce, 7207 E. Carefree Dr. (P.O. Box 734), Carefree, AZ 85337; (480) 488-3381; www.carefree-cavecreek.com.

**Casa Grande** • Midway between Phoenix and Tucson, this town of nearly 28,000 doesn't attract a big winter flock. It's in a farm belt and the area can get a bit windy. However, if you'd like to be within an hour's drive of both major urban centers, you might check it out. Winters are temperate with warm days and cool evenings. A few RV parks are in the area and more are being built. *For information: Greater Casa Grande Chamber of Commerce, 575 N. Marshall St., Casa Grande, AZ 85222-5244; (520) 836-2125; www.casagrandechamber.org.*

**Mesa-Tempe** • In the southeastern part of the Valley of the Sun, the large communities of Mesa and Tempe offer all your basic needs, with a combined population of more than half a million. Access to next-door Phoenix and Scottsdale is easy and the towns have their own cultural lures as well. Both offer fine museums and Tempe is home to Arizona State University. They're primarily year-around residential cities although they do have several RV parks and resorts. Apartments in Tempe may be a bit scarce because of the presence of ASU; all those students need winter roosts, too. *For information: Mesa Convention & Visitors Bureau, 120 N. Center St., Mesa, AZ 85201; (480) 827-4700; and Tempe Chamber of Commerce, P.O. Box 28500, Tempe, AZ 85285-8500; (480) 967-7891. www.tempe.gov.*

**Phoenix-Scottsdale** • You say you want to be in the middle of the action, with a great choice of cultural offerings, shopping, restaurants and classy resorts? Phoenix and Scottsdale *are* the Valley of the Sun, containing most of its population and its finest resorts. Most of the RV parks are on the outskirts, while apartment and condo rentals are scattered throughout the area. The Yellow Pages can help you find a place to roost. If you're a pre-season baseball fan, fly no further. Several Cactus League clubs conduct spring training in and about Phoenix; see Chapter Three, page 36. Ironically, Phoenix's Arizona Diamondbacks train in Tucson. Expect Phoenix-Scottsdale accommodations to be on the pricey side, compared with much of the rest of Arizona. *For information: Greater Phoenix Convention & Visitors Bureau, 400 E. Van Buren, Suite 600, Phoenix, AZ 85004-2290; (602) 254-6500, www. phoenixcvb.com; and Scottsdale Chamber of Commerce, 7343 Scottsdale Mall, Scottsdale, AZ 85251-4489; (480) 945-8481, www.ci.scottsdale. az.us.*

# COLORADO RIVER CORRIDOR

If you love water sports and balmy January nights, head for the river. Although the mighty Colorado has its roots in the 10,000-foot ramparts of the Rocky Mountains, it has dropped to nearly sea level by the time it reaches the Arizona-Nevada-California border. With several dams impeding its progress, it's no longer a river but a chain of lakes along this corridor. This is the warmest part of Arizona—too hot for some in summer but great for just about everyone in winter.

**Bullhead City** • Fast growing Bullhead offers toasty winter climate and less than four inches of rain a year. An added bonus is the busy Nevada casino town of Laughlin just across the water, linked by a bridge. Shuttle boats are available to hurry gamblers over from Bullhead City parking lots. Bullhead isn't attractive. It's a poorly planned and hastily assembled town of 35,000 residents, scattered along a dozen miles of Lake Mohave shoreline. However, it offers an abundance of water recreation. Dozens of RV parks rim the river, mostly on the Arizona side, with a few on the Nevada shore. *For information: Bullhead Area Chamber of Commerce, 1251 Highway 95, Bullhead City, AZ 86430; (928) 754-4121; www.bullheadcity.com.*

**Lake Havasu City** • The home of the displaced London Bridge is the first and still the largest of the Colorado River's planned winter resort communities, with a population of 42,000 and counting. Adjacent Lake Havasu offers an aquatic bounty. Many RV parks are in the immediate area, including a full service resort on Lake Havasu Peninsula. *For information: Lake Havasu Tourism Bureau, 314 London Bridge Rd., Lake Havasu, AZ 86403; (800) 242-8278 or (928) 855-4115; www.ci.lake-havasu-city.az.us.*

**Lake Mead National Recreation Area** • This isn't a community in the normal sense; it's a federal recreation area covering Arizona and Nevada shorelines of Lake Mead and Lake Mohave. If you're a water sports buff, this is the place; Lake Mead is America's largest reservoir. For those impressed by statistics, Mead and Mohave combined have more total shoreline miles than California.

There's no town on the Arizona side of the lake, although Boulder City, Nevada (population 12,600), offers all the essentials. It's an attractive community laid out in the 1930s as the construction town for Hoover Dam, and its downtown area has been preserved as an Art Deco historic site. Among its lures are an interesting museum and an historic hotel; tours are conducted at nearby Hoover Dam. Curiously, Boulder City is the only town in Nevada that prohibits gambling. However, there are plenty of casinos nearby, including one between Boulder City and the Arizona border. Las Vegas is a mere 30 miles away.

Lake Mead NRA is primarily RV country, unless you want to check into a motel room or resort for the winter. Nine marinas occupy Lake Mead and Lake Mohave shorelines. Most have NRA-operated campgrounds, plus RV parks with long-term rental spaces. Some offer lodge resorts as well. In addition, there are several motels in Boulder City. Incidentally, RV facilities book up very early in the winter season, so act accordingly. The climate at lakeside is similar to Bullhead City. Winters are warm and dry with cool evenings, and rainfall is less than four inches a year; most falls in summer. *For information: Lake Mead National Recreation Area, 601 Nevada Highway, Boulder City, NV 89005, (702) 293-8906; and Boulder City Chamber of Commerce, 1305 Arizona St., Boulder City, NV 89005, (702) 293-2034.*

**Parker** • Surrounded by the Colorado River Indian Reservation, Parker is a friendly mix of Native Americans and the rest of us Americans. It has a quiet, small-town aura, with a population just over 3,000. While not a fancy resort town, it's one of the least expensive places on the river. The area offers a huge selection of RV parking spaces. The twenty-mile "Parker Strip" between the town and Parker Dam to the north is practically wall-to-wall RV parks and resorts. They line both the Arizona and California shores. *For information: Parker Area Chamber of Commerce, 1217 California Ave., Parker, AZ 85344; (928) 669-2174; www.arizonaguide.com/parker.*

**Quartzsite** ● This curious settlement is 21 miles east of the Colorado River, on Interstate 10. The good news is that it has the cheapest RV parks in the state—probably in the country. The bad news is that it's hound-dog homely. Quartzsite is a patch of desert that has become one huge RV facility. Permanent dwellings are limited to a few houses, service stations, cafés and stores. Thousands of temporary shops are set up in tents during huge annual swap meets held from late January into February. They lure the world's largest gathering of RVers, swelling the town's population from 3,400 to several hundred thousand. The nearest full-service community is Blythe, California, 25 miles west. *For information: Quartzsite Chamber of Commerce, P.O. Box 85, Quartzsite, AZ 85346, (928) 927-5600; www.quartzsitechamber.com.*

**Yuma** ● Snowbirds nearly double Yuma's population of nearly 80,000 each winter. It's not a fancy resort town, but more of a revitalizing Main Street USA that offers a diversity of attractions along with sunny winter climate. Occupying the site of Yuma Crossing on the first cross-country trail to California, the town is rich in history and it has been designated a National Heritage Area. It's southernmost and driest of the Colorado River corridor towns, with an annual rainfall of less than three inches. Although it rims the river, most of its RV resorts are inland, along I-8 to the east. Others are across the stream, in Winterhaven, California. *For information: Yuma Convention & Visitors Bureau, 202 S. First Ave., Yuma, AZ 85364; (928) 376-0100; www. visityuma.com.*

# SOUTHERN ARIZONA

Tucson and the area south to Nogales offer fine Snowbird climes. We also recommend Sierra Vista, a bit farther east. It's located in a rather interesting area, often overlooked by Arizona visitors:

**Sierra Vista** ● This sprawling yet well planned community of nearly 40,000 is an appealing winter roost if you don't mind chilly evenings. January nights can get frosty and you may get a rare dusting of snow,0 although the winter climate is generally rather temperate. We like its location in Arizona's "Cowboy Corner," near historic sites such as Tombstone, Fort Huachuca and Chiricahua National Monument. Several mountain wilderness areas also are nearby. Tucson is but 70 miles away, and the Mexican border is close as well. Seasonal apartments are scarce; most winter accommodations are in RV parks, which are rather inexpensive. Several are concentrated in nearby Huachuca City, which is a bit on the scruffy side. *For information: Greater Si-*

erra Vista Chamber of Commerce, 21 E. Wilcox Dr., Sierra Vista, AZ 85635; (800) 288-3861 or (520) 458-6940; www.sierravistachamber.org.

**Tubac** ● A bit warmer than Sierra Vista, Tubac is a tiny, weather-worn art colony about 40 miles south of Tucson. It's rich in history as Arizona's oldest non-native settlement. Assuming you like slightly scruffy historic-artistic allure, Tubac has only one major drawback for potential Snowbirders—its winter visitor facilities are minimal. There are a few RV parks in the surrounding area; apartment/condo rentals are rare. *For information: Tubac Chamber of Commerce, P.O. Box 1866, Tubac, AZ 85646; (520) 398-2704.*

**Tucson** ● With fine cultural offerings, good restaurants, desert gardens, excellent museums and galleries, Tucson is a great Snowbird roost. Think of it as a flat San Francisco with warm sunshine. It offers a good assortment of RV parks and resorts, winter apartments and condos. Another plus: Arizona's best Mexican bordertown shopping is just 63 miles south, in Nogales. Tucson is cooler than the Colorado River corridor; January nights can be chilly although the average daytime high is a pleasant 66. *For information: Metropolitan Tucson Convention & Visitors Bureau, 110 S. Church Ave., Suite 9100, Tucson, AZ 85701; (800) 638-8350 or (520) 624-1817; www.visittucson.org.*

# JOINING THE RV CLAN?

If retirement is just down the road, you may be considering the purchase of a travel trailer, fifth-wheel unit or motorhome. They're a great boon to Snowbirds, offering most of the comforts of home in a more or less portable package.

Virtually every sunbelt chamber of commerce has lists of RV parks and mobile home resorts that cater to long-term visitors. Incidentally, the best place to find RV park and campground directories is in rec vehicle and camper supply stores, not in book stores.

The *Arizona Travel Planner* published by the state's tourist office lists scores of RV parks. For a free copy, contact the **Arizona Office of Tourism,** 2702 N. Third St., Suite 4015, Phoenix, AZ 85004-4608; (888) 520-3434 or (602) 230-7733; *www.arizonaguide.com* or *www.arizonavacationvalues.com.*

The **American Automobile Association** lists assorted Arizona campgrounds and RV parks in its *Southwestern CampBook,* although you must be a member to get one. Woodalls *North American Campground Directory* and Trailer Life's *Campground/RV Park Directory* are thick, comprehensive guides listing camping facilities in Arizona and elsewhere.

You probably know that mobile home parks are set up primarily for permanently parked units while RV parks are more for short-term visitors. In Arizona, however, both types of facilities often make exceptions to accommodate RVers for the winter. Many are combined mobile home and RV parks.

**IMPORTANT:** Many RV parks with long-term rates—particularly those near metropolitan areas—book up early for winter, so make your plans as soon as possible.

# TYPES OF REC VEHICLES

We've had considerable experience with RV living, since we used a 21-foot "Minnie-Winnie" named *Ickybod* when we researched state travel guides. Although we now do mostly city guides, we still fire up our RV when we feel the need to flee to nearby mountains and deserts. Of course, *Ick* would be a bit snug for a four to six month stay under the Arizona sun. You'll likely want something more roomy.

Rec vehicles come in seven basic types and we'll review each to help you make your choice. A major consideration is mobility once you get to your Snowbird roost. Some folks tow a "tag-along" vehicle that becomes their runabout after they're parked at an RV park. Others lean toward travel trailers or fifth-wheel units so they can use the towing rig to get about.

If you plan to buy a tag-along, check with the car dealer about its tow-ability. Some vehicles' drive trains are lubricated only when the engine is running. A solution is to get a two-wheel towing dolly that keeps the drive wheels off the ground.

**IMPORTANT:** Most states, including Arizona, require that occupants wear safety belts whenever the vehicle is in motion, and this includes RVs. It's legal in most states to ride in the back of a motorhome, fifth-wheel or camper if belts are available, although not in a towed travel trailer. Obviously, it's unsafe to be unbelted in any vehicle, and particularly to be moving about in an RV that's underway.

Now, a review of your RV choices:

## Pickup-mounted campers

This was America's original mass-produced motor home—a housing shell mounted on a pickup or truck bed.

*Advantages* ● Obviously, this is your best buy if you already own a pickup or small truck. Some camper units are equipped with jacks so you can drive out from under the shell and have use of your vehicle. (However, the support legs on most aren't very substantial; they're designed mostly for shedding and storing the camper shell at home.) Today's fancy pickups come with all the trimmings and are fairly easy to handle. They have a reasonably short wheelbase and they aren't too difficult to park.

*Disadvantages* ● You can't move between the driving and passenger compartment without stopping, although emergency access is now required on campers sold in most states. Campers have a rather high center of gravity and tend to be unstable in winds. Also, most are too snug for long-term residence.

## Motorhomes

These are built from the wheels up, onto a ready-made chassis. Most have long rear overhangs to provide more interior room on a relatively short wheelbase.

*Advantages* • Motorhomes are the vehicles of choice for most Snowbirds and other RVers. They come in all sizes from little 18-footers to 50-foot castles on wheels with all the amenities. They offer direct access between the driving and living area. They're easy to set up and most are self-contained. Pull up and park, and you're home.

*Disadvantages* • The larger and more comfortable they are, the more difficult they are to maneuver. Of course, they have power steering and brakes and the better ones have adequate horsepower. Still, the long wheelbase makes them tricky to manipulate. And forget about parallel parking! Because of long rear overhangs, the driver has to be careful not to swat a sign or passer-by when making a tight turn. Motorhomes generally are the most expensive RV rigs, foot for foot.

## Chassis mount

They're similar to motorhomes, although the unit is built onto the chassis of a van or pickup, utilizing the original cab.

*Advantages* • They're usually less expensive than motorhomes, since the builder buys mass-produced chassis-cab units. Otherwise, they offer the same advantages.

*Disadvantage* • The van wheelbase limits their size, and some of the larger rigs have ridiculously long rear overhangs, increasing the risk of slapping something in a tight turn.

## Travel trailers

These are the oldest RVs, tracing their ancestry back hundreds of years to horse-drawn gypsy carts and shepherd wagons.

*Advantages* • If you like to nest in the same place all winter, travel trailers may be your best bet. They're much less expensive, since you aren't buying a motor vehicle, and they generally offer more room per lineal foot. And of course, you have your towing rig free once you get settled in.

*Disadvantages* • Speed limit is 55 miles per hour for towed vehicles in many states. Also, most states prohibit carrying passengers in trailers. The rigs tend to be unstable in high crosswinds and winding roads. Your ride up front will be rougher, since the hitch telegraphs bumps to the towing vehicle. Finally, they're really tough to park.

## Fifth-wheel units

These are hybrids between travel trailers and campers. The rig is attached to a special hitch mounted in the bed of a pickup or truck. Fifth-wheel units cost about the same, foot-per-foot, as travel trailers.

*Advantages* ● They're more stable than a travel trailer and some states allow belted passengers to ride in them. They're easy to unhook and set up at a campground, although perhaps not quite as easy as a travel trailer. You can get very large rigs with all of the comforts, including rooms that pop out once you're parked. However, you must have a pretty hefty truck to pull it. Fifth-wheelers are easier to maneuver than trailers.

*Disadvantages* ● Once you've parked the rig, you're stuck with a truck for transportation—although some of today's rigs are quite fancy. Also, fifth-wheelers share a trailer's disadvantages in maneuvering and parking.

## Tent trailers

If you're on a tight budget, or if you have a light-duty towing vehicle, folding tent trailers may be the way to go.

*Advantages* ● They're a cut above a tent, and relatively cheap. Some of the better tent trailers even have bathrooms and showers, plus full kitchens. They tow much easier than travel trailers. Their compact, fold-down design offers little wind resistance. Some of the lower ones won't block your rear vision, particularly if you tow it with a higher profile vehicle.

*Disadvantages* ● They offer little insulation from temperature and campground noises. Although they're *relatively* easy to set up, all other types of RVs are easier.

## Van conversion

This is similar to a chassis mount, except that the living area is built into the original body shell of the van.

*Advantages* ● They're small enough to maneuver and park in town. We researched our earlier guidebooks in the original *Ickybod*, a Volkswagen pop-top, and really appreciated its maneuverability. Obviously, they get better gas mileage than bigger rigs. Pop-top versions are reasonably comfortable, once you get settled in a campground.

*Disadvantages* ● Face it, folks. Do you want to live for several months in a van without an onboard pottie or full kitchen? (Some have tiny bathrooms, although that sacrifices what little storage space is available.) Since vans have limited living space, the bed has to be put up or folded away every day. They're not practical for long-term use, except for a person who doesn't mind padding to a campground pottie.

## TRAILER REGULATIONS

All recreational vehicles require special handling skills, particularly trailers and fifth-wheel units. Because of the inherent instability of towed vehicles, most states have special laws governing them. They are fairly uniform from one state to the next and usually include these requirements:

- Safety chains are mandatory. They should be long enough to permit turning, yet short enough to keep the trailer tongue from digging into the ground if the hitch fails.
- Passengers aren't allowed to ride in travel trailers in most states.
- Size limits vary from state to state. In Arizona, a trailer can't be more than 40 feet long, eight feet wide and 13.5 feet high. Combined length of a trailer and towing vehicle can't exceed 65 feet.
- Outside mirrors are required on both sides of a towing vehicle if the trailer obstructs rear vision—which all but small tent trailers do.
- Towed rigs must have the same lighting system as any other vehicle—taillights, stoplights and turn indicators.
- Towing more than one vehicle, such as a travel trailer and a boat, is a no-no.
- The speed limit for towed vehicles is the same as for large trucks, which in most states is 55 mph.
- In Arizona, separate braking systems are required on trailers with a gross weight over 1,500 pounds. It varies from 1,500 to 3,000 pounds in other states. Trailer brakes are always a good idea, whether required or not. They help prevent jackknifing and they keep the trailer from shoving the towing vehicle forward in a sudden stop.

## HANDLE WITH CARE

Whether you're driving a motorhome or towing a trailer or fifth-wheel, follow these tips to ensure that your new home on the road stays there:

- If you're a first-timer, practice stopping and turning on familiar roads before you head out. An RV has a wider turning radius and most have long rear overhangs. They also have higher centers of gravity and they're sluggish in acceleration. Give yourself plenty of leeway when passing. RVs require longer stopping distances than cars, particularly trailers and fifth-wheel units. Incidentally, most states require all slow moving vehicles to pull over and let faster traffic pass, and many require that RVs and trailers stay to the outside lane of multiple lane highways and freeways, except when passing.
- Downshift when you're going downhill. The added weight of an RV will push you faster than you think.
- When you approach a speed bump, *crawl* over it. If you hit a speed bump at an angle, your land yacht will rock and pitch like a boat in a storm.
- ***VERY IMPORTANT!*** RVs behave very badly on muddy roads. Unlike cars and trucks, most of an RV's weight is over the rear wheels and this can act as a pendulum on a slippery surface. Dual rear wheels don't help much. You may be less likely to bog down in the mud with duals, but you'll fishtail very quickly on a slippery surface. As for snow and ice, you'd best stay in the RV park until conditions improve.

• If you're pulling a heavy trailer, get a special towing package that includes a beefed-up rear suspension and load-leveler. Otherwise, the trailer tongue will push down on your vehicle's rear, making it less stable. Also, it can tilt your headlights into the eyes of oncoming drivers. As noted above, larger trailers should have independent braking systems to avoid jackknifing in a sudden stop; most states require them.

• Remember that your rear vision is restricted when you're driving an RV or pulling a trailer, and side-view mirrors usually have blind spots. (A combined regular and concave mirror will help solve this problem.) Signal well in advance and change lanes slowly, to give vehicles around you time to react.

• Don't overload your rig. Water and fuel weigh about eight pounds per gallon, adding hundreds of pounds to the vehicle's weight. Check with the dealer for the gross vehicle weight rating, which is the maximum allowable load, including people and cargo. If you exceed this, lots of things can happen and they're all bad. You may have a blowout; your rig may lurch drunkenly on curves and accelerate on downgrades; and you won't have adequate power for hill climbing or safe passing.

• Balance your load and keep your RV's center of gravity as low as possible. Don't put heavy objects in higher cabinets or cab-over bunks.

• Be very careful of fire! Check all gas fittings and carry dry chemical extinguishers. Bear in mind that you're traveling with several gallons of Propane and gasoline. Check evacuation routes. RVs are required to have at least two exits. One may be a break-away window, so learn where it is.

• Don't give your RV a headache. The average car is just over four feet high but most RVs top out at seven feet or more.

• Keep an eye on your tail. Most RVs have long rear overhangs, and it's easy to slap something in a tight turn, or back into an object that's closer than it appears in your mirrors. Also, the distance between your rear view mirror and rear window creates a tunnel vision effect; you usually can't see a vehicle that's riding on your tail. To correct this problem, install one of those fish-eye lenses on the rear window.

• If your rig has dual wheels, periodically check the air pressure of both the inner and outer tires by pressing your thumb hard into the sidewalls. You can't always tell by the tire profile if one has gone flat, since one holds the other up. It's extremely dangerous to travel at high speeds if both duals aren't sharing the load. Also, remember that RV tires are rated to carry more air than passenger car tires; keep them at the proper pressure.

• Finally—and this is for courtesy as well as safety—stay in the right hand lane except to pass. On two-lane roads, pull over whenever possible to let faster traffic go by. An RV's width makes it difficult for those behind to see oncoming vehicles. Further, motorists following too closely may not realize that you can't see them in your side view mirrors or through your rear window.

Nothing is more exasperating than trundling behind a big motorhome or trailer rig on a two-lane highway. Drivers *do not* have the right to arbitrarily set speed limits for those behind them by poking along. And no, we're not amused by those bumper stickers that read: "I may be slow, but I'm ahead of you."

Don't force an impatient motorist into an unsafe pass. You may be the first at the scene of the accident—as a participant.

# RV SUPPORT GROUPS

When you join the RV set, you join a fraternity that has its own jamborees, caravans and clubs. You'll find that its members are a gregarious lot, quick to share information, opinions, advice, assistance and friendship. Making friends at an RV park or campground is easy; just stop by and borrow a cup of coffee. Many RV parks, particularly those catering to long-term visitors, sponsor dances and other social functions.

Incidentally, we encountered a discomforting statistic a few years ago: Ninety-six percent of all RVers are couples. The vast majority of those who have lost a mate or are single apparently stay at home. That's a shame. If you're single or widowed, don't be shy about hitting the road alone. Many second-time-around romances and good friendships have bloomed over a campground barbecue pit or bingo party.

Some rec vehicle makers, such as Airstream, promote social programs and RV gatherings for their vehicle owners. Camping groups such as Thousand Trails do the same.

A particularly useful organization for Snowbirds is the **Good Sam Club,** operated by TL Enterprises. A modest annual membership fee provides a ten percent discount on Good Sam-rated RV parks, plus free trip routing service, and a newsletter that lists upcoming caravans, camporees and other news of the RV world. Other services include RV insurance and towing, a travel agency, and mail forwarding and messenger service (for a fee). For information, contact: Good Sam Club, 2575 Vista del Mar, Ventura, CA 93001; (800) 234-3450; *www.goodsamclub.com.*

If all of this sounds like a paid commercial, it isn't. Sam probably doesn't even know that he's getting a free plug. As a matter of fact, we aren't Good Sam members since we don't often use commercial RV parks or campgrounds.

## PART TWO
# THE COMMUNITIES

We've already touched on several communities that offer good job prospects, retirement opportunities for winter roosts. What follows is a more detailed look at the state's cities and towns. However, we don't cover every single city and hamlet; we review only those which we feel offer potential—and appeal—for those contemplating Arizona in their future.

In the lists that follow, property taxes were supplied by the Arizona Department of Commerce or by individual communities. Population figures are the most recent we could find, from the last census or from community estimates.

Arizona's population is focused in two counties—Maricopa (Phoenix) and Pima (Tucson). Four out of five of the state's residents live in one or the other. Both counties also have extensive wilderness areas. Maricopa County's Valley of the Sun is surrounded by rugged mountains, and Pima County stretches west across untracked desert, nearly reaching the California border.

Much of what's left of the state's population is along the Colorado River Corridor, shared by Mohave, La Paz and Yuma counties, and in huge Coconino County in north central Arizona, covering more than 18,000 square miles. The largest cities outside the Phoenix and Tucson metropolitan hubs are Yuma with 77,500 people and Flagstaff with 57,700. As evidence of Arizona's lopsided population distribution, they rank only tenth and only eleventh in size.

# Arizona Counties

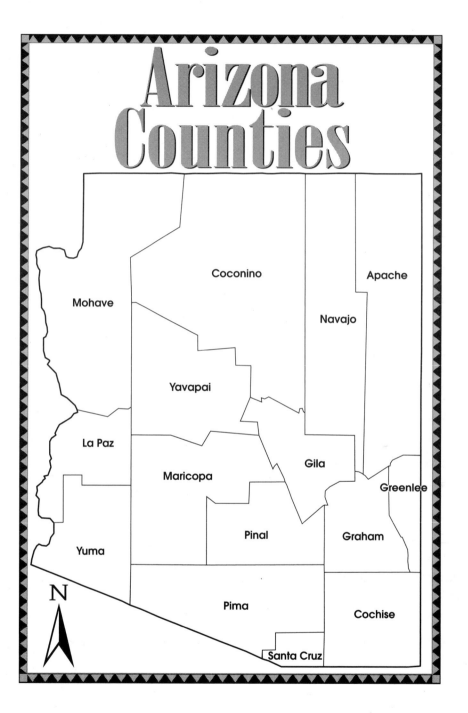

Mohave

Coconino

Apache

Navajo

Yavapai

La Paz

Gila

Greenlee

Maricopa

Pinal

Graham

Yuma

N

Pima

Cochise

Santa Cruz

## Chapter Eight

# THE WESTERN EDGE
## THE COLORADO RIVER CORRIDOR

---

This section covers communities bordering on the Colorado River, that watery divide between Arizona, Nevada and California. The chapter also includes two towns that are a few miles inland.

*Rio Colorado* isn't really a river in this area, however. With seven dams between the Grand Canyon and the Mexican border, it's more of a chain of lakes. These reservoirs may disturb environmentalists, although they provide unlimited water recreation, and that's one of the area's chief lures.

**THE WAY IT WAS** ● The Colorado is one of the most harnessed and harassed rivers in the world. Indeed, its much-diverted muddy water is the lifeblood of southwestern Arizona and much of southern California and Nevada.

It ran wild and free for untold centuries, carving the majestic Grand Canyon above and carrying rich red soil into the Gulf of California. Like all wild things, *Rio Colorado* was unpredictable. For centuries, native people tried to farm along its rich bottomlands, only to be flooded out one year and wilted by drought the next.

European and American explorers began coming upriver from the Gulf of California in the early 1800s; others passed this way overland during the 1849 California gold rush. Some chose to stay; they pushed the native inhabitants off their land and took up farming. Suffering

*Wedged into rugged Black Canyon, Hoover Dam put the mighty Colorado into harness and quickly became—from the ground and from the air—a major tourist attraction*

from the same water flow frustrations as their predecessors, these newcomers decided that the great river needed to be put into harness.

The first efforts came in 1901, when water was diverted into the Imperial Canal near Yuma to irrigate the dry but rich soils of California's Imperial Valley. However, the river didn't take to harness easily. A flood breached the canal in 1905 and the wild river changed course. For sixteen months it flowed unchecked into the Salton Basin, which was 235 feet below sea level. By the time the breach finally was closed in 1907, the Salton Basin had become the 40-mile-long Salton Sea, which still exists.

Men were more determined than ever to control the Big Red. In 1909, the Laguna Dam was completed just north of Yuma. It provided desert irrigation, and it also brought an end to river navigation. Until this time, paddlewheelers had chugged as much as 300 miles upstream from the Gulf of California to serve riverside communities.

## No more river mischief

Laguna Dam was too far downstream for effective flood control, and spring thaws continued bringing muddy overflows. To put a final cap on the river's mischief, the U.S. Bureau of Reclamation launched history's most challenging dam project, in the narrow and rocky walls of Black Canyon. In 1935, the completion of Hoover Dam—the world's highest—marked the end of the free-flowing Colorado.

Meanwhile, in another time and place, air conditioning was being perfected. In 1906, Willis S. Carrier of Buffalo, New York, developed a "dew-point control air washer," passing air through water-cooled pipes. Better refrigerants were developed in the 1920s and the true air conditioner was born. The first public use of air conditioning was in a movie theater in 1922. By the 1930s, small and relatively efficient units were being produced.

In Arizona, they couldn't have come at a better time.

**THE WAY IT IS** ● Air conditioners and dams have created a string of skinny communities and skinny lakes along the banks of the lower Colorado. They stretch from Hoover Dam south to Yuma and into Mexico.

Most of the riverside towns are unplanned and not very pretty. The subtle beauty of the desert suffers under the weight of asphalt and the glare of neon. These towns are lively places, however; glossy speed-boats skim over placid reservoirs and retirees live out their American dream of a winter place in the sun.

The corridor isn't strictly for Snowbirds. Thousands of folks crank up their air conditioners and live here the year-around. However, the area is much more popular with winter visitors. Yuma, the largest of the river towns, nearly doubles its population in winter, and scruffy little Quartzsite balloons from a couple of thousand to about 200,000. If you plan to settle permanently along Arizona's western edge, stay close to your air conditioner in July, when the average daytime high is around 108!

## BULLHEAD CITY

Named for a promontory now submerged into Lake Mohave, Bullhead City sits just above the triangle where the Arizona, Nevada and California borders merge. It's a low-rise scatter of housing tracts, modular homes and mobile home parks. This sun-warmed jumble of hasty settlement is the most northern of the string of towns along *Rio Colorado's* Arizona shorelines.

South along State Route 95, the unincorporated communities of Riviera, Fort Mohave and Golden Shores stretch Bullhead's outskirts to Interstate 40. Much of this area is within the Fort Mohave Indian Reservation.

Bullhead City wasn't incorporated until 1984, although its roots go back to 1945, when it was the construction camp for Davis Dam, immediately to the north. A mere 504 feet above sea level, it often earns the dubious honor as America's summer hot spot. Tourist officials wish people wouldn't talk about that, of course. In winter, thousands of

Snowbirds triple the town's population. About twenty RV and mobile home parks and resorts line the river's shores.

Across the reservoir, Laughlin, Nevada, is another reason for Bullhead's popularity. Back in 1966, entrepreneur Don Laughlin guessed that winter vacationers might like to pass the time pulling a few slot machine handles. He bought a broken-down bait shop and six acres of riverfront and built a small gambling parlor. His Riverside Casino prospered and expanded; more followed and a sudden city blossomed in the desert. Laughlin immodestly named it for himself.

Nearly a dozen gaming halls now line the Nevada side, beguiling Bullhead folks with the seductive glitter of neon. Laughlin even went to the expense of building a bridge to link the two cities.

**Elevation** • 504 feet

**Location** • In Mohave County on State Route 95.

**Climate** • Warm, dry winters with cool evenings; hot, dry summers. July average high is 108.2, low is 79.1; January average high is 62.2, low 41.8. Annual rainfall 4.19 inches; no snowfall.

**Population** • 33,800

**Population trend** • Gained more than 50 percent in the past ten years.

**Property tax** • (assessed at ten percent of real value) $12.83 per $100 assessed valuation.

**Economy** • Tourism fuels Bullhead's economic fires, and of course Snowbirds bring their retirement checks. Booming Laughlin employs more than 14,000 people. The Mohave Generating Station, a cooperative of four utilities, also is a major employer.

**Job prospects** • The services sector, including tourism, employs nearly 40 percent of Bullhead's work force, and much of that commutes to Laughlin. Retail trade is second with 20 percent and construction is third with fourteen percent. Job prospects are about average; many of the residents are retirees.

**Industrial facilities** • A 190-acre industrial park near the airport.

**Real estate** • The area has several planned subdivisions with amenities such as pools and tennis courts, along with conventional homes and a few condos. A typical new three-bedroom home averages about $125,000. Much of Bullhead's housing, both permanent and temporary, is in mobile home parks.

**The media** • Three newspapers—the tri-weekly *Mohave Valley News*, bi-weekly *Booster/Laughlin Leader* and the weekly *Laughlin Gambler-Bullhead City Bee*. One TV station, plus a cable company.

**Medical services** • A 68-bed hospital, a 120-bed extended care facility and a mental health clinic.

**Transportation** • Served by Greyhound. Bullhead City Airport has a 5,000 foot runway and scheduled flights by feeder lines.

*Education* • Bullhead City campus of Mohave Community College, plus elementary, intermediate and high schools.

*Local government* • Incorporated in 1984; mayor, six council members and a city manager.

*Places to stay* • Twenty-five motels, more than 20 RV parks and nine mobile home parks.

*Leisure facilities* • Three public parks, public boat launches, one 18-hole and four nine-hole golf courses.

*Tourist lures* • The biggest lure, of course, is Lake Mohave, offering assorted water sports. Laughlin's gaming parlors are another major draw. The Black Mountains to the east provide outdoor pursuits. The historic mining towns of Oatman and Goldroad are just to the east.

*Contacts* • Bullhead Area Chamber of Commerce, 1251 Highway 95, Bullhead City, AZ 86429; (928) 754-4121; *www.bullheadcity.com.*

Bullhead City Economic Development Authority, 1255 Marina Blvd., Bullhead City, AZ 86439; (928) 763-9400.

## KINGMAN

This community of more than 32,000 occupies a ruggedly attractive valley of eroded buttes and cliffs at the junction of I-40 and U.S. Highway 93. Dating from 1882, it was named for surveyor Lewis Kingman, who was plotting a rail route between Needles, California, and Albuquerque, New Mexico. However, it was silver and copper discoveries in the surrounding hills that kept the town on the map.

• FLAGSTAFF

• PHOENIX

• TUCSON

Mining declined during the 1930s and was virtually shut down as a non-essential industry during World War II. The surrounding countryside is dotted with ghost towns and semi-ghost towns worthy of exploring. They include Chloride, Cerbat, Mineral Park, Goldroad, Old Trails and Oatman.

While those towns withered, Kingman survived as a provisioning center for travelers on the Santa Fe Railway and historic U.S. Highway 66. The first path through here dates back to 1859, when Army Lieutenant Edward Beal's construction crew carved a wagon road that eventually led from Arkansas to Los Angeles. It was the first federally funded road in the Southwest. Old Route 66 roughly followed its course, although it veered northeast to Chicago.

Kingman is still an important crossroad and a popular pausing place for motorists hurrying along I-40. The Economic and Development Commission has been successful in attracting light industry and warehousing operations, and the town has seen a population jump of nearly 58 percent in the past decade. Incidentally, the town's favorite son isn't surveyor Kingman. It's the late, gravel-voiced actor Andy Devine, who was born in nearby Flagstaff and grew up here. The main street is named for him, and he's featured in a special exhibit at the local museum. Most of Kingman's business has shifted to the suburbs, so the turn-of-the-last-century downtown along old Highway 66 is being preserved as an historic district.

*Elevation* • 3,225 feet

*Location* • In Mohave County on I-40, about 50 miles northeast of the Colorado River.

*Climate* • More temperate in summer than the river towns because of its higher elevation. July average high 97.4, low 67.2; January average high 55.3, low 31.4. Rainfall 9.35 inches; snowfall 3.4 inches.

*Population* • 21,400, with a similar number in surrounding unincorporated areas.

*Population trend* • Gained nearly 58 percent in the past ten years.

*Property tax* • $9.80 per $100 assessed valuation; the rate has declined in recent years.

*Economy* • Kingman is the regional trade center for northwestern Arizona. With I-40 and the Santa Fe railway passing through town, it's an important warehousing and distribution area. An airport industrial park has attracted some light manufacturing.

*Job prospects* • Fairly good, according to the Economic Development Commission. Kingman has been successful in job creation in the manufacturing and distribution business, because of its key location and transportation infrastructure. The best prospects are in manufacturing, warehousing, retail sales, tourism and related services. More than one job in four is in wholesale and retail trade, with a similar number in the services sector.

*Industrial facilities* • Kingman Airport Industrial Park with 4,000 acres, plus various other industrial and warehousing sites.

*Real estate* • The housing market includes a mix of older homes and a few subdivisions, with the average price of a three-bedroom detached home around $70,000.

*The media* • One daily newspaper, *The Mohave County Miner* and a weekly, the *Kingman Booster*. One local TV station plus feeds from Phoenix and Las Vegas; also a cable service.

*Medical services* • A small regional hospital, several medical clinics and nursing homes.

*Transportation* • Served by Greyhound and Amtrak. Kingman Airport has two 6,800-foot lighted runways, with scheduled air service.

*Education* • Mohave Community College, plus several elementary, middle and high schools.

*Local government* • Seat of Mohave County since 1887. Incorporated in 1952; mayor, six council members and a city manager.

**Places to stay** • More than 30 motels with a total of 1,632 rooms, and several RV parks.

**Leisure facilities** • Ten public parks, two public pools, three fitness centers, a senior center and two golf courses, plus tennis, racquetball and shuffleboard courts.

**Tourist lures** • Hualapai Mountain Park and the Cerbat Mountains offer picnicking, camping and hiking. A downtown historic district includes early 20th century buildings, Locomotive Park, Historic Route 66 monuments and the excellent Mohave Museum of History and Arts.

**Contacts** • Kingman Chamber of Commerce (Powerhouse Visitor Center), 120 W. Andy Devine Ave., Kingman, AZ 86402; (928) 753-6253; *www.kingmanchamber.org.*

Economic & Tourism Development Commission, City of Kingman, 310 N. Fourth St., Kingman, AZ 86401; (928) 753-8130; *www.ci.kingman.az.us.*

Kingman 2005 Inc., 7000 Flightline Dr., Kingman, AZ 86401; (928) 757-2005; *e-mail: kng@2005@ctaz.com*

## LAKE HAVASU CITY

You've likely heard the story. The London Bridge, while not falling down, was too old and narrow to handle modern traffic, so city officials put it up for sale in 1968. They didn't really expect any buyers, but entrepreneur Robert P. McCulloch offered $2,460,000. He said he wanted to move it to the Arizona desert, where he'd purchased a piece of Lake Havasu shoreline.

About $9 million later, McCulloch had performed a most curious feat. The bridge was dismantled stone by stone and reconstructed over an Arizona sandpile. Then the sand was scooped out to create a channel between the mainland and a peninsula in Lake Havasu. Fortunately, the London Bridge did not fall down. *Voile!* McCulloch had the centerpiece for his planned city in the desert.

Lake Havasu City is the largest of the new communities along the Colorado River and the fastest growing, with a population increase of 72 percent in the past decade. It's also the best planned of the riverside towns. Local officials say "The Bridge" is Arizona's second most-visited attraction, after the Grand Canyon. An adjoining English Village offers such British lures as a London cab, double decker bus and even a proper pub.

**Elevation** • 482 feet

**Location** • In Mohave County, nineteen miles south of I-40 on State Highway 95.

**Climate** ● Warm, dry winters with cool evenings, and hot, dry summers. July average high 108.6, low 78.8; January average high 67.3, low 37.1. Rainfall 3.82 inches; no snowfall.

**Population** ● 44,200

**Population trend** ● Gained over 72 percent in the past ten years.

**Property tax** ● $11.11 per $100 assessed valuation.

**Economy** ● Tourists and retirees are the main contributors to Havasu's economy. Officials estimate that "The Bridge" lures more than a million visitors who bring $100 million to the local economy each year. Light manufacturing is gaining ground, particularly in a city-owned industrial park.

**Job prospects** ● They're average, with rather low wages, according to the local Job Service office. Best possibilities are in light manufacturing, tourism and related service jobs.

**Industrial facilities** ● City-owned light industrial & business park.

**Real estate** ● Planned subdivisions offer some of the best housing variety along the Colorado River. Prices for a three-bedroom home begin around $70,000.

**The media** ● One daily newspaper, *Today's News Herald*; the area also is served by Kingman's daily *Mohave County Miner*. Two local TV stations and cable feeds of regional stations, plus a cable TV company.

**Medical services** ● A 138-bed hospital and a 120-bed nursing home, plus several resident care and retirement homes.

**Transportation** ● Served by Greyhound and shuttle vans to the Las Vegas airport; America West Express flies from Lake Havasu Airport.

**Education** ● Lake Havasu campus of Mohave Community College, with extension courses from Northern Arizona University, plus several elementary schools, a middle school and high school.

**Local government** ● Incorporated in 1978; mayor, six council members and a city manager.

**Places to stay** ● More than a score of motels and resort hotels, short-term apartment and condo rentals, several mobile home parks and campgrounds.

**Leisure facilities** ● Four golf courses, four public parks, several tennis courts, swimming beaches and boat launches.

**Tourist lures** ● The bridge and its English Village are the main draws, of course. Water sports are popular and various watercraft rentals are available at the village. Lake Havasu State Park contains several beaches, camping and picnic areas.

**Contacts** ● Lake Havasu Tourism Bureau, 314 London Bridge Rd., Lake Havasu City, AZ 86403; (800) 242-8278 or (928) 855-4115.

Partnership for Economic Development, same address as above; (928) 505-7333.

City of Lake Havasu, 2330 McCulloch Blvd. N., Lake Havasu City, AZ 86403; (928) 453-4142; *ci.lake-havasu-city.az.us.*

# PARKER

Parker is a folksy little riverside town surrounded by the Colorado River Indian Reservation. However, it's not exclusively an Indian community, but an affable ethnic mix of Native Americans and the rest of us Americans. The town was founded in 1908 and named in honor of Eli Parker, the first Native American to fight in the Spanish-American War.

While it's not a glamorous resort, Parker offers the advantage of inexpensive home prices and some of the cheapest RV parks in Arizona. In fact, it's the recreational vehicle capital of the Colorado River Corridor.

The "Parker Strip" stretching ten miles north to Parker Dam is an almost continual swatch of RV parks, on both the Arizona and California shores. The reservoir here has a typical Native American name, Lake Moovalya. It's one of the busiest boating, water-skiing and fishing lakes on the river.

**Elevation** ● 450 feet

**Location** ● On State Route 95 in La Paz County, on Lake Moovalya, about midway between interstates 10 and 40.

**Climate** ● Warm, dry winters with cool evenings; hot, dry summers. July average high 108.6, low 78.8; January average high 67.3, low 37.1. Rainfall 3.82 inches; no snowfall.

**Population** ● 3,150

**Population trend** ● Gained less than eight percent in ten years.

**Property tax** ● $8.13 per $100 assessed valuation.

**Economy** ● Like everything else in Parker, the economy is water oriented. Most of the area's income is derived from tourism, retail sales and retirees. A Native American casino helps lure visitors.

**Job prospects** ● It's not a good market for job hunters, since growth is rather stagnant. A third of the jobs are in tourism and another fifth are in retail trades.

**Industrial facilities** ● A 100-acre industrial park, owned by the Colorado River Indian tribe.

**Real estate** ● Home prices are a good buy and property taxes are among the lowest in the state. Figure on $60,000 to $80,000 for a three-bedroom house.

**The media** ● One weekly newspaper, the *Parker Pioneer*. Two local TV stations, plus feeds from Yuma and Phoenix, and cable TV.

**Medical services** ● One small hospital.

**Transportation** ● Served by Greyhound. Avi-Suquilla Airport has a 4,800-foot lighted runway; no scheduled air service.

*Education* • Elementary and high schools; extension courses available from Yuma's Arizona Western College.

*Local government* • Incorporated in 1948; mayor, six council members and a city manager. Parker became the seat of La Paz County when it was separated from northern Yuma County in 1983.

*Places to stay* • About a score of motels, 49 mobile home and RV parks on the Arizona side and a similar number on the California shore.

*Leisure facilities* • Six parks, a public swimming pool, a senior citizens' center and an 18-hole golf course.

*Tourist lures* • Water sports abound, particularly along the Parker Strip. The Colorado River Tribes Indian Museum offers exhibits on Native American culture, plus a gift shop and library. The Blue Water Resort and Casino has 200 hotel rooms. Camping, boat launching, water sports and picnicking are available at nearby Buckskin State Park; River Island State Park and La Paz County Park.

*Contacts* • Parker Area Chamber of Commerce, 1217 California Ave., Parker, AZ 85344; (928) 669-2174; *www.arizonaguide.com/ parker; e-mail: parker.chamber@redrivernet.com.*

Town of Parker, P.O. Box 609, (1314 11th St.) Parker, AZ 85344; (928) 669-9265; *www.ci.parker.az.us.*

# QUARTZSITE

We probably should be more kind, but Quartzsite is not a pretty face. It's a rather homely town that consists mostly of a collection of desert RV parks. It dates back to 1856 when one Charles Tyson built a civilian fortress and stage stop.

Not much happened for the next century until a developer opened a service station and restaurant and began promoting an annual gem show and flea market called "The Main Event." It has grown into a series of overlapping winter swap meets and gem shows that draws upwards of 1.5 million people. Many are retirees in RVs and the town has more than 70 RV parks. Folks say that you can walk from one end of town to the other over the rooftops of RVs.

The hundreds of thousands of Snowbirders have the time of their lives with barbecues, potluck dinners and dances. Some merely unfold camp chairs on a swatch of Astroturf beside their RVs and breathe in clean desert air. Cheap rent is the town's main attraction. With dozens of RV parks competing for customers, space rent is the lowest in Arizona and perhaps in the entire country.

During much of the winter, the town resembles a huge traveling show that's about to pull up stakes. A few businesses are anchored to the desert dirt, although most of the trade is conducted out of tents and shade ramadas during the swap meets and gem shows. When the mercury starts to rise, Quartzsite shrinks to about 3,350 souls and functions mostly as a refueling stop on Interstate 10. The permanent population *is* growing, however; it nearly doubled in the past decade and more permanent buildings are cropping up.

*Elevation* ● 879 feet

*Location* ● In La Paz County, 21 miles west of the Colorado River at the junction of I-10 and Highway 95.

*Climate* ● Warm, dry winters with balmy evenings; sizzling, dry summers. July average high is 108.6 with no nearby reservoir to cool things off, low is 81; January average high 65, low 36.8. Rainfall 4.37 inches; no snowfall.

*Population* ● About 3,350.

*Population trend* ● Gained nearly eighty percent in ten years.

*Property tax* ● $13.68 per $100 of assessed valuation.

*Economy* ● Tourism is the only basis for Quartzsite's economy and most of that comes between November and April.

*Job prospects* ● They're limited to a few government jobs, plus seasonal retail work. Indicative of the economy, the largest employers are truck stops and fast food places.

*Industrial facilities* ● None.

*Real estate* ● A few homes have been built although most of the action is in RV parks.

*The media* ● No local publications or TV stations. Television feeds from Yuma and Phoenix, plus a cable system.

*Medical services* ● Three small clinics; the nearest full-scale hospital is in Blythe, California, 22 miles west.

*Transportation* ● Greyhound; nearest airports are in Parker and Blythe.

*Education* ● An elementary school and high school.

*Local government* ● Incorporated in 1989; mayor, town council and town manager.

*Places to stay* ● Three motels and scores of rec vehicle and mobile home parks.

*Leisure facilities* ● You mean other than sitting on a patch of Astroturf in front of your RV, sipping a martini? There's a large town park, a botanical garden, nine-hole golf course, a senior center and some shuffleboard courts. Some mobile parks have pools, not open to the public.

*Tourist lures* ● Other than a small museum, there isn't much, although hundreds of thousands come for the annual shows. Also, folks are lured into the surrounding hills for excellent rockhounding; the rugged Kofa Mountains to the southwest offers several scenic areas and hiking trails.

***Contacts*** • Quartzsite Chamber of Commerce, P.O. Box 85, Quartzsite, AZ 85346; (928) 927-5600; *www.quartzsitechamber.com;* e-mail: *qtzchamber@redrivernet.com.*

Town of Quartzsite, P.O. Box 2812 (465 N. Plymouth Ave.), Quartzsite, AZ 85346; (928) 927-4333; *www.ci.quartzsite.az.us.*

## YUMA

Anyone who thinks Yuma is just a place to pause for food and fuel on the long haul across the desert on Interstate 8 needs to take another look. This desert town on the banks of the Colorado River is bustin' out all over. Its old downtown area is being revitalized with new restaurants and shops, several historic buildings are being restored and a new riverfront park is in the works. Yuma Crossing State Historic Park is developing into one of the state's more interesting visitor attractions.

Downtown Yuma and its riverfront were designated in 2000 as Yuma Crossing National Heritage Area. It's one of only eighteen such areas in America and the only one in the West. The city's suburbs are busy with new housing developments. With a population pushing 80,000, Yuma is now the largest Arizona city outside the Phoenix and Tucson metropolitan centers.

*Money Magazine* rated it as one of the top places to live in the country, and the *Farmer's Almanac* said Yuma has the best climate in America. Best climate? The average maximum summer temperature is over 100 degrees. But it's a dry heat, as they say, and you can always go jump in the river.

Arizona's earliest explorers saw more barrier than beauty in the Colorado River. Then in 1699, mission founder Father Eusebio Kino found a fording place near the confluence of the Gila and Colorado rivers. "Yuma Crossing" ultimately became an important link in the first trails west, and it's now an historic site. (Kino is credited with naming *Rio Colorado* for its reddish, silt-laden waters.) In 1799, Father Francisco Tomas Garcés established two missions along the river. A presidio was built to protect Mission la Purisima Concepcion, on what is now the California side. The entire settlement, including the good padre, was wiped out in a bloody Quechan Indian uprising two years later. That finished things for the Spanish at Yuma Crossing.

Colonel Stephen Watts Kearny and frontier scout Kit Carson forded the river here in 1846, heading west to help snatch California from Mexico. During the 1849 gold rush, many argonauts used this southern route to avoid the barrier of the Sierra Nevada range to the north.

*Yuma Territorial Prison is one of that city's many historic attractions; this watchtower was built over the prison reservoir.*

A few returned to this area, attracted by nearby gold strikes and the agricultural potential along the river's rich bottomlands.

The hamlet of Colorado City was established here in 1854. Historians tell us—with a sly grin—that the town's first permanent resident was a shady lady named Sarah Bowman, who ran a combined restaurant and bawdy house. The river flexed its muscles in 1862, washing Colorado City into the Gulf of California, bordello and all. Another town, called Arizona City, was built on higher ground. The name later was changed to Yuma, after the local native tribe.

Water diversion from the Colorado provided an agricultural base for Yuma's economy and the town took hold. The military was attracted during World War II by the area's cloud-free days and wide open spaces and two bases are still here—a Marine Corps air station and the U.S. Army Yuma Proving Grounds.

**Elevation** ● 138 feet

**Location** ● In Yuma County, on Interstate 8 along the Colorado River, 25 miles north of the Mexican border.

**Climate** ● Warm, dry winters with cool evenings; hot, dry summers. July average high 106.6; low 73.6; January average high 68.4, low 36.8. Rainfall 2.99 inches (the lowest in Arizona); no snowfall.

**Population** • nearly 80,000

**Population trend** • Gained 36 percent in the past ten years.

**Property tax** • $15.02 per $100 of assessed valuation.

**Economy** • It's a mix, from military bases to Snowbirds to agriculture to tourism. More than 166,000 acres of crops are watered by the Colorado River and agriculture is a billion dollar a year industry.

**Job prospects** • Some industries and warehousing operations have been lured to Yuma, although most of the jobs are in retail trade and services. The border town of San Luis to the south is a major twin-plant manufacturing center, although most of those jobs and local field work are taken by Mexican "guest workers."

**Industrial facilities** • Several industrial parks have been built and others are planned as Yuma pushes to attract more light and heavy industry and warehousing.

**Real estate** • Prices are on the rise; a new three-bedroom house starts at about $150,000.

**The media** • The *Yuma Daily Sun* and the weekly *Valley Foothills News*. Two local TV stations, plus cable TV.

**Medical services** • A fully-equipped hospital and an emergency care unit; several medical clinics and extended care facilities.

**Transportation** • Greyhound and Amtrak stop here. Yuma International Airport is served by scheduled airlines.

**Education** • Arizona Western College, six vocational schools, five private schools, plus several elementary, middle and high schools.

**Local government** • The seat of Yuma County, it was incorporated in 1873; mayor, six council members and a city administrator.

**Places to stay** • More than 30 motels with over 2,000 rooms, and a dozen or more RV parks. Some parks are in town; others are along the river, and eastward along I-8.

**Leisure facilities** • Fifteen public parks, five golf courses, three public pools, an adult recreation center, plus tennis courts and such.

**Tourist lures** • Yuma offers three museums (see Part Three, Chapter Thirteen), plus the Yuma Territorial Prison State Park, Yuma Crossing State Historic Park and Fort Yuma's Quechan Museum on the California side.

**Contacts** • Yuma Convention & Visitors Bureau, 202 S. First Ave., Yuma, AZ 85364; (928) 376-0100; *www.visityuma.com; e-mail: rbeadle@visityuma.com.*

Yuma County Chamber of Commerce, 377 S. Main St., Yuma, AZ 85364; (928) 782-2567; *www.yumachamber.org; e-mail: info@yumachamber.org.*

City of Yuma, 180 W. First St., Yuma, AZ 85364; (928) 783-1271; *www.ci.yuma.az.us.*

Greater Yuma Economic Development Corporation, 377 S. Main St., AZ 85364; (928) 783-0193; *www.gyedc.org; e-mail: gr8teryuma@aol.com.*

## Chapter Nine
# NORTHWESTERN ARIZONA
## BENEATH THE MOGOLLON RIM

If you explore northwestern Arizona in search of a possible future home site, you may think you've taken a wrong turn and wound up in the Pacific Northwest. Approaching Flagstaff, the area's largest city, you'll see great stands of ponderosa pines carpeting Coconino National Forest. On the horizon, the serrated San Francisco Peaks thrust more than 12,000 feet skyward.

The great Colorado Plateau occupies much of northwestern Arizona, lifting it 7,000 feet or more above sea level and pushing much of the land into a conifer zone. The Grand Canyon was created when this tableland gradually uplifted while the Colorado River carved down through its layered rock. However, that simplistic explanation doesn't satisfy some geologists. They subscribe to a "stream piracy theory," saying that two rivers flowing in opposite directions began carving the canyon's primeval course. Each originated high in a ridgeline of the Colorado Plateau which is dome shaped and tilted to the south. Then the northbound stream formed a lake. It eventually backed over ridge and the southern stream "pirated" it to form a single southbound Colorado River. That's all speculation, of course. However it got there, the Grand Canyon is the stunning cornerstone to this corner of Arizona.

The Colorado Plateau, ranging from 4,000 to 9,000 feet, extends down from the Grand Canyon and drops off abruptly at the 200-mile-long Mogollon Rim. It's a wonderfully mixed land of alpine lakes, volcanic peaks and red rock canyons.

**THE WAY IT WAS** • The area's first settlers were drawn to these high, cool pine forests around 15,000 to 20,000 years ago. Sharing the land with antelope, bison and a native camel, they migrated with the seasons to hunt and forage. About 4,000 years ago, they began rudimentary agriculture, growing a balanced protein diet of corn, squash and beans.

From these early tribes evolved the Sinagua (*si-NAU-wa*), who settled around present-day Flagstaff and south through Oak Creek Canyon around 1000 A.D. Although they occupied much of the forested Colorado Plateau, their name in Spanish means "without water." It was a reference to the dry, porous volcanic soil in the plateau's eastern region, where their abandoned villages were first noted by Spanish explorers. An advanced society, the Sinagua farmed, built irrigation canals and constructed elaborate adobe pueblos above ground and in the niches of protective cliffs and canyons.

Then curiously, by the time those Spanish travelers passed through here in the sixteenth century, the Sinagua had gone. Were they driven out by drought, disease or the arrival of warlike Athabaskans from the north? Archaeologists can only speculate. Thousands of ruins have been found to prove that they were here; nothing has been found to confirm why they left. It's likely that the present-day Hopi are their descendants.

White migration to the region didn't begin until the middle of the 1800s. Settlers were drawn by minerals, harvestable forests and potentially rich farmlands. The first permanent community was Prescott, selected as the site for Arizona's territorial capital in 1863. Four years later, it lost the capital to Tucson and finally to Phoenix. However, mining and lumbering continued to draw settlers.

From Prescott, settlement spread northward, through the fertile Verde Valley and Sedona's beautiful Oak Creek Canyon to the ponderosa pine fringes of Flagstaff and Williams.

**THE WAY IT IS** • Despite its beauty, much of northwestern Arizona is thinly populated. Most of its citizens are focused along a narrow north-south corridor from Prescott through Sedona to Flagstaff. Coconino County, which covers much of this area, has only 116,000 residents and nearly half of those live in Flagstaff, the area's largest city. Grand Canyon National Park, national forests and several Native American reservations occupy much of the land.

The Arizona Strip, a region north of the canyon—and therefore isolated by it—is one of the least populated areas of the state. It's occupied by a few hardy Mormon settlements, high prairie and ranches, some fine stands of pine and not much else.

Northwestern Arizona's lower reaches offer good potential for relocating families and year-around retirees who don't mind an occasional snowfall and cold winter nights. Folks who miss the four seasons but don't miss blizzards should like this area's more gentle winters.

# CAMP VERDE

If you like small town living, you may like to retire to historic Camp Verde. The oldest settlement in the Verde Valley, it was established in 1865 as an Army fort to protect settlers from native reprisals, since they were pushing them off their lands. Remnants of the garrison are preserved in Fort Verde State Historic Park.

The town is rather ordinary looking, although it's in a good location, just off a major interstate highway and within a short drive of several tourist lures. It's popular with the horsy set. Incidentally, non-Spanish speaking folks may like to know that *verde* means green, and it refers to the green swatch of the Verde River flowing through the valley.

**Elevation** • 3,133 feet

**Location** • In Yavapai County, just off Interstate 17, about 85 miles north of Phoenix.

**Climate** • Warm to hot summers; cool winters. July average high 101, low 63; January average high 56.5, low 29. Rainfall 13 inches; no snowfall.

**Population** • 9,800

**Population trend** • Gained more than 50 percent in the past .

**Property tax** • (assessed at ten percent of real value) $12.67 per $100 assessed valuation.

**Economy** • Construction, tourism and light industry form Camp Verde's rather limited economic base.

**Job prospects** • They're about average, according to the Camp Verde Chamber of Commerce. Many residents commute to nearby Cottonwood and Sedona to work, since Camp Verde isn't a significant commercial center.

**Industrial facilities** • Several small industrial sites are available.

**Real estate** • Homes are rather inexpensive, perhaps $65,000 for a typical three-bedroom unit. A few new subdivisions are being built in the surrounding Verde Valley. A 42-unit low income senior housing project is available for retirees.

**The media** • One bi-weekly newspaper, *The Bugle & Journal*; TV via relay from Flagstaff and Phoenix.

**Medical services** • Hospital in Cottonwood; some medical clinics in Camp Verde.

**Transportation** • Nearby I-17 brings Greyhound. Air service is available from Sedona and Flagstaff.

**Education** • Elementary, middle and high school, plus one private school.

***Local government*** • Incorporated in 1986; mayor, six council members and a town manager.

***Places to stay*** • Three motels and several campgrounds.

***Leisure facilities*** • Two recreation centers and a swimming pool, large senior center, tennis courts and a horse arena.

***Tourist lures*** • Fort Verde State Historic Park, plus the other Verde Valley attractions (see Cottonwood below). Also, it's a short drive to Sedona, Oak Creek Canyon and Flagstaff.

***Contacts*** • Camp Verde Chamber of Commerce, P.O. Box 3520, Camp Verde, AZ 86322; (928) 567-9294.

Town of Camp Verde, P.O. Box 710 (473 S. Main St.), Camp Verde, AZ 86322; (928) 567-6631; *cvaz.org.*

# COTTONWOOD

About the same size as Camp Verde, Cottonwood is the commercial center of the Verde Valley. It's actually a town with two faces. Newer Cottonwood is a typical collection of small shopping centers and subdivisions, while Old Cottonwood offers a handful of false front stores that house native crafts shops, antique stores and a couple of curio shops.

The town dates from the 1870s when soldiers from nearby Camp Verde were stationed here. A group of settlers followed, and named their hamlet for a nearby stand of cottonwoods along the Verde River.

Clarkdale is a smaller town just to the south, with an old style business district and a more interesting history. It was built as a model company town in 1914 to house workers for a large smelter that processed copper ore from Jerome, which is perched on the side of nearby Mingus Mountain. The smelter has been shut for decades and today's Clarkdale is a quiet little place with an old fashioned "Main Street USA" feel. A much newer model community, Verde Valley Ranch, is being built nearby, with 1,200 homes, a golf course, a lake and river access, boosting Clarkdale's population. It's a project of the Phelps Dodge Corporation, which once was a major player in Jerome-Clarkdale mining activities.

***Elevation*** • 3,300 feet

***Location*** • In Yavapai County, in the heart of the Verde Valley, about twenty miles southwest of Sedona.

***Climate*** • Warm summers, mild to chilly winters. July average high 98.4, low 66; January average high 58.2, low 28.4. Rainfall 12.21 inches; snowfall five inches.

***Population*** • Cottonwood 9,800; Clarkdale 3,500

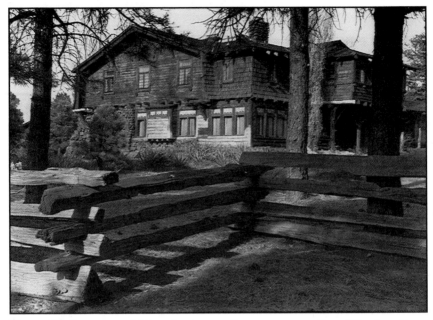

*Flagstaff offers several historic sites and museums, such as Riordan State Historic Park, which preserves the estate of a wealthy pioneer family.*

**Population trend** ● Cottonwood gained more than 50 percent and Clarkdale nearly 60 percent in the past decade.

**Property tax** ● $10.39 per $100 assessed valuation in Cottonwood and $10.99 in Clarkdale.

**Economy** ● Since Cottonwood is the trade center for the Verde Valley, its economy is rooted in the retail, services and tourism. Retired people make up 25 percent of the Cottonwood-Clarkdale population.

**Job prospects** ● Cottonwood offers a rather tepid employment market, according to the local Job Service office. Most positions are in retail sales, tourism and other service areas. Many residents commute to tourist-related, restaurant and retail jobs in Sedona.

**Industrial facilities** ● Two industrial parks near the airport.

**Real estate** ● This is where folks come when they can't afford Sedona. The price of a three-bedroom home starts around $100,000.

**The media** ● Bi-weekly *Verde Independent*. TV via feeds from Flagstaff and Phoenix, plus a cable TV company.

**Medical services** ● A modern, well-equipped hospital and several medical clinics.

**Transportation** ● The Greyhound stops at Camp Verde, fifteen miles away. Cottonwood Airport has a 4,250-foot lighted runway with charter service and rental cars.

**Education** ● Verde Valley campus of Yavapai College, plus the usual elementary, middle and high schools.

**Local government** • Incorporated in 1960; mayor, six council members and a city manager.

**Places to stay** • About ten motels offering an inexpensive alternate to Sedona's pricey resorts; a few campgrounds and RV parks.

**Leisure facilities** • Four public parks, a recreation center, a senior center, two golf courses, public pool, tennis courts and such.

**Tourist lures** • Cottonwood is a good base for exploring nearby attractions such as Sedona and Oak Creek Canyon, Tuzigoot National Monument, Montezuma's Castle National Monument, Fort Verde State Historic Park and the rustically historic mining town of Jerome.

**Contacts** • Cottonwood Chamber of Commerce, 1010 S. Main St., Cottonwood, AZ 86326; (928) 634-7593.

City of Cottonwood, 827 N. Main St., Cottonwood, AZ 86326; (928) 634-5526; *www.ci.cottonwood.az.us.*

# FLAGSTAFF

Flagstaff is the most versatile small city in Arizona, both for visitors and potential new residents. Northern Arizona University provides cultural opportunities while fine museums and historic buildings preserve the area's past. It's the seat of government for huge Coconino County, Arizona's second largest, covering 18,629 square miles.

Within a day's drive of the city are seven national parks and monuments, including several intriguing Native American ruins. Flagstaff gets nippy in winter since it's the highest and most northerly of northwestern Arizona's larger towns. Snow is not unusual although severe storms are rare.

If you like the great outdoors, you'll find it in abundance, since Flagstaff sits at the foot of the San Francisco Peaks, crowned by Mount Humphreys, the tallest mountain in Arizona. The state's largest ski area, the Arizona Snowbowl, is cradled in these ramparts, and the area abounds with hiking trails, fishing lakes and campgrounds. Downtown Flagstaff is a mix of turn-of-the-century and modern. The historic district along old Route 66 is undergoing a major renaissance, blossoming with trendy cafés, boutiques and specialty shops.

White settlement of the region didn't begin until the 1870s. After several false starts, sheepherder Thomas Forsythe McMillan and family arrived, concluded that it was good sheep country and stayed. By 1880, the area's population had swelled to 67. The railroad came through two years later and Flagstaff's future was assured.

The town's curious name came from a flagpole that may or may not have existed. Some historians say that limbs were stripped from a tall

Ponderosa and a flag was hoisted on July 4, 1876, to honor the centennial of America's independence. Others insist that the pole was a marker to guide travelers headed west. Later, according to local history buffs, the tree was chopped down and used as firewood at Sandy Donahue's Saloon. So much for historic preservation. Twice in three years, the new settlement was burned and rebuilt. Fortunately, there was plenty of lumber in the area. The city was incorporated in 1894.

Tourism is a major industry in Flagstaff, and government employment play a significant role in the local economy. Northern Arizona University is its largest employer, with a staff of 2,500.

**Elevation** • 6,905 feet

**Location** • In Coconino County, on interstates 40 and 17, midway between Arizona's eastern and western borders.

**Climate** • Warm summers, cool to cold winters. July average high 81.1, low 50.6; January average high 42.2, low 14.6. Rainfall 19.8 inches; snowfall 109 inches.

**Population** • 57,700

**Population trend** • Gained fifteen percent in the past ten years.

**Property tax** • $11.99 per $100 assessed valuation.

**Economy** • Although tourism is the main industry, government services, light manufacturing and education are important as well, and several high tech companies have located here. With the presence of Lowell Observatory and a U.S. Geological Survey Landsat office, space science also figures in the economic picture.

**Job prospects** • The employment situation is "very competitive," according to the local Job Service office. Best prospects are in construction, retail sales, high tech, tourism and other service jobs.

**Industrial facilities** • Four large industrial parks.

**Real estate** • Based on the nationwide index of 100, housing costs in Flagstaff are slightly above average, rated at 118.6. A good selection is available in older homes, new subdivisions, townhouses and condos. The market is "very active," according to the local board of realtors.

**The media** • The daily *Arizona Sun* is the local newspaper. Local TV stations, cable feeds from Phoenix and Los Angeles and a cable company.

**Medical services** • A modern full-service hospital and several medical clinics.

**Transportation** • Served by Greyhound and Amtrak. Pulliam Airport has a 7,000-foot runway, with daily scheduled service by America West and feeder airlines. Also, van service is available to the international airport in Phoenix.

**Education** • Northern Arizona University has been rated as one of the best affordable schools in America. Other facilities include Coconino Community College, eight private schools, several elementary, middle and high schools.

**Local government** • Seat of Coconino County since 1891. Incorporated in 1894; mayor, six council members and a city manager.

**Places to stay** • More than 60 motels with nearly 5,000 rooms, a youth hostel and several RV parks and campgrounds, including camping in the surrounding Coconino National Forest.

**Leisure facilities** • Three public pools, 29 parks, an ice rink, symphony orchestra, six recreation centers, one public and several private golf courses, tennis courts and the nearby Arizona Snowbowl for winter sports. Many NAU facilities are open to the public.

**Tourist lures** • Flagstaff is Arizona's best located city for sightseeing. It's a short drive to the Grand Canyon, Oak Creek Canyon, the outdoor lures of the San Francisco Peaks and Arizona Snowbowl, plus Sunset Crater, Wupatki, Tuzigoot, Montezuma's Castle and Walnut Canyon national monuments. Local lures include the outstanding Museum of Northern Arizona, Coconino Center for the Arts, the Lowell Observatory and Riordan State Historic Park.

**Contacts** • Flagstaff Chamber of Commerce, 101 W. Route 66, Flagstaff, AZ 86001; (928) 774-4505; *www.flagstaffchamber.com* or *www.flagstaffchamber.org; e-mail: chamber@flagstaff.az.us.*

City of Flagstaff, 211 W. Aspen St., Flagstaff, AZ 86001; (928) 774-5281; *www.flagstaff.az.us.*

Greater Flagstaff Economic Council, 1300 S. Milton Rd., S-125, Flagstaff, AZ 86001-6354; (928) 779-7658.

# JEROME

If you like an idle pace and weather-worn history, you might consider Jerome for retirement. Don't go there looking for work, however. Although it once was a boomtown of copper production, things are pretty quiet these days. It's basically a rustic hillside town frozen in time, popular with history buffs, tourists and a few resident artists.

● FLAGSTAFF

● PHOENIX

●TUCSON

Historians say Jerome never was pretty. Cantilevered into the slopes of Cleopatra Hill, halfway up Mingus Mountain, it was one of Arizona's largest and wildest mining camps. In 1903, a visiting *New York Sun* reporter called Jerome "the wickedest town in America."

Its terraced streets were lined with saloons and bawdy houses. Sloping yards sprouted tailing dumps and mining gear instead of rose bushes. Homes were so steeply terraced, claim old-timers, that you could look down your neighbor's chimney. Slides were common and the town jail skidded several dozen feet downhill, where it remains to this day. Smelters belched pollution. Nearly a mile underground, men stood in boot-deep water, groveling for copper ore in humid 100-degree heat. Dozens died from falls, blasts and other miscalculations.

The bawdy houses and smelters are gone, along with the miners and most of the littered mining machinery. Jerome survives today as an attraction for visitors fascinated by its wicked past. It has lured a rather youthful population of artists and shopkeepers, as well. Instead of old miners dozing in the sun, one is more likely to see pretty young entrepreneurs or bearded artists. The weathered business district is terraced on three levels as the highway switchbacks through town. Galleries, curio shops and antique shops occupy many of its old buildings. Red and green scars are still evident in the hillsides, where miners dug for gold, silver and copper.

The first claim was filed on Mingus Mountain in 1876. Prospectors found a little gold and silver and a lot of copper. In 1883 the United Verde Copper Company built a smelter and the boom began; at its peak, Jerome bustled with 15,000 citizens. In less than 80 years, a billion dollars worth of copper, gold, silver, lead and zinc was rooted from 80 miles of tunnels beneath the town. Alternately leveled by fire and rebuilt, tough old Jerome thrived until 1953, when the last copper mine was shut down. The population dwindled to 150, then slowly climbed to its present number as tourists began coming to town.

*Elevation* • 5,248 feet

*Location* • In Yavapai County, on the slopes of Mingus Mountain, above the Verde Valley west of Cottonwood.

*Climate* • Warm summers, cool to chilly winters. July average high 89.2, low 67.1; January average high 49.8, low 32.2. Rainfall 17.95 inches; snowfall 24.9 inches.

*Population* • about 330

*Population trend* • Although up from its all-time low of several decades ago, it lost about 18 percent in the past ten years.

*Property tax* • $11.44 per $100 assessed valuation.

*Economy* • Tourism.

*Job prospects* • There aren't many, unless you want to open a boutique or gallery, or work in one. Three of four jobs in town are tied to tourism.

*Industrial facilities* • None.

*Real estate* • Three-bedroom home prices start around $65,000, although there aren't many available. Century-old fixer-uppers occasionally reach the market and old Victorian style homes can for more than $200,000.

*The media* • No local newspaper; TV arrives by relay from Phoenix, Prescott and Flagstaff.

*Medical services* • The nearest are in Cottonwood.

*Transportation* • Again, nearest facilities are in Cottonwood.

*Education* • One elementary school.

**Local government** ● Incorporated in 1899; mayor and six council members.

**Places to stay** ● A few motels and bed and breakfast inns, including the stylish Inn at Jerome.

**Leisure facilities** ● Three parks and an archives research center.

**Tourist lures** ● Jerome is the main lure, with several museums, Jerome State Historic Park, an art center in a former brick school complex, several boutiques and restaurants dressed in period décor.

**Contacts** ● Jerome Chamber of Commerce, P.O. Box K, Jerome, AZ 86331; (928) 634-2900.

Jerome Historical Society, P.O. Box 156, Jerome, AZ 86331; (928) 634-5477.

Town of Jerome, P.O. Box 335, Jerome, AZ 86331; (928) 634-7943; *e-mail: jeromeaz@verdenet.com.*

# PAGE

This is the dark horse on our list of recommended Arizona communities. At the top of the state next to the Utah border and tucked into a niche carved out of the Navajo Nation, Page is often overlooked. Yet it offers several pluses—recreational facilities and water play on Lake Powell, a dry climate, low property taxes and a tidy looking town.

Sitting high on a sandstone shelf above Lake Powell and Glen Canyon Dam, Page thrives on the tourist business lured by Glen Canyon National Recreation Area. More than three million people a year come to play on the reservoir. This arid plateau isn't particularly attractive, although this planned community has a neat, clean-swept look. It was created in 1956 as the construction town for Glen Canyon Dam, with features such as underground utilities and a cluster of public schools rimmed by the main residential area.

East of Page is the core of the local economy—the huge coal-fed Navajo Generating Plant, operated by Phoenix' Salt River Project and other partners. Once a target of environmentalists for supposedly polluting the skies above the Grand Canyon, the plant recently completed a $430 million installation of "scrubbers" to reduce its emissions. Consuming 24,000 tons of coal a day brought by rail from mines eighty-five miles away, it produces enough electricity for a city of three million people.

*Elevation* ● 4,380 feet

*Location* ● In Coconino County, between the Navajo Reservation and Glen Canyon National Recreation Area.

**Climate** • Very dry; warm to hot summers, chilly to cold winters. July average high 97, low 71; January average high 45, low 24. Rainfall 4.78 inches; snowfall 4.9 inches.

**Population** • 7,000

**Population trend** • Little movement; it gained 3.2 percent in the past decade.

**Property tax** • $7.03 per $100 assessed valuation.

**Economy** • Tourism and public utilities balance the local economy. More than three million people visit Glen Canyon National Recreation Area each year.

**Job prospects** • They're good only in tourist services and public utilities. Seventy percent of the jobs are tied to these sources. The local chamber of commerce says that Page's overall job prospects are "about average."

**Industrial facilities** • A 102-acre industrial park.

**Real estate** • Three-bedroom homes average about $135,000, according to the chamber.

**The media** • One weekly newspaper, the *Lake Powell Chronicle*. Television feeds from Phoenix and Salt Lake City, plus a local cable company.

**Medical services** • A small full-service hospital, two medical clinics and a mental health facility.

**Transportation** • Page Airport, with a lighted 5,500-foot runway. Scheduled service to Phoenix, Denver and Salt Lake City, plus charter service.

**Education** • A campus of Coconino Community College, two elementary, one junior high and one high school.

**Local government** • Founded as a construction town in 1956, Page was incorporated in 1975; mayor, six council members and a city manager.

**Places to stay** • About 20 motels and resort hotels, including waterside resorts on Lake Powell; three bed & breakfast inns, several RV parks, NRA and private campgrounds.

**Leisure facilities** • Three public parks, two golf courses, senior citizen center, teen center and tennis courts.

**Tourist lures** • Glen Canyon National Recreation Area embraces adjacent Lake Powell and Glen Canyon Dam, offering boating, camping, picnicking, fishing and such. The Navajo and Hopi reservations with their great variety of attractions are next door, and both rims of the Grand Canyon are a few hours drive west. Also, Page isn't far from the canyonlands of Utah, just to the north.

**Contacts** • Page-Lake Powell Chamber of Commerce, P.O. Box 727 (664 N. Navajo St.), Page, AZ 86040; (888) 261-PAGE or (928) 645-2741; *pagelakepowellchamber.org;* e-mail: *info@pagelakepowell-chamber.org.*

City of Page, P.O. 1180 (697 Vista Ave.), Page, AZ 86040; (928) 645-8861; *www.ci.page.az.us.*

# PAYSON

This mountain retreat in a woodsy setting below the Mogollon Rim might tempt you if you don't mind getting wet and a bit chilly in winter. Although it has historic roots, Payson is a rather ordinary looking town, with typical strip malls and clusters of shopping centers and a few planned subdivisions. Its forested setting and mountainous backdrop of the Mogollon Rim add scenic allure.

Well off Arizona's main traveled routes, it's popular as a summer retreat for Phoenicians fleeing the desert sizzle. As such, it has a considerable number of lodgings for a rather small town. It's enjoying a growth surge, gaining more than 60 percent in the past decade; many of the new residents are retirees.

Payson first saw life when prospectors found a bit of gold in nearby creek bottoms in 1881. They didn't find much, although the town grew as a ranching center. Author Zane Gray loved the timbered land above Payson and below "The Rim." He built a hunting cabin there, where he wrote many of his books. His cabin was an historic site until it was destroyed by fire. The local Payson museum has an extensive exhibit on the author. Although most of Payson is modern, a few old buildings along Main Street recall the town's cowboy past.

***Elevation*** ● 4,930 feet

***Location*** ● In Gila County, 94 miles northeast of Phoenix.

***Climate*** ● Warm summers, cool to chilly winters. July average high 92.5, low 58.5; January average high 53.1, low 23.7. Rainfall 20.77 inches; snowfall 25.1 inches.

***Population*** ● 14,200

***Population trend*** ● Gained 62.6 percent in the past ten years.

***Property tax*** ● $11.32 per $100 assessed valuation.

***Economy*** ● Retirement and tourism provide Payson's economic base. More than 60 percent of its population is retired. The community has an active senior center and senior recreation program.

***Job prospects*** ● Payson's Economic Development Corporation is working to attract light industry and job prospects are about average. Best bets, according to the local Job Service office, are in retail sales, tourism and other service jobs.

***Industrial facilities*** ● Two light industrial parks.

***Real estate*** ● Housing ranges from older homes in downtown Payson to several woodsy subdivisions and summer cabins. Prices for a three-bedroom home start around $85,000 to $100,000.

***The media*** ● Three weeklies, the *Mogollon Advisor*, *Rim Country News* and *Payson Roundup*. Cable feeds from Phoenix.

***Medical services*** • A small hospital, medical clinics and three nursing homes.

***Transportation*** • Payson airport has a lighted 5,000-foot runway with charter service available.

***Education*** • A community college plus the usual elementary, middle and high schools.

***Local government*** • Founded in 1881 and incorporated in 1973; mayor, six council members and a town manager.

***Places to stay*** • About 20 motels and lodges, a dozen RV parks and campgrounds, plus camping in adjacent Tonto National Forest.

***Leisure facilities*** • A senior center, public golf course, three public parks, tennis courts and a small zoo.

***Tourist lures*** • Tonto National Forest provides the usual hiking, camping, picnicking, fishing and such. The Museum of the Forest has exhibits on Zane Gray and local history, and a Native American casino on the edge of town offers gaming. Tonto Natural Bridge north of Payson has been expanded and improved as a state park.

***Contacts*** • Rim Country Regional Chamber of Commerce, P.O. Box 1380, Payson, AZ 85547; (928) 474-4515; *www.rimcountrychamber.com; e-mail: rcrc@rimcountrychamber.com.*

Town of Payson, 303 N. Beeline Highway, Payson, AZ 85541; (928) 474-5242.

# PINE & STRAWBERRY

Pine and Strawberry are small pine-clad villages a few miles north of Payson, tucked under the Mogollon Rim. Both communities date back to the 1880s although their appearance now is essentially alpine modern. A post office was established at Pine in 1884 and named for the surrounding piney forests. Strawberry, settled about the same time, got its pleasing name from wild strawberries that grow in the area.

They're both fast-growing although their economy depends heavily on weekend visitors, second-home dwellers from Phoenix and retirees.

***Elevation*** • Pine 5,448 feet; Strawberry 6,047 feet

***Location*** • In Gila County, thirteen miles north of Payson and 110 miles northeast of Phoenix.

***Climate*** • Warm summers, cool to chilly winters, July average high 92.5, low 58.5; January average high 53.1, low 23.7, Rainfall 20.77 inches; snowfall 25.1 inches.

***Combined population*** • about 2,500

***Population trend*** • Gained about 25 percent in the past decade.

*Property tax* • $13.41 per $100 assessed valuation.

*Economy* • Primarily tourism and recreation; not much real economic growth.

*Job prospects* • They are very limited; the few available service jobs are rather seasonal, since Pine and Strawberry are primarily summer retreats. They offer better prospects for retirement than for employment.

*Industrial facilities* • None, although light industry is being sought.

*Real estate* • Three-bedroom home prices range from $100,000 to $200,000, according to the chamber of commerce.

*The media* • The weekly *Payson Roundup* is distributed here. TV relays from Phoenix, Tucson and Prescott.

*Medical services* • One clinic and three nursing homes; other services in Payson.

*Transportation* • Shuttle bus service to Payson and Phoenix; Payson Airport is fifteen miles south.

*Education* • An elementary and middle school; high school students commute to Payson.

*Local government* • Both communities unincorporated; services provided by Gila County.

*Places to stay* • Six motels and four RV parks, plus Forest Service campgrounds in the surrounding mountains.

*Leisure facilities* • Pine has a public park; other facilities are in nearby Payson.

*Tourist lures* • See Payson listing.

*Contacts* • Rim Country Regional Chamber of Commerce, P.O. Box 1380, Payson, AZ 85547; (928) 474-4515; *www.rimcountrychamber.com; e-mail: rcrc@rimcountrychamber.com.*

Gila County Board of Supervisors, 1400 E. Ash St., Globe, AZ 85501; (928) 425-3231.

# PRESCOTT

If we were looking for a woodsy place to relocate a family or to retire, we'd be hard-pressed to choose between Prescott and Flagstaff. While Flagstaff is on a major freeway and railway and closer to the Grand Canyon, Prescott is a more attractive town and it's closer to Phoenix.

So, flip a coin.

Friendly natives may gently correct you when you say "Pres-kott." It's "PRESS-kit," with the last syllable bitten

• FLAGSTAFF

• PHOENIX

• TUCSON

off smartly. Even local radio announcers, alleged guardians of proper pronunciation, say it that way.

Once you've learned the language, townsfolk will boast of PRESS-kit's idyllic location, between the dry high desert and the cool pines of PRESS-kit National Forest. It's cooler in summer than Sedona, they'll tell you, and not nearly so crowded. PRESS-kit has several art galleries, they point out, and an active performing arts center.

Two colleges and an aeronautical university provide an academic base. The town has a several museums and the whole of the Bradshaw Mountains for a playground. History? Why, PRESS-kit was where Arizona began! Territorial capital, it was. Hadn't you heard?

When Arizona was sliced free from New Mexico to become its own territory in 1863, the new governor—John N. Goodwin—began casting about for a capital site. The mineral-rich central highland seemed most logical, so a temporary capital was set up first at Fort Whipple, then on Granite Creek to the south. The town of Prescott was platted in 1864 and a sturdy log and whipsaw-board governor's mansion was constructed. The fort was moved here to protect the new capital. However in 1867, before something fancier than an oversized log cabin could be built, the capital was shifted to Tucson. Prescott citizens lured it back briefly in 1877 before it settled for good in Phoenix.

No matter, the people said. Who wanted all that political ruckus and traffic, anyhow? The town has done just fine without it, as a trading, ranching and lumbering center.

Prescott today looks more like a vintage New England village than a Southwestern community. The bold, Doric-columned Yavapai County Courthouse occupies a large town square. Early American style homes and occasional Victorians line streets shaded by mature trees. Many business buildings are of sturdy brick. The downtown area appears prosperous despite a commercial exodus to suburban shopping centers. An abundance of motels, restaurants and a few curio shops and antique stores serve the thousands of tourist drawn to this contented, tree-shaded community.

Don't be fooled by Prescott's Eastern look, however. The town is decidedly Western, with several cowboy shops and galleries. Locals claim that their annual Frontier Days is America's oldest rodeo, dating back to 1888.

*Elevation* • 5,347 feet

*Location* • In Yavapai County, on State Route 89, about midway between Phoenix and Flagstaff.

*Climate* • Warm summers, cool to chilly winters. July average high 89, low 58; January average high 50, low 20. Rainfall 18 inches; snowfall 20.6 inches.

*Population* • About 36,000

*Population trend* • Gained 27.6 percent in the past decade.

*Property tax* • $9.67 per $100 assessed valuation.

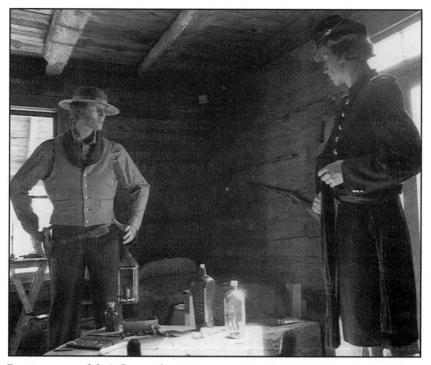

*Prescott served briefly as the Arizona territorial capital and exhibits at the Sharlot Hall Museum recall those days. Mannequin soldiers discuss politics in the log cabin style governor's "mansion."*

**Economy** • Prescott offers a good economic balance of tourism, education, light manufacturing and retail sales, with lumbering and ranching in the surrounding areas.

**Job prospects** • Most in demand are skilled trades and clerical jobs. Four of ten jobs are in the services area, mostly tourism, while retail trade is second and construction is third. Manufacturing is in fourth place, although it's gaining as new light industries are drawn to the area.

**Industrial facilities** • Five industrial parks.

**Real estate** • Older homes and new planned developments comprise the town's realty mix. Average price of a new three-bedroom is $240,000, although many older ones are less.

**The media** • The *Daily Prescott Courier* and the weekly *Prescott News*. Local TV stations plus feeds from Phoenix and cable TV.

**Medical services** • A regional medical center, 358-bed veterans' hospital and domiciliary, six nursing homes, four home care services and an adult day care center.

**Transportation** • Served by Greyhound. Ernest A. Love Field has two runways with scheduled air service.

**Education** • Embry-Riddle Aeronautical University, Yavapai Community College, Prescott College (private four-year liberal arts), five private schools, six public elementary, two middle and one high school.

***Local government*** • Seat of Yavapai County. Incorporated in 1881; mayor, six council member and a city manager.

***Places to stay*** • About 30 motels, nineteen bed and breakfast inns, several national forest campgrounds, six private campgrounds and RV parks.

***Leisure facilities*** • Several public parks, a small zoo, three public pools, two golf courses, several art galleries, a roller skating rink, plus tennis and racquetball courts.

***Tourist lures*** • Surrounding Prescott National Forest offers the usual outdoor pursuits. The town has several museums, including the outstanding Sharlot Hall Museum that includes the original territorial governor's mansion; the Phippen Museum of Western art and the Smoki Museum of Native American lore.

***Contacts*** • Prescott Chamber of Commerce, P.O. Box 1147 (117 W. Goodwin St.), Prescott, AZ 86302; (800) 266-7534 or (928) 445-2000.

City of Prescott, P.O. Box 2059 (201 S. Cortez St.), Prescott, AZ 86302; (928) 445-3500; *www.cityofprescott.net.*

## SEDONA

It's no coincidence that three of our favorite Arizona towns—Prescott, Flagstaff and Sedona—are in the state's north central area. The scenery's beautiful, summers are sunny, winters are mild and each is a well rounded community with a stable economy, many cultural offerings and interesting attractions.

Sedona is the most affluent of the three and it's certainly in a striking setting, surrounded by the red rock palisades of Oak Creek Canyon. It's one of the most striking civic settings in the world. When Frank Lloyd Wright first laid eyes on the canyon, he said simply: "Nothing should ever be built here."

Obviously, his advice was ignored. The canyon is dotted with campgrounds and small resorts; Sedona in the lower end is busy with art galleries, gift shops and large resorts. It has been estimated that as many as four million people a year pass through Oak Creek Canyon and Sedona. Good grief, that's only second to the number of visitors to the Grand Canyon!

Sedona is one of the largest and most popular resort areas in Arizona. Its posh spas rival those of Scottsdale, Phoenix and Tucson and they're in more impressive settings. Sedona lures natives as well as outsiders, particularly Phoenicians seeking solace from the summer

*The Coffeepot is one of the most striking red rock formations in the Sedona-Oak Creek Canyon area.*

sun. They return in the fall to admire the saffron leaves of sycamore, aspen and cottonwood along Oak Creek. Sunlight and shadows play off red sandstone buttes. We find it hard to believe that all who live here don't drop whatever they're doing each evening to admire the sunset.

Despite its tempting beauty, the area didn't attract permanent white settlement until 1876 when one James Thompson began farming here. A Pennsylvania Dutch couple, Carl and Sedona Schnebly, arrived in 1901 and built a boarding house. The following year, they petitioned for a post office, which they offered to operate from their lodge. Carl had two suggestions for the town's name—Schnebly's Station and Oak Creek Crossing. The post office department rejected them, saying they were too long to fit on a cancellation stamp. So Carl's brother Ellsworth told him to name the town for his wife.

A fortunate suggestion, for it's difficult to picture an art colony called Schnebly's Station. Early in the last century, Hollywood movie makers were attracted by the area's handsome rock formations. The first film was a silent version of Zane Gray's *Call of the Canyon*. Artists began settling in, drawn by the isolation and beauty. Then resort builders arrived. They put an end to the isolation but more or less protected the setting.

Sedona has grown considerably in recent decades, more than doubling its population since 1976. Surprisingly, it wasn't incorporated until 1988. While not a model of urban planning, the town still retains much of its early-day charm. There are no highrises to block those orange-hued rocks and no neon to compete with the canyon's light-and-shadow shows. The community is split between Coconino and Yavapai counties. The original site in Coconino county—which locals call "Uptown Sedona"—hasn't changed much in the past 30 years.

Most of the growth is concentrated south on Highway 179 (still in Coconino County) and southwest along 89A on the Yavapai County side. Although these new areas are a bit sprawled, developers have taken a cue from Uptown and resisted neon and highrises. Route 89A through "new" Sedona is lined with spur streets leading to planned residential areas with predictable names like Shadows Estates, Settlers Rest, the Palisades, Western Hills, Rolling Hills and Mystic Hills.

The town is unabashedly tourist-oriented and it is upscale tourism, for the most part. More than two dozen galleries display fine examples of Western and other contemporary art. About 300 artists live here. Performing arts thrive as well. Musicales and plays are presented at the Sedona Arts Center. Each summer, the community sponsors the Jazz on the Rocks Festival and the Sedona Chamber Music Festival.

*Elevation* ● 4,500 feet

*Location* ● In lower Oak Creek Canyon, 30 miles south of Flagstaff; divided between Coconino and Yavapai counties.

*Climate* ● Warm summers and temperate winters with occasional frost. July average high 95.1, low 65.1; January average high 55, low 29.7. Rainfall 17.15 inches; snowfall 8.8 inches.

*Population* ● 10,500; about 17,000 in the two-county area.

*Population trend* ● Gained 32 percent in the past decade, mostly on the Yavapai County side.

*Property tax* ● $8.11 in the Coconino County section and $10.23 in Yavapai County.

*Economy* ● Tourism and affluent retirees fuel Sedona's economy.

*Job prospects* ● More than half the jobs are in retail sales, tourism and related services. There isn't much available in the professions or skilled trades. Most people don't come here to earn money; they come here *with* money.

*Industrial facilities* ● Tourism *is* the industry.

*Real estate* ● Sedona is easy to love but difficult to afford. Three-bedroom home prices start around $300,000 and those with any sort of view go considerably higher.

*The media* ● The twice weekly *Sedona-Red Rock News*. Television feeds from Flagstaff, Prescott and Phoenix, plus a local cable company.

*Medical services* ● An outpatient medical clinic with emergency services; hospitals are in Cottonwood and Flagstaff.

*Transportation* ● Sedona's airport has a 5,100-foot lighted runway, with air charter service.

*Education* ● Extension courses provided by Yavapai Community College; seven private schools, plus the usual public schools.

*Local government* ● Incorporated in 1988; government services shared by Coconino and Yavapai counties.

**Places to stay** • Dozens of motels plus several world-class resorts; nearly 3,000 rooms available. Three RV parks and several national forest campgrounds in Oak Creek Canyon.

**Leisure facilities** • A community center, art center; numerous parks in Oak Creek Canyon; golf and tennis at area resorts.

**Tourist lures** • Sedona and its setting are the chief lures, of course. The four million annual visitors take jeep trips into red rock country, hike the canyons, attend music and art festivals and browse the boutiques and galleries. Dozens of miles of hiking trails wind about the red rock ramparts. Scenic drives are popular and Red Rock State Park offers hiking, ranger programs and a fine interpretive center.

**Contacts** • Sedona-Oak Creek Canyon Chamber of Commerce, P.O. Box 478, Sedona, AZ 86339; (928) 204-1123; *www.visitsedona.com; e-mail: info@sedonachamber.com.*

City of Sedona, 102 Roadrunner Dr., Sedona, AZ 86336; (928) 282- 3113; *www.city.sedona.net.*

# VERDE VILLAGE

The planned community of Verde Village was established in 1970, primarily as a retreat for retirees and summer weekenders fleeing Valley of the Sun heat. Three-fourths of its residents are retired. During the 1980s, it was the fastest growing community in the Verde Valley and one of the fastest in Arizona. Things have slowed down a bit since, although it still gained more than 20 percent in the past five years.

Cottonwood and Yavapai County provide virtually all of Verde Village's services. See the Cottonwood listing on page 123 for more details.

**Elevation** • 3,300 feet

**Location** • In Yavapai County, adjacent to Cottonwood in the Verde Valley.

**Climate** • Warm summers, mild to chilly winters. July average high 98.4, low 66; January average high 58.2, low 28.4. Rainfall 12.21 inches; snowfall five inches.

**Population** • About 10,100

**Population trend** • Gained about 35 percent in the past decade.

**Property tax** • $10.39 per $100 assessed valuation.

**Contacts** • Cottonwood Chamber of Commerce, 1010 S. Main St., Cottonwood, AZ 86326; (928) 634-7593.

City of Cottonwood, 827 N. Main St., Cottonwood, AZ 86326; (928) 634-5526; *www.ci.cottonwood.az.us.*

# WILLIAMS

Think of Williams as a small, slower paced Flagstaff. Like its larger brother, it's rimmed by national forests, with four seasons and easy access to northwestern Arizona's natural attractions. Unlike Flagstaff, it chugs along at an idle pace, with very little growth and few prospects for job-seekers. Retirees might find its woodsy setting attractive, although winters are cold. This is your place if you're the outdoor type seeking small town living. You can golf in summer and hit the slopes at the Williams Ski Area in winter.

Williams is the closest town to the South Rim of the Grand Canyon, and its chamber likes to boast about that. In fact, it calls itself the Williams-Grand Canyon Chamber of Commerce. A vintage steam train chugs visitors between the town and that grand gorge.

The small business district is caught in a pleasant 1930s time warp. Other than several motels, it has changed little from the days when it was an important pause on the Santa Fe Railway and old Route 66. Cattle ranching began in the area in the late 1870s, and the railroad arrived in the 1880s to haul logs for the local timber industry.

The town and its main street are named for randy old mountain man and guide William S. "Bill" Williams. He prowled these parts for a quarter of a century until the Utes got him in 1849. To honor his spirit, townsfolk dress up as mountain men and shady ladies and stage frontier celebrations over Memorial Day and Labor Day weekends.

*Elevation* • 6,770 feet

*Location* • In Coconino County, 30 miles west of Flagstaff on I-40; 60 miles south of the Grand Canyon.

*Climate* • Temperate summers, mild to cold winters. July average high 83.1, low 54.8; January average high 44.3, low 21.3. Rainfall 21.21 inches; snowfall 75.8 inches.

*Population* • just under 3,000

*Population trend* • Gained 12 percent in the past decade.

*Property tax* • $9.63 per $100 assessed valuation.

*Economy* • The town's slow-paced economy is dependent primarily on tourism, with a bit of lumbering, mining and ranching.

*Job prospects* • They're very scarce; tourist jobs here are seasonal.

*Industrial facilities* • One small industrial park.

*Real estate* • There's little in the way of new construction. Homes are mostly old and mostly in the $50,000 to $90,000 range.

**The media** ● One weekly, the *Williams News*. Television via relay from Flagstaff and Phoenix.

**Medical services** ● An emergency medical center; nearest hospital is in Flagstaff.

**Transportation** ● Greyhound bus service. The historic Grand Canyon Railway runs between Williams and the canyon. Williams Municipal Airport has a 6,000-foot runway; charters available.

**Education** ● An elementary, middle and high school.

**Local government** ● Incorporated in 1901; mayor, six council members and a city manager.

**Places to stay** ● About 25 motels and the historic Fray Marcos Hotel; several RV and trailer parks, plus campgrounds in the surrounding Kaibab National Forest.

**Leisure facilities** ● Community center, five public parks, a golf course, riding stables, aquatic center, tennis courts and the Williams Ski Area.

**Tourist lures** ● The Grand Canyon, obviously, is the biggest lure, closely followed by the Grand Canyon Railway that takes vintage rail buffs there. A deer farm and petting zoo is just outside of town, and the surrounding national forest lures the outdoor set.

**Contacts** ● Williams-Grand Canyon Chamber of Commerce, 200 W. Railroad Ave., Williams, AZ 86046; (928) 635-4451; *www.williamschamber.com; e-mail: info@williamschamber.com.*

City of Williams, 113 S. First St., Williams, AZ 86046; (928) 635-1494; *www.ci.williams.az.us.*

### Chapter Ten
# METROPOLITAN MIDDLE
## PHOENIX AND THE VALLEY OF THE SUN

---

**T**he Valley of the Sun, a great desert basin rimmed by ruggedly handsome peaks, is the economic, political and social heart of Arizona. More than three of five Arizonans live in Maricopa County, which includes the Valley of the Sun and desert regions southwest of there. Most of the valley's 21 communities have merged together like thin pancake batter, creating an urban megalopolis 30 miles across. It's beginning to resemble a desert version of the Los Angeles basin.

Despite its urban sprawl, the area still retains some of the flavor of frontier Arizona. It's a delightfully curious mix of Old West and New Wave. You can pull on your Levi's and eat cowboy steaks or wrap yourself in society's most sophisticated trappings and nibble daintily on *foi gras*.

**THE WAY IT WAS ●** In a state rich with Spanish, Mexican and cowboy lore, the settlement of the Phoenix basin was rather routine. Even its founder had a boring name—John Smith. Native Americans farmed the area for several centuries, diverting water from the Salt River. Judging from archaeological sites, their population may have reached 100,000. Then they mysteriously vanished around 1400 A.D., abandoning their irrigation canals.

Later Pima Indians noted the deserted ditches and called their builders "Hohokam," which means "gone away" or "used up."

This Sonoran Desert basin dozed in the sun until pioneer John Smith started a hay camp in 1864. Former Confederate soldier Jack Swilling arrived three years later and formed a company of unemployed miners to dig out the abandoned Hohokam canals. The group soon had a fine wheat and barley crop growing. One of the settlers, an educated Englishman named Darrel Duppa, named the settlement "Phoenix." He predicted that a great city would rise from the site of the former Indian camp, as the fabled Phoenix bird rises from its own ashes every 500 years.

This Phoenix didn't take that long.

The area grew quickly, particularly after the Roosevelt Dam was completed on the Salt River in 1911, encouraging agricultural expansion. Then the valley got a share of water from the Central Arizona Project as new diversion dams were completed on the Colorado River. The Phoenix bird really took off, like the roadrunner with Wile E. Coyote on its tail. It has never looked back.

World War II brought the military, seeking year-around weather for flight and combat training. At war's end, all of that sunshine tempted many GIs to return.

**THE WAY IT IS** • The valley has become a major urban center with attendant congestion and even occasional smog. In less than 50 years, this busy region has made the transition from barley fields and cow ponies to planned subdivisions and helicopter traffic spotters. The 2000 census revealed that Phoenix was America' second fastest growing large city, after Las Vegas, with a growth rate of 34 percent. It hurried into the new century as the sixth largest city in the country, with a population topping 1.3 million.

Phoenix is the urban core of a glop of 21 fused-together communities. Many of these peripheral towns have grown even faster than their leader. The statistical growth champ between 1990 and 2000 was Marana, which swelled by 520 percent, from 2,187 to 13,556. Other county growth hogs were Surprise (what an appropriate name!), 333 percent, Gilbert, 277 percent; Peoria, 114 percent; and Fountain Hills, 101 percent. The county gained nearly a million new residents during that period, increasing its population by more than 40 percent. More than a third of these were in Phoenix. With a total population approaching three million, the Valley of the Sun is one of America's largest urban centers.

In listing the cities of Arizona's metropolitan core, we include some communities that are outside the Valley of the Sun. A few are beyond the valley's outer fringes to the west and northeast, and others are south, along the Interstate 10 corridor between Phoenix and Tucson. Actually, no one has specifically defined the Valley of the Sun's boundaries, although it's generally regarded as the desert basin encompassed by hills surrounding greater Phoenix. The term "Valley of the Sun" is an invention of local boosters, not cartographers.

# PHOENIX

It's great that the Phoenix bird rose to build a new city over Hohokam canals. But did the old bird have to get this big? During the 1980s, it led the nation in population gain, then its Sunbelt rival Las Vegas took over the statistical lead in the 1990s. In total numbers, however, Phoenix is nearly four times larger than Glitter City. In late 1995, it surpassed Los Angeles, not in population but in total land area.

Phoenix is not only growing; it's rebuilding and improving. In the closing years of the last century, a $1.1 billion downtown renewal project brought a new convention center, art center, a baseball stadium for the Arizona Diamondbacks, science and history museums, performing arts theater, aquatic center and public parks and plazas.

The Phoenix bird is thus providing a total environment for urban living. Even with a few growing pains, it's one of the cleanest, safest and most appealing large cities in America. Tourists love it, too, and about fourteen million come to Phoenix and next-door Scottsdale every year.

Of course, with all of this growth and all of these visitors comes traffic congestion. Public transit is pretty much limited to buses; the city has no rail commute system. However, major freeway expansion in recent years has eased traffic congestion somewhat. Interstates 10 and 17 form a cross near the heart of the city and cross-town freeways are easing the drive to and from the suburbs. A beltway system currently under construction will girdle the Valley of the Sun. And amazingly, in one of the largest cities in America, in an urban core of high rises and busy sidewalks, you can still find a place to park!

*Elevation* • 1,117 feet

*Location* • In Maricopa County; the geographic and economic heart of the Valley of the Sun.

*Climate* • Warm to hot summers; balmy winters with some chilly evenings. July average high 104.4, low 78.3; January average high 64.6, low 38. Rainfall 6.74 inches; rare traces of snow.

*Population* • 1,400,000

*Population trend* • Gained 34 percent in the past decade.

*Property tax* • (assessed at ten percent of real value) Varies with the area; averages $16.76 per $100 assessed valuation.

*Economy* • It's versatile, vibrant and growing. Tourism and other services, retail trade and manufacturing produce most of the income, employing nearly 600,000 people, accounting for two-thirds of the jobs. Phoenix is the nation's third largest producer of electronics.

**Job prospects** • Job selection is wide and prospects generally are quite good. Phoenix is definitely the employment core of the Valley of the Sun. Its total labor force exceeds its total population because tens of thousands commute from the suburbs. Tourism and other services employ the most people, followed by retail trade and manufacturing. Thousands of seasonal tourist jobs open up during the fall-winter-spring visitor season. Since Phoenix is the state capital, the government is a major employer.

**Industrial facilities** • They're extensive, with numerous industrial parks, many with air or rail service.

**Real estate** • Housing is likewise varied, with homes ranging from $80,000 in older southwest Phoenix. Prices start around $125,000 for a three- bedroom home in the newer developing areas and go well beyond. The city's overall housing cost is higher than most of the rest of the state, yet much lower than many other urban areas. Home prices are about half what they are in Los Angeles and San Francisco .

**The media** • The daily *Arizona Republic* plus 50 smaller newspapers and other periodicals in the metropolitan area. Eight local TV stations and a full-service cable company.

**Medical services** • More than twenty hospitals, two psychiatric hospitals and numerous clinics and extended care facilities.

**Transportation** • Served by Greyhound and Amtrak. Sky Harbor International Airport is the ninth busiest in America, with a thousand arrivals and departures daily. It's home base for America West Airlines and it's served by more than twenty other carriers, including all major U.S. airlines. Eleven other airports are in the area.

**Education** • Arizona State University is in nearby Tempe; Phoenix has more than 80 technical and business colleges, three religious colleges and five community colleges, plus numerous public elementary, middle and high schools.

**Local government** • Incorporated in 1881; became the state capital in 1889. The city government is operated by a mayor, an eight-member council and a city manager.

**Places to stay** • Nearly 200 resorts, motels and hotels with more than 20,000 rooms; dozens of mobile home and RV parks.

**Leisure facilities** • An extensive assortment of spare time lures— public swimming pools, golf courses, tennis courts, 47 art galleries and 138 public parks, including seven huge wilderness parks in the surrounding mountains. Phoenix is among the world's leaders in total acreage of public park lands.

**Tourist lures** • Only the Grand Canyon draws more visitors to Arizona. Tourist attractions include the excellent Heard Indian Museum, science, technology and history museums and scores of other archives. Other lures include the Arizona State Capitol Museum, Desert Botanical Garden, Heritage Square with historic homes, and the highly regarded Phoenix Zoo. Of course, many visitors come just for the sun—to luxuriate in luxury resorts.

*Contacts* ● Community and Economic Development Office, City of Phoenix, 200 W. Washington St., 20th Floor, Phoenix, AZ 85003-1161; (602) 262-5040.

Greater Phoenix Convention and Visitors Bureau, 400 E. Van Buren St., Suite 600, Phoenix, AZ 85004-2290; (877) CALL-PHX or (602) 254-6500; *www.phoenixcvb.com.*

Phoenix Economic Growth Group, 400 N. Fifth St., Room 1625, Phoenix, AZ 85004; (602) FOR-PHNX or (602) 253-9747.

Phoenix Chamber of Commerce, 201 N. Central, Suite 2700, Phoenix, AZ 85073; (602) 495-2183.

Greater Phoenix Economic Council, Two N. Central Ave., Suite 210, Phoenix, AZ 85004; (602) 256-7700; *www.gpec.org.*

## APACHE JUNCTION

This town on the outer eastern edge of the Valley of the Sun came of age in the last two decades as a Snowbird and retirement retreat. Apache Junction has nearly a hundred RV and mobile home parks. With the completion of the Highway 60 freeway, it's also a bedroom community for the greater Phoenix-Scottsdale area. Its population boomed during the past five years.

Scattered over ruggedly scenic desert below the legendary Superstition Mountains, the town sits at the junction of the Apache Trail (State Highway 88) and U.S. 60. It's the gateway to the Salt River Canyon recreation area, the Superstitions and Tonto National Forest.

The "Trail" was carved through the rough Salt River Canyon early in this century as a construction road for the Theodore Roosevelt Dam. Completed in 1911, the dam is the cornerstone of the Salt River Project, providing water to the Valley of the Sun. In the 1920s, Highway 60 was cut through the Pinal Mountains to the south, linking Phoenix with the copper mines of the Globe-Miami area.

Apache Junction was born in 1922 when entrepreneur George Cleveland Curtis put up a tent and started peddling sandwiches and water to travelers at the intersection of the two routes.

*Elevation* ● 1,715 feet

*Location* ● In Pinal County near the foothills of the Superstition Mountains, at the junction of highways 60, 88 and 89.

*Climate* ● Hot, dry summers; warm, mild winters. July average high 104.3, low 74.2; January average high 64.9, low 35.6. Rainfall 7.52 inches; rare traces of snow.

*The Superstition Mountains form a dramatic backdrop for the community of Apache Junction.*

**Population** • 32,800

**Population trend** • Up more than 75 percent in the past decade.

**Property tax** • (assessed at ten percent of real value) $17.18 per $100 assessed valuation.

**Economy** • It's based almost entirely on the three R's of Arizona growth—recreation, retirement and real estate. Its popularity as a retirement area and a bedroom community to the Valley of the Sun has led to a moderate boom in home construction.

**Job prospects** • They aren't very good, although it's a nice place to live if you're willing to commute to work—or if you don't have to work. Retail trades, services and public administration comprise most of the work force.

**Industrial facilities** • Two small industrial parks.

**Real estate** • Several planned communities, including senior villages, have been built in recent years. An average three-bedroom detached home is from $100,000 and up.

**The media** • The weekly *Apache Junction Independent*. TV provided by Phoenix, plus relays from Tucson and cable channels.

**Medical services** • A few medical clinics; nearest hospitals are in Mesa, eight miles west.

**Transportation** • Served by Greyhound; nearest airport is Phoenix Sky Harbor.

**Education** • Apache Junction campus of two-year Central Arizona College, plus four elementary, one junior high and one high school.

**Local government** • Incorporated in 1978; mayor, six council members and a city manager.

***Places to stay*** • A few motels and many mobile home and RV parks.

***Leisure facilities*** • Four public parks including a 1,600-acre multi-use park, a public swimming pool, senior center and racquetball and tennis courts.

***Tourist lures*** • The Superstition Mountains, home to the legendary Lost Dutchman Mine, are in the town's back yard. Lost Dutchman State Park offers camping, picnicking and hiking. Reservoirs of the Salt River Canyon and old Western style towns such as Tortilla Flat and Goldfield also draw visitors.

***Contacts*** • Apache Junction Chamber of Commerce, P.O. Box 1747, Apache Junction, AZ 85217-1747; (480) 982-3141; *www.apachejunctioncoc.com; e- mail: chamber@ci.apache-jct.az.us.*

Department of Development Services, City of Apache Junction, 1001 N. Idaho Rd., Apache Junction, AZ 85217; (480) 671-5083; *www.ajcity.net.*

# ARIZONA CITY

Invented in 1960 as a planned community midway between Phoenix and Tucson, Arizona City offers a recreational lake, golf course and parks. It sits amidst rich agricultural fields of the Santa Cruz Basin midway between Phoenix and Tucson. Although the population is small, its percentage of increase is nearly 75 percent in the past five years.

***Elevation*** • 1,505 feet

***Location*** • In Pinal County near the Interstate 10 and I-8 junction; about eight miles south of Casa Grande.

***Climate*** • Warm to hot summers; warm winters with cool evenings. July average high 105, low 75.1; January average high 67, low 35.7. Rainfall 8.45 inches; rare traces of snow.

***Population*** • Approximately 4,500

***Population trend*** • Gained nearly 75 percent in the past ten years.

***Property tax*** • $18.25 per $100 assessed valuation.

***Economy*** • It's based largely on agriculture, light industry and retail, with some retirees.

***Job prospects*** • Average to good. The town is working to attract smokeless industries and has had some success. Agriculture is still active in the area.

***Industrial facilities*** • Two small industrial parks.

***Real estate*** • Virtually all homes are in planned developments, since this is a new city. Prices for a three-bedroom home range from $70,000 to $80,000.

***The media*** • The weekly *Arizona City Independent*, and the *Daily Dispatch* from nearby Casa Grande; TV via cable.

***Medical services*** • One medical center.

***Transportation*** • Also see Casa Grande.

***Education*** • Central Arizona College near Casa Grande; an elementary and high school in Arizona City.

***Local government*** • Unincorporated; government services provided by Pinal County.

***Places to stay*** • Six motels and three RV parks in the area.

***Leisure facilities*** • An 18-hole golf course, small recreational lake and community center.

***Tourist lures*** • Not many. Nearby Picacho Peak State Park, site of the westernmost battle of the Civil War, offers camping, picnicking and hiking. Casa Grande National Monument is also is nearby.

***Contact*** • Arizona City Chamber of Commerce, P.O. Box 5, Arizona City, AZ 85223; (520) 466-5141; *www.arizonacitychamber.org;* e-mail: *azchamber@cgmailbox.com.*

# AVONDALE

This is the largest of several small communities on the western rim of the Valley of the Sun, known locally as West Valley. It's also the fastest growing town in the area, gaining more than 120 percent population in the past ten years. If you don't care for the fused together metroglop of greater Phoenix, you might like to settle out here. One can still find open desert between the borders of Avondale, Goodyear, Buckeye and Litchfield Park. Go a short distance farther west and you'll find only miles and miles of mostly uninhabited desert—all the way to the California border.

The demographics of these communities are similar. Percentage wise, they're growing much faster than the ballooning suburbs of Phoenix, although they're starting from a much smaller numeric base. This growth is spurred in part by a pilot training center and Lockheed-Martin facility adjacent to the nearby Phoenix-Goodyear Airport. The towns offer a balanced economy of manufacturing, retailing and a bit of agriculture. Avondale was developed by the Goodyear Tire and Rubber Company, which came here initially to grow cotton for tire treads, then it started an aviation facility. A post office was opened in 1911 and the town was incorporated in 1946.

***Elevation*** • Approximately 1,000 feet

***Location*** • In Maricopa County on the western edge of the Valley of the Sun just off I-10; about twenty miles from downtown Phoenix.

**Climate** ● Warm to hot summers; balmy winters with cool evenings. July average high 106.8, low 75.3; January average high 66.9, low 35.8. Rainfall 7.56 inches; rare traces of snow.

**Population** ● About 36,500

**Population trend** ● Gained 122 percent in the past ten years.

**Property tax** ● $14.53 per $100 assessed valuation.

**Economy** ● Nearby Phoenix-Goodyear Airport, Luke Air Force Base, farming, light industry and retailing provide a balanced economic base.

**Job prospects** ● There's considerable employment diversity among these fringe towns and job prospects range from average to good.

**Industrial facilities** ● Several industrial parks are in the area.

**Real estate** ● Avondale's growth has spurred the local construction industry. A variety of housing is available, from older homes starting around $80,000 to master planned communities and "ranchettes" that range well beyond $200,000.

**The media** ● The weekly *West Valley View* covers the local scene; dailies come from Phoenix. TV also is from Phoenix and a cable company serves the area.

**Medical services** ● A midsize hospital is twelve miles away; Avondale has a nursing center and small medical clinics.

**Transportation** ● A regional bus system links Avondale to nearby cities and Phoenix. The Phoenix-Goodyear Airport, operated by the city of Phoenix, is nearby, with an 8,500-foot runway. Sky Harbor International Airport is about twenty miles east.

**Education** ● Estrella Mountain Community College, plus the usual elementary and middle schools and two high schools.

**Local government** ● Incorporated in 1946; mayor, seven-member council and a city manager.

**Places to stay** ● Four motels, a resort and several RV parks in the area.

**Leisure facilities** ● Six public parks, seven golf courses, an auto race track, community center and senior center, plus tennis, racquetball and handball courts.

**Tourist lures** ● It's a family town, not a tourist town. Locals like the solitude of the surrounding desert, not yet devoured by asphalt. It's a short drive to the many tourist and cultural offerings of the Valley of the Sun.

**Contacts** ● Southwest Valley Chamber of Commerce, 289 N. Litchfield Rd., Goodyear, AZ 85338; (623) 932-2260; *www.southwestvalleychamber.org;* e- mail: *info@southwestvalleychamber.org.*

Economic Development Department, City of Avondale, 525 N. Central, Avondale, AZ 85323; (623) 932-6183; *www.avondale.org.*

# BUCKEYE

Beginning life as a farming town in 1888, Buckeye got its nice name from the Buckeye Canal, one of the first modern irrigation ditches in the state. This town west of Phoenix was one of the slowest growing communities in the valley until it was carried aloft by industrial developments around nearby Avondale, Goodyear and Litchfield Park. It then became one of the area's fastest growing towns in the first years of the new century. However, it still manages to maintain a small town atmosphere.

• FLAGSTAFF

• PHOENIX

• TUCSON

*Elevation* • 890 feet

*Location* • In Maricopa County, on the far western edge of the Valley of the Sun just south of Interstate 10; about 30 miles from Phoenix.

*Climate* • Warm to hot summers; balmy winters with cool evenings. July average high 107.3, low 74.3; January average high 67.1, low 34.3. Rainfall 7.08 inches; rare traces of snow.

*Population* • 10,700

*Population trend* • Gained 47.4 percent in the past ten years.

*Property tax* • $12.83 per $100 assessed valuation.

*Economy* • Light manufacturing, retail and services, construction and some agriculture.

*Job prospects* • Average to above average prospects, with the growth of industries in the surrounding communities.

*Industrial facilities* • Several industrial parks.

*Real estate* • Several new subdivisions are a-building, and a few older homes are on the market. Prices range from $90,000 to $200,000 for three- bedroom dwellings.

*The media* • The weekly *Buckeye Valley News* and *West Valley View*. Daily news and TV programming comes from Phoenix and a local cable company.

*Medical services* • A 24- hour emergency medical center and clinic; eight hospitals within 36 miles.

*Transportation* • Served by Greyhound. General aviation and charter service at Buckeye Municipal Airport; Sky Harbor International is about 35 miles away.

*Education* • Several elementary schools and two high schools.

*Local government* • Incorporated in 1929; mayor, six-member council and town manager.

*Places to stay* • Several motels and three RV parks.

*Leisure facilities* • Seven public parks, a community center, two 18-hole golf courses, and tennis, racquetball and handball courts.

***Contacts*** • Buckeye Valley Chamber of Commerce, 508 E. Monroe Ave., Buckeye, AZ 85326; (623) 386-2727; *www.buckeyevalleychamber.org.*

Town of Buckeye Planning & Economic Development, 100 N. Apache Rd., Buckeye, AZ 85326; (623) 386-4691.

# CAREFREE & CAVE CREEK

Sitting on the far northeastern fringes of the Valley of the Sun, these hamlets are twins in location only. As the cute name suggests, Carefree is a modern planned community. It appeals primarily to retired folks and commuters to Phoenix and Scottsdale. Cave Creek is on the rustic side, a Western style town that began as a mining camp in the 1870s.

Both communities occupy an attractive rocky desert setting, surrounded by rockier hills. They rate high on our list of desirable Arizona villages, particularly for retired folks. However, temporary winter facilities are rather limited for Snowbirds. The two hamlets balance one another nicely. One can luxuriate in luxury resorts such as the Boulders and shop at stylish boutiques in Carefree, and then get a cowboy steak at a restaurant-saloon in Cave Creek. However, Cave Creek isn't totally rustic; several modern subdivisions occupy its cactus- studded desert hills.

Interstate 17, a few miles west, offers a quick 25-minute trip to downtown Phoenix. For serious shopping and dining, upscale Scottsdale is a few miles south of Carefree.

***Elevation*** • Carefree 2,500 feet; Cave Creek 2,200 feet

***Location*** • In Maricopa County, 25 miles northeast of Phoenix.

***Climate*** • Warm to hot summers; mild winters with some chilly evenings. July average high 102, low 75.4; January average high 62, low 38.8. Rainfall 12.35 inches; rare traces of snow.

***Population*** • Carefree 3,000; Cave Creek 4,000

***Population trend*** • Carefree is quickly outpacing Cave Creek; it gained 76.6 percent in the past decade, compared with the older city's 27.5 percent.

***Property tax*** • $9.39 per $100 of assessed valuation.

***Economy*** • It's pretty much based on tourism and desert living. The towns aren't working to attract industry.

***Job prospects*** • They're quite limited since the focus here is retirement and commuting to Phoenix and Scottsdale.

***Industrial facilities*** • None.

***Real estate*** • Housing is expensive in this highly desirable area, ranging from $200,000 and up.

**The media** • One weekly, the *Foothills Sentinel* and a monthly, the *Carefree Enterprise*. Daily newspapers and TV service from Phoenix, plus a cable company.

**Medical services** • A 24-hour emergency care facility and small clinics; extensive facilities in Scottsdale and Phoenix.

**Transportation** • Nearest commercial transit is in Scottsdale and Phoenix; Sky Harbor International Airport is about 25 miles away. Carefree has a general aviation facility with a 4,100-foot runway.

**Education** • The usual public schools.

**Local government** • Cave Creek was incorporated in 1986 and Carefree in 1984. Council-manager government in Cave Creek; mayor, six council members and a town administrator in Carefree.

**Places to stay** • Two resorts and a few bed & breakfast inns.

**Leisure facilities** • Two community centers, an adult center, three public parks and three golf courses, plus many more in the Paradise Valley and Scottsdale area.

**Tourist lures** • Folks come here mostly for the striking rocky desert scenery, the boutiques of Carefree and the frontier ambiance of Cave Creek, which also has an interesting historic museum. The surrounding desert rises into the wilds of Tonto National Forest.

**Contacts** • Carefree/Cave Creek Chamber of Commerce, 7207 E. Carefree Dr. (P.O. Box 734), Carefree, AZ 85337; (480) 488-3381; *www.carefree-cavecreek.com*.

Town of Carefree, 100 Easy St., Carefree, AZ 85377; (480) 488-3686; *www.carefree.org*.

Town of Cave Creek, 37622 N. Cave Creek Rd., Cave Creek, AZ 85331; (480) 488-1400; *www.cavecreek.org*.

# CASA GRANDE

A thriving working class town, Casa Grande was named for a large Hohokam adobe about twenty miles away. It was established in 1879 as a way station on a railroad being built to link Phoenix and Tucson. Incorporated in 1915, it's the largest community in Pinal County. Once primarily an agricultural community, the town is working to attract industry and retail trade.

The surrounding area is essentially irrigated desert. The countryside isn't particularly attractive, although the area is tidy, the climate's nice and homes are affordable. The town is becoming popular with retirees, and it offers two senior centers and several mobile home parks. A few Snowbirds light here as well, drawn by the relatively inexpensive facilities.

***Elevation*** • 1,398 feet

***Location*** • In Pinal County off I-10 between Phoenix and Tucson.

***Climate*** • Warm to hot summers; dry, balmy winters with cool evenings. July average high 106.2, low 76; January average high 66, low 35. Rainfall 8.12 inches; rare dustings of snow.

***Population*** • 27,300

***Population trend*** • Gained 32.2 percent in the past decade.

***Property tax*** • $14.75 per $100 assessed valuation.

***Economy*** • Originally agricultural based, it's shifting toward light industry and the services sector. Retail trade is the largest employer, followed by services and manufacturing.

***Job prospects*** • They best possibilities are in retail sales, tourist-related work and light industry.

***Industrial facilities*** • Five industrial parks, most with rail access.

***Real estate*** • There's a modest amount of new home construction in the area, plus some older houses on the market, with prices of a three-bedroom ranging from $70,000 to $90,000.

***The media*** • One daily newspaper, the *Casa Grande Dispatch*. TV relays from Phoenix, plus a local cable company.

***Medical services*** • A regional medical center, 116-bed hospital, long-term care facility and several clinics.

***Transportation*** • Served by Greyhound. Casa Grande Airport has two 5,200-foot runways.

***Education*** • Signal Peak campus of Central Arizona Community College is east of Casa Grande; one private elementary school plus public elementary, middle and high schools.

***Local government*** • Incorporated in 1915; mayor, six council members and a city manager.

***Places to stay*** • Since Casa Grande is on the heavily traveled Phoenix-Tucson corridor, it has several motels with a total room count of nearly 700, and several RV parks.

***Leisure facilities*** • Eighteen public parks, four golf courses within ten miles, a fitness center, tennis courts, two public pools and two senior centers.

***Tourist lures*** • This is a good base of operations for exploring north and south because of its midway location between Arizona's two metropolitan centers. Casa Grande Ruins National Monument and the fine Gila River Indian Arts and Craft Center are nearby.

***Contacts*** • Casa Grande Chamber of Commerce, 575 N. Marshall, Casa Grande, AZ 85222-5244; (800) 916-1515 or (520) 836-2125; *www.casagrandechamber.org; e-mail: chamber@casa grande.com.*

City of Casa Grande Planning & Development Department, 510 E. Florence Blvd., Casa Grande, AZ 85222; (520) 421-8637; *ci.casa-grande.az.us.*

Greater Casa Grande Valley Economic Development Foundation, 201 E. Third St., Casa Grande, AZ 85222; (520) 836-6868; *e-mail: casagrnd@cybertrails.com.*

# CHANDLER

This is another of the Valley of the Sun's authentic boomtowns, zooming from 29,673 in 1980 to nearly 90,000 in 1990 and 176,581 at the turn of the century. A small town two decades ago, it is now the sixth largest city in Arizona. All of this adds up to an abundance of new housing, good job prospects and a generally upscale economy.

Chandler doesn't have the cultural and tourist offerings of other valley communities, but no matter. Everything is within a few minutes' drive. Tempe's Arizona State University, for instance, is just across the freeway.

The town began in the early 1890s when Canadian-born veterinarian Alexander John Chandler staked out a 1,800-acre ranch. A ambitious entrepreneur, he brought in irrigation water and then subdivided and sold off parcels for small farms. He went on to establish a resort, bank and other properties to become his namesake town's leading citizen. There's not much agriculture left today, however. The primary crop is subdivisions.

*Elevation* ● 1,210 feet

*Location* ● In Maricopa County, southeast of Phoenix.

*Climate* ● Warm to hot summers; balmy winters. July average high 103.8, low 76.4; January average high 65, low 37.3. Rainfall 8.42 inches; rare traces of snow.

*Population* ● 186,875

*Population trend* ● Gained nearly 100 percent since 1990.

*Property tax* ● $13.25 per $100 assessed valuation.

*Economy* ● Active and diversified, with a mix of construction, high tech industries, retail trade and service jobs.

*Job prospects* ● Space age firms like Intel Corporation, Motorola, Ryobi Outdoor Products and Speedfam International offer good potential, along with construction and retailing. Also, it's a short drive to the even larger Phoenix job market.

*Industrial facilities* ● Fifteen industrial parks, many with rail and air service.

*Real estate* ● Prices for three-bedroom detached homes range from $100,000.

*The media* ● The daily *Chandler Tribune* and weekly *Chandler Independent*. Phoenix provides local television, and Chandler has a cable company.

*Medical services* ● Full service Chandler Regional Hospital and several small medical clinics.

***Transportation*** • Served by Greyhound. Two local airports have lighted runways; Phoenix Sky Harbor International is fifteen miles away.

***Education*** • Private elementary and high schools and numerous public elementary, middle and high schools; ASU campus nearby.

***Local government*** • Incorporated in 1920; mayor, six council members and a city manager.

***Places to stay*** • Several hotels and motels with a 1,700 total room count.

***Leisure facilities*** • Four golf courses, five public pools, various parks and playing fields, large tennis complex and racquetball courts.

***Tourist lures*** • Most are elsewhere, although Chandler has a nicely done historical museum.

***Contacts*** • Chandler Chamber of Commerce, 25 S. Arizona Place, Chandler, AZ 85225; (480) 963-4571.

City of Chandler Economic Development Division, 215 E. Buffalo St., Chandler, AZ 85225; (480) 782-3030; *www.chandleraz.org.*

# FLORENCE

Sitting off to the eastern side of the Phoenix-Tucson corridor, Florence is a pleasant surprise. It's one of Arizona's oldest towns, dating from 1866 when one Levi Ruggles laid out a townsite near a ford in the Gila River. This is a handsome place today, with fine nineteenth century homes in the Florence Townsite National Historic District. All are listed on the National Register of Historic Places. With its quiet pace, it's becoming popular with retirees.

The Western flavor downtown, with false front stores and sidewalk overhangs, seems right out of a cowboy movie set. In fact, it has been used by Hollywood film makers. Movie cowboy legend Tom Mix is linked to the area, although for an unfortunate reason. He slammed his Cord sports car into a ditch seventeen miles south of Florence in 1940 and died at the wheel; a monument marks the spot.

Despite its laid back lifestyle, Florence isn't exactly sleeping in the sun. Population has more than doubled in the past decade. It's the seat of Pinal County and its 1891 courthouse is an architectural gem—a red brick structure with gingerbread trim and a hexagonal clock tower. The town also is home to the Arizona State Prison, built in 1909 to replace the aging Yuma Territorial Prison.

***Elevation*** • 1,493 feet

***Location*** • In Pinal County, midway between Phoenix and Tucson on U.S. Highway 79.

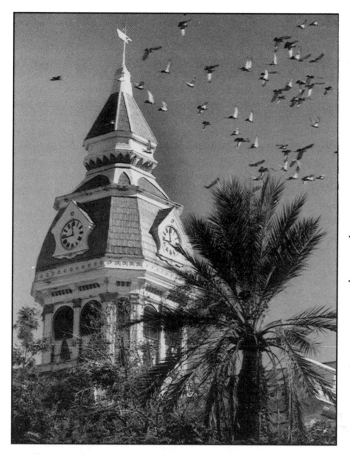

*Birds of a feather (pigeons in this case) flock about the elaborate clocktower of the Pina County Courthouse in Florence.*

**Climate** • Warm to hot summers; balmy winters with cool evenings. July average high 106.1, low 74; January average high 66.8, low 36.1. Rainfall 9.5 inches; occasional traces of snow.

**Population** • 17,225

**Population trend** • Gained 132 percent in the past decade.

**Property tax** • $16.85 per $100 assessed valuation.

**Economy** • It's heavily focused on public administration, because of its county seat status and the adjacent state prison; these facilities account for more than half of the local payroll.

**Job prospects** • Construction, services and retail trades offer potential, with the current growth trend. Largest employers are the county government and Arizona State Prison.

**Industrial facilities** • No major industrial parks.

**Real estate** • Three- bedroom home prices range from $80,000 to $150,000.

**The media** • One weekly, the *Florence Reminder*; daily news coverage is provided by the *Casa Grande Dispatch*. TV relays from Phoenix and Tucson, plus cable.

***Medical services*** • A full-service hospital, a nursing home and a residential care home.

***Transportation*** • Nearest airport is in Coolidge, ten miles away; no scheduled air or bus service.

***Education*** • The usual public schools; no private ones.

***Local government*** • Seat of Pinal County since 1875. Incorporated in 1908; mayor, six council members and a town manager.

***Places to stay*** • A few motels and two RV parks.

***Leisure facilities*** • A senior center, three public parks and a pool, a golf course and tennis courts.

***Tourist lures*** • The historic downtown district draws visitors, along with the courthouse and McFarland State Historic Park, which honors the former U.S. Senate majority leader, Arizona governor and chief justice of the Arizona supreme court. Casa Grande Ruins National Monument is nearby.

***Contacts*** • Greater Florence Chamber of Commerce, P.O. Box 929, Florence, AZ 85232; (520) 868-9433; www.florenceaz.org.

Pinal County Development Board & Visitors Center, Box 967 (135 N. Pinal St.), Florence, AZ 85232; (888) 469-0175 or (520) 868-4331.

Town of Florence, P.O. Box 2670 (755 N. Main St.), Florence, AZ 85232; (520) 868-7500; *www.ci.florence.az.us; e-mail: florence@town. florence.az.us.*

# FOUNTAIN HILLS

An upscale planned community started in 1970, Fountain Hills is carefully laid over a rugged desert panorama. It was created by Lake Havasu City's McCulloch Properties of London Bridge fame, and designed by Charles Wood Jr., who also fashioned the original Disneyland layout.

Fountain Hills is much more stylish than either of these; there's no London Bridge and no fairyland castle. However, since McCulloch likes to have a gimmick, this community boasts the world's tallest fountain as its focal point. It spurts skyward from a nicely landscaped lake, and the town is built around it.

Although many retired people are drawn to Fountain Hills, it has a rather low median age of 37. Many residents are professionals who commute to work in the Valley of the Sun. Like the fountain, its population is shooting skyward.

***Elevation*** • 1,520 to 3,000 feet

***Location*** • In Maricopa County, 30 miles northeast of Phoenix and a few miles east of Scottsdale.

***Climate*** • Warm to hot summers; balmy winters with some cool evenings.

July average high 105.1, low 74.2; January average high 66.7, low 36.4. Rainfall 8.06 inches; occasional traces of snow.

**Population** ● 21,190

**Population trend** ● Doubled in the past ten years.

**Property tax** ● $10.44 per $100 assessed valuation.

**Economy** ● It's essentially an upper middle class bedroom town, with small businesses and services as its economic core.

**Job prospects** ● Most jobs are elsewhere; Fountain Hills is populated mostly with commuters and retirees.

**Real estate** ● Housing is predictably expensive in this upscale town. Three-bedroom detached homes start around $180,000 and shoot skyward from there.

**The media** ● The weekly *Times of Fountain Hills* and monthly *Sentinel*. Daily newspapers and TV from Phoenix, plus a cable company.

**Medical services** ● Two family health centers and a walk-in clinic; other facilities in Scottsdale, plus a Mayo Clinic four miles west.

**Transportation** ● Mesa and Scottsdale airports are thirteen miles away and Phoenix Sky Harbor is 24 miles.

**Education** ● The usual public schools.

**Local government** ● Incorporated in 1989; governed by the Town of Fountain Hills Council.

**Places to stay** ● A few local motels and a upscale golf resorts, plus numerous hotels, motels and RV parks in adjacent communities.

**Leisure facilities** ● Two public parks, a public golf course and two golf resorts, an equestrian center, community center and several public tennis courts.

**Tourist lures** ● Some come to see that tall fountain, while the surrounding desert draws hikers and seekers of solitude. McDowell Mountain Regional Park is just north of town; Saguaro Lake and Canyon Lake of the Salt River Project are northeast.

**Contact** ● Fountain Hills Chamber of Commerce, P.O. Box 17598, Fountain Hills, AZ 85268; (480) 837-1654; *www.fhchamberofcommerce.org; e-mail: frank@fhchamberofcommerce.org.*

# GILBERT

To call Gilbert a dynamic growth area is an understatement. It was the fastest growing city in the nation in the decade of the eighties, leaping from 6,000 to nearly 30,000. It more than tripled in size in the 1990s and strode into the new millennium with a population of 122,360.

Still, it works to preserve its small town environment and quality of life, according to the Chamber of Commerce: "The town has successfully woven its agricultural heritage into a diverse economic tapestry that includes strong retail and manufacturing sectors. This has resulted in one of the highest median household incomes in the area."

Gilbert isn't all new. It dates back to an 1890 homestead filed by William A. Gilbert and it was incorporated in 1920. However, it dozed for decades as a small farming community until it caught the Valley of the Sun growth bug in the 1980s.

*Elevation* • 1,273 feet

*Location* • In Maricopa County's southeast corner, next door to Chandler and about twenty miles from downtown Phoenix.

*Climate* • warm to hot summers; balmy winters with cool evenings. July average high 104.3, low 80; January average high 64.9, low 35.6. Rainfall 7.66 inches; occasional traces of snow.

*Population* • Approximately 127,000

*Population trend* • Gained 277 percent in the past decade.

*Property tax* • $13.08 per $100 assessed value.

*Economy* • A pro-growth attitude, broad employment base with several high tech industries and expanded shopping centers add fuel to Gilbert's economic engine.

*Job prospects* • It offers one of Arizona's best job markets, with a low unemployment rate and a diversified economy. Employment opportunities range from high tech and light industry to construction, retail and services.

*Industrial facilities* • More than a dozen industrial parks, many with rail and air service.

*Real estate* • The average sale price of a new home in recent years was about $176,000, according to the chamber of commerce.

*The media* • The weekly *Gilbert Independent* and daily *East Valley Tribune.* TV from Phoenix and a local cable company.

*Medical services* • One hospital in adjacent Chandler and four in Mesa, plus several clinics in Gilbert.

*Transportation* • Served by Valley Metro regional bus system. Chandler and Mesa municipal airports are nearby; Phoenix Sky Harbor is nineteen miles northwest.

*Education* • Chandler/Gilbert Community College, Mesa Community College and Arizona State University are all within a short commute. Gilbert has the full range of public and charter schools.

*Local government* • Incorporated in 1920; mayor, six council members and a town manager.

*Places to stay* • Several motels and RV parks in Chandler and Mesa.

*Leisure facilities* • Five golf courses, fourteen public parks including a skate park, recreation center, two public pools and many tennis and racquetball courts.

*Tourist lures* • While not a tourist town, Gilbert is not far from the Superstition Mountains and Salt River Canyon; the many lures of Phoenix- Scottsdale are within a short drive.

*Contacts* • Gilbert Chamber of Commerce, P.O. Box 527, Gilbert, AZ 85299-0527; (480) 892-0056, *www.gilbertaz.com; e-mail: info@gilbertchamber.com.*

Economic Development Department, Town of Gilbert, 1025 S. Gilbert Rd., Gilbert, AZ 85296, (480) 545-6865; *www.gilbertaz.com.*

## GLENDALE

Another of the mushroomburbs of the Valley of the Sun, Glendale is a mix of residential areas, shopping centers and manufacturing. Nearby Luke Air Force Base, the nation's largest fighter training facility, provides civilian employment; it was annexed by Glendale in 1995. Electronics, precision metal working and casting, and aerospace activities add to the job base.

Like Chandler and Gilbert, Glendale's main asset is growth. It began rather modestly as a farming settlement by the Illinois Church of the Brethren in 1892 and it progressed rather slowly until it caught the growth bug of recent decades. It's now Arizona's fourth largest city.

Despite its explosive growth and the resultant newness, downtown Glendale is historically charming, with lots of antique shops, tearooms and such. A jolly little trolley takes visitors about the Catlin Court Historic District, where old homes have been converted into specialty boutiques.

*Elevation* • 1,100 feet

*Location* • In Maricopa County, northwestern area of the Valley of the Sun.

*Climate* • Warm to hot summers; mild winters. July average high 104.4, low 78.3; January average high 64.6, low 38. Rainfall 6.74 inches; rare traces of snow.

*Population* • about 225,000

*Population trend* • Increased by 48 percent in the past ten years.

*Property tax* • $16.72 per $100 assessed valuation.

*Economy* • It's rolling right along, and it spans the spectrum from metal fabricating to light manufacturing and services and retail. One of the world's largest shopping malls opened here in 1994, with 1.3 million square feet of retail space.

*Job prospects* • They're generally excellent and they cover a broad range, including manufacturing, aerospace, communications, precision metal working, chemicals, electronics, warehousing, services and retail sales. Luke Air Force Base is Glendale's largest employer. Among major corporations with facilities here are Honeywell, Bechtel, Parker Hannifin and K-B Toys.

*Industrial facilities* ● Numerous industrial parks and factories.

*Real estate* ● A three- bedroom home ranges from $90,000 to $100,000 and beyond.

*The media* ● Two weeklies, *The Glendale Star* and *The Prospector*, plus the monthly *Arrow*. Daily newspapers and TV from Phoenix; local cable service.

*Medical services* ● Three hospitals, six nursing homes and several medical clinics; other facilities in surrounding communities.

*Transportation* ● Served by Greyhound. Glendale Airport has a 5,350-foot lighted runway; Phoenix Sky Harbor is about 30 miles away.

*Education* ● Glendale Community College, several technical schools and the usual public schools.

*Local government* ● Incorporated in 1910; mayor, six-member council and city manager.

*Places to stay* ● Several motels and business-oriented hotels and a number of RV parks, plus other facilities in surrounding communities.

*Leisure facilities* ● Sixty-one public parks, three golf courses, a tennis center, seven public swimming pools and two roller skating rinks.

*Tourist lures* ● Glendale is known as the "Antique Capital of Arizona" and its old style downtown district with more than 90 specialty shops is popular with visitors.

*Contacts* ● Glendale Chamber of Commerce, P.O. Box 249, Glendale, AZ 85311; (800) ID- SUNNY or (623) 937-4754.

Glendale Office of Tourism, 5800 W. Glenn Dr., Suite 140, Glendale, AZ 85301; (623) 930-4500; *www.glendaleaz.com* and *www.ci.glendale.az.us.*

# GOODYEAR

If the name sounds familiar, it's because this little town was established by the Goodyear Tire and Rubber Company in 1916—not to make tires but to raise cotton for tire cords. Originally, the town was going to be called Egypt. Goodyear soon had thousands of acres under cultivation, and the firm later located its aircraft division here; Lockheed-Martin arrived in later years. Although it remained small for decades, Goodyear is experiencing a serious growth surge.

● FLAGSTAFF

● PHOENIX

● TUCSON

This is another of those small communities on the western edge of the Valley of the Sun that appeals to people who want to see more desert than asphalt. It isn't ruggedly handsome desert like that around Scottsdale and Fountain Hills, although it has some open green space and the Estrella and White Tank mountains are nearby, offering hiking and picnicking.

**Elevation** • Approximately 1,000 feet

**Location** • In Maricopa County, on the western fringe of the Valley of the Sun, known locally as the Southwest Valley; seventeen miles from Phoenix.

**Climate** • Warm to hot summers; mild winters. July average high 106.8, low 75.3; January average high 66.9, low 35.8. Rainfall 7.56 inches; occasional trace of snow.

**Population** • About 23,000

**Population trend** • More than doubled in the past ten years.

**Property tax** • $12.88 per $100 assessed valuation.

**Economy** • The economic base is centered around the Phoenix-Goodyear Airport. The Airline Training Center Arizona, operated by Lufthansa, trains commercial airline pilots and the Lockheed Martin facility is adjacent, occupying a million-square-foot campus.

**Job prospects** • With large employers such as Lockheed Martin, Rubbermaid and Poore Brothers, area job prospects are varied and generally plentiful.

**Industrial facilities** • More than 2,000 acres of industrial property, some with parks, in an area known as the Western Maricopa Enterprise Zone.

**Real estate** • Several master-planned communities are in the area, with prices for a three-bedroom home ranging from $100,000 to $450,000.

**The media** • The weekly *West Valley View*. Daily news and TV programming comes from Phoenix and a local cable company.

**Medical services** • A 24- hour emergency clinic and medical plaza; a 192-bed hospital is twelve miles away.

**Transportation** • Bisected by I-10 and served by Greyhound. Phoenix-Goodyear Municipal Airport has an 8,500-foot lighted runway. Sky Harbor is about 25 miles east, reached by regional transit.

**Education** • Estrella Mountain Community College, plus the usual public schools.

**Local government** • Incorporated in 1946; mayor, six-member council and city manager.

**Places to stay** • A few motels, small hotel and a large resort.

**Leisure facilities** • Ten golf courses, several public parks, a community center, pool and tennis courts; Estrella Mountain Regional Park is nearby.

**Tourist lures** • Phoenix International Raceway is nearby and the lures of Phoenix-Scottsdale are less than an hour's drive.

**Contacts** • City of Goodyear, 190 N. Litchfield Rd., Goodyear, AZ 85338; (800) 872-1749 or (623) 932-3910.

Southwest Valley Chamber of Commerce, 289 N. Litchfield Rd., Goodyear, AZ 85338; (623) 932-2260; *www.southwestvalleychamber.org; e-mail: info@southwestvalleychamber.org.*

# LITCHFIELD PARK

This town west of Phoenix was established by the Goodyear Tire and Rubber Company in 1918 and named for the firm's vice president Paul W. Litchfield; it was first called Litchton and then Litchfield Park. It was he who had conceived the idea of raising cotton in adjacent Goodyear for tire cords. Litchfield Park was designed as a model company town and much of that careful community blueprint is still evident.

Growth has been slow until recently; it's beginning to pick up because of new facilities at nearby Phoenix-Goodyear Airport and westward spread of the ever-expanding Phoenix economy. However, it is still one of the Valley of the Sun's slower growing communities; most growth is immediately beyond the town limits.

**Elevation** • About 1,000 feet.

**Location** • In Maricopa County, just north of Goodyear, on the western edge of the Valley of the Sun.

**Climate** • Warm to hot summers; mild winters. July average high 106.8, low 75.3; January average high 66.9, low 35.8. Rainfall 7.56 inches; occasional trace of snow.

**Population** • about 4,000

**Population trend** • Gained 15.3 percent in the past ten years.

**Property tax** • $14.98 per $100 assessed valuation.

**Economy** • The economic base is diversified to include light industry, retail trade and services. The nearby Litchfield Naval Air Facility and Phoenix- Goodyear Airport are important economic elements.

**Job prospects** • The unemployment rate is rather low and nearby industries such as Rubbermaid, McKesson and a large grocery distribution center and luxury desert resort provide job possibilities.

**Industrial facilities** • Several industrial parks are nearby.

**Real estate** • Construction activity is very active around Litchfield Park although little is happening within the planned community. Prices for new homes start above $100,000; older homes within the town are very scarce and rather pricey.

***The media*** • The weekly *West Valley View;* daily news and TV programming comes from Phoenix and a local cable company.

***Medical services*** • A full service hospital is twelve miles east of town.

***Transportation*** • Served by Greyhound. Phoenix-Goodyear Municipal Airport has an 8,500-foot lighted runway. Sky Harbor is about twenty miles east.

***Education*** • Extension courses from Maricopa Community College in nearby Goodyear; the usual public schools in the area.

***Local government*** • Founded in 1918; incorporated in 1987; mayor, six-member council and city manager.

***Places to stay*** • The large Wigwam Resort; motels and RV parks in nearby communities.

***Leisure facilities*** • Six public parks, three golf courses and a public swimming pool.

***Tourist lures*** • World Wildlife Zoo and White Tank desert park are nearby.

***Contacts*** • City of Litchfield Park, 214 W. Wigwam Blvd., Litchfield Park, AZ 85340; (623) 935-5033, *www.litchfield-park.org.*

Southwest Valley Chamber of Commerce, 289 N. Litchfield Rd., Goodyear, AZ 85338; (623) 932-2260; *www.southwestvalleychamber.org; e-mail: info@southwestvalleychamber.org.*

# MESA

One of Arizona's economic boomtowns, Mesa ranks third in population after Phoenix and Tucson. Its gained more than 100,000 residents between 1990 and 2000, second only to Phoenix in total population growth.

This is a well-balanced city, with a good industrial, cultural and recreational mix. It sits on the eastern edge of the Valley of the Sun, with easy access to the outdoor lures of Tonto National Forest. Downtown Phoenix, Scottsdale and Arizona State University are just to the west.

Mesa was settled by a group of Mormons who set up camp on a bluff above the Salt River in 1877. They weren't very original in picking a name for their settlement; *mesa* means flat-topped hill or table in Spanish. Like the pioneers of neighboring Phoenix, they cleaned out old Hohokam canals along the river and soon had themselves a thriving little farming town. Those early Mormons wouldn't recognize their creation today; sprawl has buried most of the farm fields. However, downtown Mesa is quite attractive, with Spanish-style colonnade sidewalks, brick crosswalks and streets lined with palm and orange trees.

**Elevation** • 1,225 feet

**Location** • In Maricopa County, fourteen miles east of Phoenix.

**Climate** • Warm to hot summers; mild winters. July average high 104.3, low 74.1; January average high 64.9, low 35.6. Rainfall 7.52 inches; occasional trace of snow.

**Population** • 415,000

**Population trend** • Gained nearly 40 percent in the past ten years.

**Property tax** • $11.11 per $100 assessed valuation.

**Economy** • Mesa's economy is broad-based and solid. Seven of *Fortune Magazine's* top five hundred companies are located here. Production ranges from propulsion equipment and helicopters to food high tech and electronics.

**Job prospects** • With a thriving economy and a low jobless rate, this is a good place to find work. Among its chief employers are McDonnell Douglas Helicopters, General Motors Proving Grounds and Motorola.

**Industrial facilities** • More than twenty industrial parks, plus several large manufacturing complexes.

**Real estate** • A variety of homes is available, from conventional subdivisions to planned communities to condos and townhouses. Home prices for a three- bedroom detached unit start around $100,000 and range well beyond $150,000.

**The media** • The daily *Mesa Tribune* and the weekly *Mesa Independent*. Phoenix and a local cable company furnish the television.

**Medical services** • Four hospitals, eighteen extended care and convalescent homes and several medical clinics.

**Transportation** • Served by Greyhound. Falcon Field has a lighted 4,300-foot runway; Phoenix Sky Harbor is twelve miles west of Mesa.

**Education** • Mesa Community College, the east campus of Arizona State University, the usual public schools plus several private schools.

**Local government** • Incorporated in 1883; mayor, six-member council and city manager.

**Places to stay** • About 70 hotels and motels, plus many RV and mobile home parks with more than 30,000 total spaces.

**Leisure facilities** • Numerous public parks, 40 golf courses in the area, ten public pools, plus tennis, handball and racquetball courts.

**Tourist lures** • Mesa has five museums, including the excellent Mesa Southwest Museum downtown, and the Champlin Fighter Museum and Commemorative Air Force Museum at Falcon Field. The Chicago Cubs do their spring training here in February and March.

**Contacts** • Mesa Chamber of Commerce/Mesa Convention & Visitors Bureau, P.O. Box 5820 (120 N. Center St.), Mesa, AZ 85211-5820; (800) 283-6372 or (480) 827- 4700; *www.mesachamber.com.*

City of Mesa Economic Development, 100 N. Center, Mesa, AZ 85201; (800) 290-6372 or (480) 644-2398; *www.ci.mesa.az.us.*

Planning Department, City of Mesa, 55 N. Center St., Mesa, AZ 85201; (480) 644-2185.

## PARADISE VALLEY

If you like awesome rocky desert scenery and you can afford the prices, this can indeed become your paradise. There's little work available; folks come here either to retire or to commute to high-paying jobs elsewhere. Situated in a high desert basin between Scottsdale and Carefree, Paradise Valley is the Beverly Hills of the Valley of the Sun. It's a contented scatter of expensive homes, estates tucked into rough-hewn foothills and an occasional resort.

It was established in the late 1880s as a farming community by settlers who diverted water from a tributary of the Salt River. By the post-World War II years, most of the farms had been bought up as homesites by the more prosperous folks of growing Phoenix.

*Elevation* • 1,421 feet

*Location* • In Maricopa County, north of the Phoenix Mountains, between Scottsdale and Carefree-Cave Creek.

*Climate* • Warm to hot summers; mild winters. July average high 104.1, low 80.9; January average high 64.5, low 42.6. Rainfall 8.40 inches; snowfall very rare.

*Population* • About 14,000

*Population trend* • Gained 15 percent in the past ten years.

*Property tax* • $12.54 per $100 assessed valuation.

*Economy* • Residents bring their own economy in the form of fat bank accounts. Most folks work elsewhere or they can afford not to work at all. The town has a small business and commercial district.

*Job prospects* • Not much to offer; unemployment is low become most residents are retired or they commute to jobs outside.

*Industrial facilities* • None.

*Real estate* • Homes rival those of Sedona as the most expensive in Arizona, starting around $200,000 and going into the millions for walled estates and mini-ranches. As the old saying goes, "If you have to ask the price..."

media • Two weeklies, the *Paradise Valley Voice* and *Paradise Valley Independent*. Phoenix stations and cable companies provide TV.

*Medical services* • Three hospitals in the area; two emergency centers and five extended care facilities.

*Transportation* • Mostly BMWs and Mercedes. Scheduled air service from Scottsdale Municipal Airport (feeder lines) and Phoenix Sky Harbor, about fifteen miles away.

*Education* • A mix of private and public schools.

*Local government* • The Town of Paradise Valley, which doesn't encompass all of the valley, was incorporated in 1961, with a mayor, six-member council and town manager.

*Places to stay* • The valley offers some of Arizona's most elegant resorts, plus a few smaller hotels and upscale motels.

*Leisure facilities* • Sixteen parks, eight golf course, two swimming pools, plus various tennis and racquetball courts at the resorts.

*Tourist lures* • Visitors come here mostly to envy the posh estates, or to stay at the resorts. Nearby North Mountain Park and Squaw Peak offer picnicking and hiking.

*Contact* • North Phoenix Chamber of Commerce, 2737 E. Greenway, Suite 10, Phoenix, AZ 85032-4391; (480) 482-3344; *www.northphoenixchamber.com; e-mail: info@northphoenixchamber.com.*

# PEORIA

Once a quiet farming town on the northwestern edge of the Valley of the Sun, Peoria has been caught up in the greater Phoenix growth surge, more than doubling its population during the past decade.

The town was established in 1885 when four farming families bought land shortly after the completion of the Arizona Canal, which brought water to this area of the Valley of the Sun. They named it for their hometown of Peoria, Illinois, of which it bears absolutely no resemblance. Despite its rapid growth, it retains some of its small town characteristics and open desert and a few farms remain on the fringes.

*Elevation* • About 1,100 feet

*Location* • In Maricopa County, 20 miles northwest of Phoenix.

*Climate* • Warm to hot summers; mild winters. July average high 106.3, low 74.7; January average high 66.5, low 35. Rainfall 7.65 inches; rare traces of snow.

*Population* • 117,200

*Population trend* • Gained 114 percent in the past decade.

*Property tax* • $14.76 per $100 assessed valuation.

*Economy* • City officials are very pro-growth. The Peoria Economic Development Group is working to draw both business and industry and several new office buildings have arisen.

*Job prospects* • With its industrial, medical, business and retail growth, Peoria offers above average employment opportunities. The services industry is the largest employer, followed by retailing, manufacturing and construction.

*Industrial facilities* ● Two industrial parks with rail access.

*Real estate* ● A good selection of homes is available, with prices for a three-bedroom ranging from $100,000 to $150,000.

*The media* ● Two weeklies, the *Peoria Times* and *The Westsider*. Daily news and TV from Phoenix and a local cable company.

*Medical services* ● Four hospitals and five extended care facilities within a five-mile radius.

*Transportation* ● Glendale Municipal Airport is adjacent to Peoria; Phoenix Sky Harbor is about 25 miles away.

*Education* ● Glendale Community College and the western campus of Arizona State University are nearby. Peoria has the usual public schools.

*Local government* ● Incorporated in 1954; mayor, six-member council and a city manager.

*Places to stay* ● Seven motels or small hotels and a couple of RV parks.

*Leisure facilities* ● Seventeen public parks, a community center, large sports complex, three golf courses, two public pools and several tennis courts, plus soaring, the space-oriented Challenger Learning Center and a mockup old Western town.

*Tourist lures* ● Peoria is a residential and business center, so tourists don't flock here. Lake Pleasant Regional Park is fifteen miles north, providing fishing, boating and swimming.

*Contacts* ● Peoria Chamber of Commerce, P.O. Box 70, Peoria, AZ 85380; (800) 580- 2645 or (623) 979-3601; *www.peoriachamber.com*.

City of Peoria, 8401 W. Monroe St., Peoria, AZ 85345; (623) 773-7300; *www.peoriaaz.com*

Peoria Economic Development Group, Inc., 10601 N. 83rd Dr., Peoria, AZ 85345; (623) 486-2011.

# SCOTTSDALE

When we first visited this mountainous desert region 30 years ago, Scottsdale was a quiet cowboy style hamlet. As we explored its Western wear stores, art galleries and curio shops, words like "quaint" and "charming" came to mind. Those shops still exist, although they're surrounded by suburban sprawl. Scottsdale has become the Valley of the Sun's most fashionable large community.

When Phoenix began spilling northward, Scottsdale went on its own annexation binge in self defense. It grew from a square mile in 1951 to 185 square miles today! Yet it remains one of the Valley of the Sun's most inviting towns, with some of the area's most opulent resorts. Scottsdale's growth, although rapid, has been more controlled than most other cities. It retains much of the Southwest and Santa Fe style architecture that visitors remember when the town was much smaller. Since it's on the outer edge of the Phoenix megalopolis, a brief drive north takes you into a desert that is still free of subdivisions and service stations.

The craggy Camelback Mountain, so named because it resembles a kneeling camel, offers a dramatic backdrop to the city. Most of the posh resorts are tucked into its foothills, while others are in the rock-rimmed Paradise Valley to the north.

All of this upscale sprawl had rather humble beginnings. In 1894, Rhode Island banker Albert G. Utley arrived, subdivided 40 acres of desert and sold off lots. Utleydale or Utleyburg didn't sound right, so he named the new town for former Army chaplain Winfield Scott, an early resident who did much to encourage settlement. Through the years, it became famous as a charming little Western town, way out in the desert beyond Phoenix. Horses had the right-of-way and hitchin' rails stood before false-front stores. Scottsdale prided itself in being one of America's most Western towns. Much of that flavor is now buried in suburban sprawl, although Old Town Scottsdale still retains that yesterday look.

**Elevation** • 1,260 feet

**Location** • In Maricopa County, just northeast of Phoenix.

**Climate** • Warm to hot summers; mild winters. July average high 104.8, low 77.5; January average high 64.8, low 37.6. Rainfall 7.05 inches; rare traces of snow.

**Population** • 210,000

**Population trend** • Gained 55.8 percent in the past ten years.

**Property tax** • $10.58 per $100 of assessed valuation.

**Economy** • It's a mix of tourism, upscale shopping and financial services. Some of the valley's finest retail malls and boutiques are here and—for some odd reason—so are many of the area's largest new car dealers.

**Job prospects** • Other than the tourist industry, most of Scottsdale's employment base is clerical and white collar. About 65 percent of the jobs are in retailing, finances and services.

**Industrial facilities** • Several light industrial complexes.

**Real estate** • Scottsdale embraces some of the valley's most expensive homes, right up there with Fountain Valley and Paradise Valley. Plan on starting in the high $100,000's.

**The media** • One local daily, the *Scottsdale Progress;* telly feeds come from next-door Phoenix.

**Medical services** • Four hospitals, several clinics and emergency medical centers and a psychiatric hospital.

**Transportation** • Scottsdale Municipal Airport, with an 8,250-foot runway, has commuter hops to Sky Harbor, just ten miles away. And yes, that does seem odd. Presumably, they don't serve in-flight meals.

*Education* • Scottsdale Community College, plus several private schools and the usual public schools.

*Local government* • Founded in 1888; mayor, six-member council and city manager.

*Places to stay* • More than 70 resorts, motels and lodges, including some of the most elegant resorts in Arizona; limited RV facilities.

*Leisure facilities* • About 30 golf courses in the area—some public and some at resorts, plus 28 parks, three public pools, more than a hundred art galleries and many tennis, racquetball and handball courts—on and off the resort properties.

*Tourist lures* • The drive from Scottsdale through Paradise Valley to Carefree/Cave Creek provides some of the finest desert vistas in the American West. Mountain parks in the area offer picnicking and hiking. Old Town Scottsdale is popular for its fine shops, galleries and restaurants, a history museum and the Scottsdale Center for the Arts.

*Contacts* • Scottsdale Chamber of Commerce, 7343 Scottsdale Mall, Scottsdale, AZ 85251; (480) 945-8481.

City of Scottsdale Economic Development Division, 7447E. Indian School Rd., Scottsdale, AZ 85251; (480) 994-7989; *www.ci.scottsdale.az.us.*

# SUN CITY & SUN CITY WEST

The world's largest senior community, Sun City covers a patch of low, landscaped desert northwest of Phoenix. It was founded by the Del E. Webb company in 1960 and reached its planned capacity in the 1980s, although growth continues on the periphery. Newer Sun City West has grown from zero to more than 30,000 since it started in 1978. A third Webb community, Sun City Grand, was established recently.

Sun City residents enjoy a comfortable, self-contained lifestyle, with golf courses, swimming pools, recreation centers, crafts classes and social clubs. And it's home to the Sundome Center for the Performing Arts.

*SIDE NOTE:* Although Webb is famous as a creator of retirement communities, historians find him more interesting for another reason. He was the contractor for Bugsy Siegel's Fabulous Flamingo in Las Vegas in 1946. The project ran way over budget and fell months behind schedule, and Bugsy was accused of skimming funds. Although none of this was Webb's fault, he became mighty nervous during construction delays, so Siegel reportedly told him: "Don't worry, Del, we only kill each other." A few months after the Flamingo opened, Bugsy's comment became his prophesy; he was gunned down in his girlfriend Virginia Hill's mansion in Bel Air.

***Elevation*** • About 1,000 feet

***Location*** • In Maricopa County, twenty miles northwest of Phoenix.

***Climate*** • Warm to hot summers; mild winters. July average high 106.3, low 65.2; January average high 66.5, low 35. Rainfall 7.65 inches; rare traces of snow.

***Population*** • Sun City 52,000; Sun City West 30,000.

***Population trend*** • Sun City gained 27 percent and Sun City West 46 percent in the past ten years.

***Property tax*** • $14.92 per $100 of assessed valuation in Sun City and $10.67 in Sun City West.

***Economy*** • It's based almost entirely on retirement income, which supports a small services and retailing industry.

***Job prospects*** • Very few; most folks come here to *quit* working.

***Industrial facilities*** • None.

***Real estate*** • Prices start around above $100,000 and climbing beyond $200,000. Detached homes, cluster homes and duplexes are available. To live here, at least one family member must be 55 or older, and none can be younger than 18.

***The media*** • The weekly *Sun City Independent*; daily newspaper and TV from Phoenix and cable companies.

***Medical services*** • Hospitals in Sun City and Sun City West and others in the area; several extended care facilities in the area.

***Transportation*** • Served by Greyhound. Glendale and Phoenix-Goodyear airports are nearby. Phoenix Sky Harbor is 40 minutes southeast, served by Super Shuttle and Airport Express.

***Education*** • Rio Salado Community College offers adult classes here. Public schools are in adjacent towns.

***Local government*** • Both Sun City and Sun City West are unincorporated; administrative services are provided by homeowners associations and by Maricopa County.

***Places to stay*** • A few motels and RV parks within a few miles of the two retirement communities; Sun City Grand offers overnight lodging for prospective buyers.

***Leisure facilities*** • Seven recreation centers in Sun City and four in Sun City West; eight area golf courses, the Sundome Center for the Performing Arts; plus extensive senior-oriented recreational activities, with swimming pools, golf, tennis and health clubs.

***Tourist lures*** • Very little within the communities. An attractive desert park with the mundane name of White Tank Mountain provides hiking and picnicking, ten miles west. Lake Pleasant Regional Park is fifteen miles west of the retirement communities, offering boating, hiking, swimming, riding and picnicking.

***Contacts*** • Sun City Visitors Center, P.O. Box 2481 (9903 W. Bell Rd.), Sun City, AZ 85372, (800) 437-8146 or (623) 977-5000; *www.visitsuncity.com; e-mail: s.cvisitorctr@aol.com.*

Sun City Grand, R.H. Johnson Blvd. (off Grand Avenue), Surprise, AZ 85374; (623) 546-7200; *www.suncity.com/grand.*

Sun City West Visitors Center, 13823 W. Camino del Sol, Sun City, AZ 85375; (623) 214-8629; *www.suncity.com/west*

Northwest Valley Chamber of Commerce, 12425 W. Bell Rd., C-305, Surprise, AZ 85374; (623) 583-0692; *www.northwestvalley.com.*

## TEMPE

Arizona State University dominates both the cultural and economic life of this fast-growing suburb. More than 70 percent of Tempe's residents are college educated, and the large 44- thousand student campus functions as the area's cultural center. ASU is the fourth largest research university in the nation.

Tempe began life in 1872 when Charles Trumbull Hayden opened a general store and flour mill on the banks of the Salt River. He called the place Hayden's Ferry. Well-traveled Englishman Darrel Duppa, who had given Phoenix its imaginative name, commented in 1878 that this area resembled the Vale of Tempe in Thessaly, Greece, and the name took hold.

Many of the town's early buildings, including Hayden's home, have been preserved in the Old Town section near the ASU campus. The look of Tempe is a pleasant mix of contemporary and Western rustic, with palm-lined streets and shaded sidewalks.

In addition to its role as the Valley of the Sun's major cultural center, Tempe offers a diversified economy of manufacturing and retail services. It's considered the state's "Tech Oasis" with more than 200 high tech companies.

*Elevation* • 1,105 feet

*Location* • In Maricopa County, just southeast of Phoenix.

*Climate* • Warm to hot summers; mild winters. July average high 104.3, low 73.4; January average high 65.5, low 35.4. Rainfall 7.63 inches; rare traces of snow.

*Population* • 160,000

*Population trend* • Gained 11.7 percent in the past ten years.

*Property tax* • $13.22 per $100 of assessed valuation.

*Economy* • Manufacturing forms Tempe's broad economic base, with retailing, services and—obviously—the huge campus of Arizona State University making major contributions. More than 20 percent of the Valley of the Sun's high tech jobs are in Tempe.

*Job prospects* • They're usually rather good. One job in three is in the services sector. Manufacturing and high tech accounts for about

22 percent of the paychecks, followed by retail trades with 17 percent. ASU is the community's largest single employer.

**Industrial facilities** • They're extensive; Tempe has 71 industrial parks, offering space for heavy and light industry and warehousing. ASU operates a large research park.

**Real estate** • Starting price for a three-bedroom home is around $110,000.

**The media** • The daily *Tempe News Tribune* and the weekly *New Times*. TV and cable from Phoenix.

**Medical services** • One hospital, two extended care units and several medical clinics.

**Transportation** • Served by Greyhound. Sky Harbor International Airport is next door, actually closer to Tempe than to any other Valley of the Sun city.

**Education** • ASU is a commanding presence, as the country's fifth largest university campus, with 43,000 students. Tempe also is home to Lamson Junior College, three private Christian schools plus eight private elementary and high schools, and the usual public schools.

**Local government** • Incorporated in 1894; mayor, six-member council and city manager.

**Places to stay** • More than 40 hotels and motels, plus several mobile home and RV parks.

**Leisure facilities** • Forty-eight public parks, four public pools, five golf courses, plus tennis and racquetball courts, various playing fields and a community center. Its recreational focal point is Rio Salado Town Lake & Tempe Beach Park with boating, picnicking and trails.

**Tourist lures** • Arizona State University campus is attractive and worth a visit, offering several galleries and museums and the Frank Lloyd Wright designed Gammage Auditorium. Tempe also has three museums, including the excellent Arizona Historical Society Museum.

**Contacts** • Tempe Chamber of Commerce, Box 28500, Tempe, AZ 85285-8500; (480) 967- 7891

City of Tempe Economic Development, 31 E. Fifth St., Tempe, AZ 85281; (480) 350-8036; *www.tempe.gov.*

## WICKENBURG

This may be the cutest little cowboy town in Arizona. Wickenburg *works* at being Western, with balconied store fronts, boardwalks and a friendly down-home attitude. "Tie up, come in and swap stories," invites a sign outside Ben's Saddlery. The town calls itself the dude ranch capital of the world, and real cowboys still ride herd in the surrounding high desert. The small downtown area is cutely Western. Century-old false-front stores tempt visitors with cowboy clothing, native crafts and curios. It also has a few antique stores and several galleries sell paintings and sculptures.

Gold, not cattle, put the town on the map. In 1863, an Austrian named Henry Wickenburg hitched his hopes to an ornery burro and began prospecting in the nearby hills. He struck it rich with the Vulture Mine. Some say he picked up a rock to throw at a vulture—or at his stubborn mule—and the rock was veined with gold. Either version of the story sounds like campfire talk. However, one truth is undeniable: Gold mines in the area yielded $30 million between 1863 and 1900. Miners needed water to wash their diggin's, so they settled along the banks of the Hassayampa River and Wickenburg was born.

Ore from 80 mines poured into town, along with the usual ration of drifters, rascals and fallen angels. At its prime, Wickenburg was the third largest city in Arizona, and one of the wildest. Folks were too busy seeking gold to build a jail, so they simply chained the bad guys to a large mesquite tree. During visiting hours, prisoners' relatives would come out and have a picnic. The tree still stands, at Tegner Street and Wickenburg Way.

As the mines played out, cattlemen began running their herds in the brushy desert. Easterners, reading newspaper reports and dime novels about the Wild West, came out to see what all the excitement was about. Dude ranching, born in Montana, quickly spread to Arizona. Wickenburg and Tucson were early dude ranch centers, and they still are. Nowadays, of course, folks call them guest ranches.

*Elevation* ● 2,100 feet

*Location* ● In Maricopa County, 58 miles northwest of Phoenix on U.S. Highway 93/60.

*Climate* ● Warm to hot summers; mild winters. July average high 103.6, low 69.7; January average high 63.3, low 30. Rainfall 10.77; rare traces of snow.

*Population* ● About 5,500

*Population trend* ● Grew about 12.6 percent in the past ten years.

*Property tax* ● $11.46 per $100 of assessed valuation.

*Economy* ● Tourism has replaced gold and cattle as the town's reason for being. Indeed, 75 percent of Wickenburg's jobs are directly tied to visitor services. The town attracts a few retirees and Snowbirds, and a little gold still trickles down from the hills.

*Job prospects* ● Despite a low unemployment rate, Wickenburg's job potential is average or below. Growth, which generates jobs, is rather slow and the locals seem to like it that way.

*Industrial facilities* ● A small light industry park.

*Real estate* ● A few modern subdivisions are a-building and the average three-bedroom home starts around $175,000.

*The media* ● The weekly *Wickenburg Sun*; Phoenix provides the dailies and the TV, although there's a local cable company.

**Medical services** • One hospital and two extended care facilities.

**Transportation** • A lighted, 5,000-foot runway at Wickenburg airport; no scheduled service; charters available.

**Education** • Two private Christian schools and the usual public schools.

**Local government** • Incorporated in 1909; mayor, six-member council and town manager.

**Places to stay** • Several motels, five guest ranches, and a dozen mobile home parks and two RV parks.

**Leisure facilities** • A community center, youth center, five public parks, two golf courses, a public pool and several tennis courts.

**Tourist lures** • Wickenburg has several historic buildings in the downtown and one of the finest small archives in the West—the Desert Caballeros Western Museum. Several ghost towns sleep in the nearby hills, while saguaro cactus and Joshua trees thrive in the surrounding desert. Hassayampa River Reserve protects a riparian woodland.

**Contacts** • Wickenburg Chamber of Commerce, 216 N. Frontier St., Wickenburg, AZ 85390; (800) 942-5242 or (928) 684-5479; *www.wickenburgchamber.com; e-mail: info@outwickenburgway.com.*

Town of Wickenburg, 155 N. Tegner St., Suite A, Wickenburg, AZ 85390; (928) 684-5451; *www.ci.wickenburg.az.us.*

# YOUNGTOWN

The grandaddy of senior villages, Youngtown was started in 1954 by the Youngtown Land and Development Company. Although it's the world's first planned retirement town, it has remained small and compact while next door Sun City and Sun City West have mushroomed. It's an attractive, neatly groomed town with an active retail core and typical planned community amenities such as a clubhouse, lake, four parks, cactus gardens and a health club.

**Location** • In Maricopa County, about twenty miles northwest of Phoenix.

**Elevation** • Approximately 1,000 feet.

**Climate** • Warm to hot summers; mild winters. July average high 106.3, low 74.7; January average high 66.5, low 35. Rainfall 7.65 inches; rare dustings of snow.

**Population** • 3,200

**Population trend** • Little change in recent years although a new subdivision adjacent to Youngtown will increase the population substantially.

**Property tax** • $9.02 per $100 of assessed valuation.

**Economy** • It's retirement based, with its income derived from pensions, savings and investments.

**Job prospects** • Mostly, Youngtown's residents work at retirement. More than half the town's few jobs are in the service, financial and retail sectors.

**Industrial facilities** • A cosmetics factory is nearby.

**Real estate** • Home prices start around $80,000 to $90,000 for a two or three-bedroom unit.

**The media** • Served by the weekly *Sun City Independent*; daily news from Phoenix, which also provides TV service; a local cable company is available as well.

**Medical services** • One extended care facility; hospitals in surrounding communities.

**Transportation** • Served by Greyhound. Glendale and Phoenix-Goodyear airports are nearby; Sky Harbor is 28 miles away.

**Education** • Rio Salado Community College offers adult education classes in nearby Sun City. Public schools are in adjacent towns.

**Local government** • Incorporated in 1960; mayor/manager and six-member council.

**Places to stay** • One hotel and two motels.

**Leisure facilities** • Clubhouse, lake, four parks and a desert botanical garden; the seasonal Agua Fria River flows past the development.

**Tourist lures** • Lake Pleasant Regional Park is fifteen miles west, with boating, hiking, swimming, riding and picnicking.

**Contacts** • Town of Youngtown, 12030 Clubhouse Square, Youngtown, AZ 85363; (623) 933-8286.

Northwest Valley Chamber of Commerce, P.O. Box 1519 (12425 W. Bell Rd., Suite 305), Surprise, AZ 85374; (623) 583-0692; *www.northwestvalley.com*.

**Chapter Eleven**

# TUCSON & BEYOND
## THE SOUTHEAST & FAR EAST

**W**e begin our final community chapter with a quick lesson in what's left of Arizona's geography. Although eastern Arizona represents a large chunk of the state, much of it is rather thinly populated. High prairie and mountains cover a good part of the area, with chilly winters that might discourage potential retirees. Tucson, Green Valley and Sierra Vista in the southeast are major exceptions.

As you head southeast from the Valley of the Sun, the land slopes gradually upward. If you follow I-10 from Phoenix, you'll gain more than a thousand feet by the time you reach Tucson, although this is still desert terrain. Heading east from Tucson, you'll encounter scattered mountain clusters, floating like alpine islands on a high prairie. If you then go northeast, you hit more prairie and mountains. An evergreen belt between Clifton and Springerville in east central Arizona resembles the Pacific Northwest, although it's not nearly as wet. West of there, in the White Mountains, are more evergreen forests. To the north, you'll encounter high prairie around Holbrook and Winslow. Continuing north, you will reach the huge Navajo-Hopi Reservation, occupying the state's northeastern corner.

The rumpled regions of eastern Arizona offer much for the wanderer, hiker, hunter and fisherperson. However, except for bustling Tucson and a few nearby communities, the region's potential for job-hunters is limited. On the other hand, retirees might be attracted to some of the charming old towns in this area. We like several of them—sturdy, no-nonsense places like Clifton, Globe, Holbrook, Safford and

Winslow. Most are cast in pleasant time warps with turn-of-the-last-century neighborhoods and brick business districts, although some have started growing a bit.

**THE WAY IT WAS** ● Arizona's historic roots began in the southeast when Spanish padres and explorers came in search of souls and gold. Franciscan Father Marcos de Niza entered this region in 1539, then 30-year-old conquistador Francisco Vásquez de Coronado followed a year later in his legendary quest for the fabled golden cities of Cibola. He probably traveled up the San Pedro River Valley just east of Sierra Vista.

In 1700, Father Eusebio Francisco Kino established Mission San Xavier at the native village of Bac, near today's Tucson. South of there, the military garrison of Tubac was founded in 1752 to put down a Pima rebellion, and a presidio was erected at Tucson in 1775.

Americans began settling the southeast after the 1848 Treaty of Guadalupe Hidalgo ceded much of Arizona to the United States. However Tucson remained part of Mexico until the Gadsden Purchase of 1854, which gave the state its present southern border.

Of course, the area's original residents insisted that neither country owned the land. It was *theirs* and they fought valiantly to keep from losing it to the intruders. Apache warriors Cochise and Geronimo gained international fame for their stubborn resistance—a fame somewhat distorted by novelists and movie producers. Not until Geronimo's final surrender in 1886 was southeastern Arizona considered "safe" for settlement.

Some of the settlers proved to be considerably less civilized than those they displaced. During the late 1800s, wild mining camps and cowboy towns produced copper, beef and violence. The most publicized single event in Western history occurred in a Tombstone alley in 1881. Virgil, Wyatt and Morgan Earp and their friend Doc Holliday advanced on five rowdies; they challenged them to fight and then opened fire at point-blank range. The gunfight at the O.K. Corral lasted only 30 seconds and claimed three lives. It has since consumed thousands of pages of pulp fiction and endless reels of movie film. One reason for its enduring fame was that gunfighter-lawman Wyatt Earp later became a dime novelist, extolling his own virtues.

**THE WAY IT IS** ● The eastern third of Arizona offers interesting contrasts. While Tucson is the state's second largest city, the southeastern corner has few residents and the far east is one of the least populated areas of the state. The northeast is dominated by Native American reservations. Outside of Tucson, the region's only large communities are Green Valley and Sierra Vista; both are in the southeast.

With its mountains, national monuments and historic sites, the southeast has emerged in recent years as a popular tourist destination. Some newcomers have chosen to stay, attracted by the benign climate and inexpensive housing of places like Green Valley, Sierra Vista and Bisbee. In the mountains north and east of here, a few retirees are discovering such hamlets as Pinetop, Lakeside, Springerville and Show Low. Springerville and Safford are commercial centers, offering modest potential for job seekers.

Our community list begins with Tucson, one of our favorite Arizona cities. Although it's a major urban center, it is quite different from Phoenix. Tucson is history, old money and tradition. Phoenix is new wave, fast paced, new money and very pro-growth. Although Tucson is growing as well, life is a bit slower here. Tucson is quite proud of its past, while Phoenix focuses mostly on its future. There is, in fact, a lively rivalry between the two metropolitan centers.

They're quite similar geographically; both occupy desert basins surrounded by rugged mountains. Tucson is 1,300 feet higher, so it's a bit cooler despite its more southerly location. The biggest difference is—well—bigness itself. Phoenix is nearly three times as large and its many suburban cities make the metropolitan larger still. By contrast, Tucson is an urban island with few communities on its periphery.

# TUCSON

Sitting in a cactus garden and surrounded by five mountain ranges, Tucson is one of America's most versatile cities. In winter, you can work on your suntan at poolside, then drive to the Mount Lemmon ski area and strap on the sticks. The city offers a generous mix of cultural activities, visitor attractions and shopping, with an excellent academic overlay provided by the University of Arizona.

Although Tucson was in Mexican territory after the signing of the Treaty of Guadalupe Hidalgo, it was in American hands. Members of the Mormon Battalion had occupied it during the Mexican War two years earlier and they weren't about to give it up. Then the 1854 Gadsden Purchase formalized its status as an American possession.

However, Tucson's history reaches well beyond that period. When Father Kino visited in 1687, he found Tohono O'odham Indians living in a village they called *Stjukshon* (Stook-shon). It means "blue water at the base of a black mountain," referring to springs in the now-dry Santa Cruz River and Sentinel Peak. The Spanish altered it to *Tucson*, which initially was pronounced "TUK-son." Kino returned in 1700 to establish Mission San Xavier (pronounced *Ha-vee-YAY* or *Ha-VEER*) in the Indian village of Bac.

The town of Tucson was started in 1775 by a wandering Irishman who was scouting for the Spanish crown. Settlers began moving into the area and the original inhabitants naturally objected. They went on the warpath and a presidio was built to protect the intruders. This was the first walled city in America—although it was still part of Spain.

After the Gadsden Purchase, Tucson continued growing as a ranching and provisioning center. A Butterfield Stage stop was opened in 1857 and the town's cantinas became notorious hangouts for drifters, outlaws and randy cowpokes. Folks said the outpost was so primitive that stage passengers who spent the night had to sleep in a "Tucson bed"—using their stomach for a mattress and their back for a blanket.

The pueblo suffered the indignity of capture by rebel Texas troops during the Civil War. They were evicted by a pro-Union California battalion after the Battle of Picacho Pass in 1862—the war's westernmost conflict. Tucson lured the territorial capital from Prescott in 1867, only to have it taken away ten years later. By the turn of the last century, this was a busy if still somewhat remote town of 10,000. World War II brought thousands of servicemen to Davis-Monthan Army Air Corps Base. Many of them liked the idea of January suntans and returned.

Tucson boomed after the war and—like its larger neighbor to the north—galloped off in all directions. Today, this vast carpet of commerce covers 500 square miles—more than metropolitan L.A. However, much of this land is taken up in large desert preserves, such as 17,000-acre Tucson Mountain Park.

Today's Tucson wears its Spanish heritage rather handsomely. Red tile and flat roofed pueblo architecture predominates. The town has more good Mexican restaurants than you can shake a tortilla at. Mexican arts and crafts add color to curio shops. Many signs are bilingual, since nearly 30 percent of Pima County's citizens are Hispanic.

Tucson's growth during the nineties was slower than Phoenix and its growth still lags behind the Valley of the Sun. However, it isn't exactly sitting still. From 1990 to 2000, its population increased by 20 percent, from 405,371 to 486,699.

*Elevation* • 2,390 feet

*Location* • In Pima County, 110 miles southeast of Phoenix and 90 miles north of Mexico.

*Climate* • Warm to hot summers; mild winters with some chilly evenings. July average high 100.1, low 73.3; January average high 66, low 36.7. Rainfall 10.73 inches; occasional traces of snow.

*Population* • about 500,000

*Population trend* • Gained 20 percent in the past decade.

*Property tax* • (assessed at ten percent of real value) $17.39 per $100 assessed valuation.

*Economy* • Manufacturing, tourism, government jobs (mostly at Davis-Monthan Air Force Base) and high tech industries provide the bricks for Tucson's economic foundation. The largest single employer is the University of Arizona.

*Job prospects* • Major employment areas are in tourism and other services, accounting for a fourth of the jobs. Retail sales, manufacturing and transportation offer potential as well. Best job possibilities are in high tech, computers, aircraft maintenance, electronics and communications, according to the local Job Service office.

**Industrial facilities** ● They range from heavy fabricating plants to space age electronics firms. Several industrial parks offer complete facilities, including rail and air.

**Real estate** ● Tucson's housing is varied, ranging from older homes in the downtown area to elegant gated communities in the foothills. Much of the architecture, both old and new, is Spanish and pueblo style. Prices for a three-bedroom home start around $100,000.

**The media** ● Two dailies, the *Arizona Daily Star* and *Tucson Citizen*, plus a few weeklies and shoppers; nine TV stations and cable.

**Medical services** ● Several hospitals and clinics, including fine facilities at the University of Arizona's medical school.

**Transportation** ● Reached by Greyhound and Amtrak. Tucson International Airport is served by more than a dozen airlines.

**Education** ● The University of Arizona is the community's academic and cultural focal point. Other schools include Tucson branches of the business and management-focused University of Phoenix, Pima Community College, ten business and vocational schools, more than a hundred private and parochial schools and the usual public schools.

**Local government** ● The seat of Pima County, incorporated in 1877; mayor, six-member council and city manager.

**Places to stay** ● More than 150 hotels, motels and resorts, including some of most elegant in the state; also several dude ranches in the surrounding desert. Dozens of RV and mobile home parks.

**Leisure facilities** ● Twenty-eight public and private golf courses, 128 city and county parks including huge Tucson Mountain Park, about 20 museums and galleries, 23 municipal pools, plus tennis, racquetball and handball courts.

**Tourist lures** ● Mission San Xavier del Bac, the much-heralded Arizona-Sonora Desert Museum, Saguaro National Park, Old Tucson western movie town, Mount Lemmon ski area, regional mountain parks and numerous other attractions. Several museums and galleries are on the campus of the University of Arizona.

**Contacts** ● City of Tucson Economic Development, P.O. Box 27210, Tucson, AZ 85726-7210; (520) 791-5093; *www.ci.tucson.az. us/oed.*

Tucson Metropolitan Chamber of Commerce, P.O. Box 991 (465 W. St. Mary's Rd.), Tucson, AZ 85702; (520) 792-1212; *tucsonchamber.org.*

Greater Tucson Economic Council, 33 Stone Ave., Suite 800, Tucson, AZ 85701; (520) 882-6079; *www.futurewest.com.*

Metropolitan Tucson Convention & Visitors Bureau, 110 S. Church Ave., Suite 9100, Tucson, AZ 85701; (800) 638-8350 or (520) 624-1817; *www.visittucson.org.*

## BISBEE

This sturdy old mining town is cantilevered into the steep flanks of Mule Pass
Gulch. Like Jerome, Bisbee is the sort of
place where your upper neighbor can
look down your chimney. The post office
department complains that it's too steep
for mail delivery.

Headframes and tailing dumps mark
the slopes; corrugated buildings shelter
smelters and stamp mills. Hillsides have
been ripped away to expose orange, rust
and gray-green wounds. You *know* this is
mining country. Coming into Bisbee, you
see something even more dramatic—the great terraced cavity of the
Lavender Pit Mine. It's so close it appears ready to swallow the town.

Why do we recommend Bisbee as a place to settle? It's rich in history, it has a classic nineteenth century downtown area, handsome old
homes and a temperate year-around climate. Further, it's a short hop
to Mexico and Tucson. The surrounding terrain is varied, since Bisbee
is on a topographic bridge between the Sonoran Desert and eastern
high country. However, the job market is very weak, so it's more practical as a retirement community.

Although it emerged as a mining center, Bisbee didn't burst into
glory overnight. It grew steadily and sturdily as big corporations
gouged deep into the earth for copper, gold, silver, lead and zinc.
Army Scout Jack Dunn filed a claim in the area in 1877, then he
brought in one George Warren as a partner. Warren cheated Dunn out
of his share, found some investors, and eventually sold to a conglomer-
ate headed by Judge DeWitt Bisbee of San Francisco. The group
formed the Copper Queen Mine Company and eventually merged with
the large Phelps Dodge Corporation.

Reveling in this wealth, the town grew as a sort of vertical San
Francisco, with plush Victorian homes, fine restaurants and—of
course—bordellos. Brewery Gulch was Bisbee's version of San Francisco's Barbary Coast, with more than 50 drinking, gambling and
whoring establishments. At its peak, Bisbee was the world's largest
copper mining town, with 20,000 residents. Phelps Dodge operated
the underground Queen Mine and the Lavender open pit mine until
1975 when falling copper prices closed those operations.

Logic says Bisbee should have withered and died, but retirees and
tourists began coming, drawn by the mild climate and sturdy charm of
the old town. Boutiques, galleries and antique shops were opened in
the red brick and tufa stone buildings. Bed & breakfast inns prolifer-
ated. The Queen Mine, unable to process copper economically, is processing visitors by offering underground tours. The town even attracts a

few movie companies, since the hillside buildings can become—with a little creative camera work—a bit of Old Spain, Greece or Mexico.

**Elevation** • 5,490 feet

**Location** • In Cochise County, just above the Mexican border.

**Climate** • Warm summers; cool winters with chilly evenings. July average high 89.3, low 64.5; January average high 56.9, low 33.7. Rainfall 16.21 inches; snowfall 4.54 inches.

**Population** • About 6,000

**Population trend** • Relatively stable; slight population loss in the past five years.

**Property tax** • $14.19 per $100 assessed valuation.

**Economy** • Tourism and light manufacturing have stabilized the town since the big mines shut down.

**Job prospects** • They aren't strong since growth is rather stagnant. Best prospects are in retail and wholesale trades, tourist and other service jobs. The local Job Service office rates employment prospects as "below average."

**Industrial facilities** • Several small industrial parks are available, including one at the airport. Nearby Naco has a "twin plant" operation on both sides of the border. However, it employs Mexican "guest workers" in all but management posts.

**Real estate** • Three-bedroom detached homes range from $55,000 upwards. Restored or restorable Victorians go for much more.

**The media** • The daily *Bisbee Review* and two weeklies, the *Bisbee Observer* and *Bisbee Gazette*. TV service from Tucson, plus cable.

**Medical services** • A hospital with combined acute care and long term care capabilities.

**Transportation** • Bridgeport Transport runs buses to Tucson. Bisbee Municipal Airport has a 5,990-foot lighted runway; no scheduled air service.

**Education** • Cochise Community College is seventeen miles east; Bisbee has an elementary, middle and high school.

**Local government** • Incorporated in 1905; mayor, six council members and a city manager.

**Places to stay** • Three motels and three historic hotels, thirteen bed & breakfast inns; eight campgrounds and RV parks.

**Leisure facilities** • Seven public parks, a golf course, galleries and boutiques, tennis courts and two ball parks.

**Tourist lures** • Three museums and more than twenty art galleries and antique shops in Bisbee's historic downtown area. Public underground tours at the Queen Mine, driver-narrated trolley tours and viewing areas at the Lavender open pit mine.

**Contacts** • Bisbee Chamber of Commerce, P.O. Box BA (31 Subway St.), Bisbee, AZ 85603; (866) 2-BISBEE or (520) 432-5421; *www.bisbeearizona.com; e-mail: info@bisbeearizona.com.*

City of Bisbee, 118 Arizona St., Bisbee, AZ 85603; 432-5446.

# CATALINA

Although it's a rather ordinary looking community, Catalina occupies a very impressive setting—tucked into the foothills of the Santa Catalina Mountains above Tucson. It's primarily a retirement area; the planned senior villages of Saddle-Brooke and Sun City Vistoso are four miles away. The town was established in the 1950s by land developers as a series of planned residential areas. It experienced considerable growth in its earlier decades although it has slowed down in recent years.

**Location** ● In Pima County, about twenty miles north of Tucson on Highway 77.

**Elevation** ● 3,100 feet

**Climate** ● Warm summers; mild winters with cool evenings. July average high 93.2, low 67.3; January average high 57.7, low 34.3. Rainfall 16 inches; occasional traces of snow.

**Population** ● About 6,000

**Population trend** ● Gained about 16 percent in the past ten years.

**Property tax** ● $15.45 per $100 assessed valuation.

**Economy** ● There isn't much of an economic base; Catalina is mostly retirement oriented, with a few small businesses.

**Job prospects** ● Not very good since it's primarily a retirement community. Most working folks commute to nearby Tucson.

**Industrial facilities** ● None

**Real estate** ● Housing is cheaper than in Tucson, which is one of the area's big draws. Prices for detached homes begin around $80,000 in Catalina. In the nearby retirement communities of SaddleBrooke and Sun City Vistoso, they start a bit higher.

**The media** ● The semi-monthly *Catalina Oracle*. Daily newspapers and TV relays from Tucson, plus a local cable company.

**Medical services** ● One county clinic; the nearest hospitals are in Tucson.

**Transportation** ● No commercial transport or airport; Tucson International is about 25 miles south.

**Education** ● A public elementary and middle school; the nearest high school is nine miles away.

**Local government** ● Village council with nine elected representatives.

**Places to stay** ● Three resorts within a ten-mile radius.

**Leisure facilities** ● A public swimming pool, park and a combined recreation and senior center.

**Tourist lures** ● Nearby Catalina State Park offers hiking, camping, picnicking and such. Hiking trails extend into the Santa Catalina Mountains of Coronado National Forest.

**Contact** ● Catalina Village Council, P.O. Box 8674, Catalina, AZ 85738; (520) 887-0608.

## CLIFTON & MORENCI

One of Arizona's early mining towns, Clifton was platted in 1873. There are two theories concerning its name, depending on your historian: It's a derivation of "Clifftown" for the surrounding bluffs, or it was named after the Clifton copper mine; Henry Clifton was an early investor in the area. Morenci (*mor-EN-cee*), established in 1884, was named for the Michigan home town of an early mine official.

The Phelps Dodge Corporation came to the area in 1882 and—through the generations—it bought mining companies and claims until it was the sole operator. It eventually bought the town of Morenci, and then dismantled it because it sat on rich copper deposits. But no matter; company officials built a prim new community in 1969, with a shopping center, theater, swimming pool, motel, restaurants, video store—all of humanity's basic needs. Phelps Dodge now owns 22,000 acres and employs more than half of the area's population.

**Elevation** ● 3,466 feet

**Location** ● Greenlee County in southeastern Arizona.

**Climate** ● Warm summers; chilly winters with cool evenings. July average high 101.4, low 71.3; January average high 61.2, low 31.1. Rainfall 12.06 inches; occasional traces of snow.

**Population** ● Clifton 2,600; Morenci 2,072

**Population trend** ● Little change; Morenci gained about ten percent and Clifton lost about eight percent.

**Property tax** ● $7.89 per $100 assessed valuation.

**Economy** ● Based primarily on copper mining, ranching, agriculture and a little tourism.

**Job prospects** ● A few available in mining, with the large Phelps Dodge operation; otherwise the job outlook is quite limited.

**Real estate** ● Not much on the market; homes begin around $60,000.

**Media** ● The weekly *Copper Era* and *Courier*; television via cable service.

**Medical services** ● One 24-hour emergency care clinic.

*Industrial facilities* • No industrial parks.

*Transportation* • No commercial transit; general aviation at Greenlee County Airport.

*Education* • An elementary, middle and high school.

*Local government* • Clifton incorporated 1873; Morenci in 1882. Mayor, six-member council and city manager in Clifton; Morenci is essentially a company town, with a council and mayor.

*Places to stay* • Three motels, two bed & breakfast inns and a boarding house.

*Leisure facilities* • Six public parks, a golf course, tennis courts and a swimming pool; each community has a swimming pool.

*Tourist Lures* • Hiking, rockhounding and hunting in the surrounding mountains.

*Contacts* • Greenlee County Chamber of Commerce, 100 N. Coronado Blvd., Clifton, AZ 85533; (928) 865-3313.

Town of Clifton, P.O. Box 1415, Clifton, AZ 85533; (928) 865-4146.

# GREEN VALLEY

An empty swatch of high desert of the Santa Cruz River Valley south of Tucson has emerged as a carefully planned community, primarily of senior citizens. Established in 1964, Green Valley has become one of Arizona's largest retirement communities. Some folks from Tucson unkindly refer to it as "Wrinkle City."

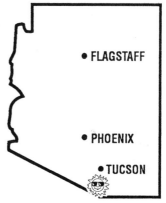

More than just a senior village, it offers shopping centers and other amenities that make air-conditioned desert living quite pleasant. Its location is appealing as well, between Tucson and the twin towns of Nogales, Arizona and Mexico. The Mexican Nogales offers the best shopping of any Arizona border town.

*Elevation* • 2,900 feet

*Location* • In Pima County, 25 miles south of Tucson on Interstate 19.

*Climate* • Warm to hot summers; mild winters with some cool evenings. July average high 101.3, low 68.4; January average high 67.1, low 31. Rainfall 10.86 inches; snowfall rare.

*Population* • 27,500

*Population trend* • Gained 22 percent in the past ten years.

*Property tax* • $11.87 per $100 assessed valuation.

*Economy* • Most of it is based on retirement income, since 85 percent of its residents are pensioned. A handful of workers commute north to Tucson.

***Job prospects*** • The town doesn't offer much more than service, retail and clerical jobs. The Green Valley Chamber of Commerce describes employment prospects as "below average."

***Industrial facilities*** • None

***Real estate*** • Most homes are set into attractive park-like complexes, rimmed by common areas or golf courses. Prices for a three-bedroom home start around $120,000.

***The media*** • The twice-weekly *Green Valley News & Sun.* Tucson provides daily newspaper and TV service, and there's a local cable company.

***Medical services*** • Two extended care facilities.

***Transportation*** • An area bus company runs between Tucson and Nogales, stopping in Green Valley. Tucson International Airport is 23 miles north.

***Education*** • An elementary and middle school; high school students go to Sahuarita, three miles north.

***Local government*** • Unincorporated; services provided by Pima County and various homeowners' associations.

***Places to stay*** • Three hotels and a bed & breakfast inn.

***Leisure facilities*** • Typical senior village amenities—seven golf courses, several swimming pools, ten recreation centers tennis, courts, putting greens and a driving range.

***Tourist lures*** • The Titan Missile Museum is next door, and historic Tubac and Tumacacori National Monument are 30 miles south. Madera Canyon, twelve miles southeast, is particularly noted for bird-watching; it also offers picnicking, hiking and camping.

***Contact*** • Green Valley Chamber of Commerce, P.O. Box 566 (270 W. Continental, Suite 100), Green Valley, AZ 85622; (520) 625-7575; *www.greenvalleyazchamber.com; e-mail: cvchamber@aol.com.*

# HOLBROOK

The seat of sparsely populated Navajo County, Holbrook is an ordinary looking community alongside the Little Colorado River with an old fashioned, clean-swept downtown. It's noted mostly as a gateway to Petrified Forest National Park and the huge Navajo-Hopi Reservation. It has several motels and restaurants and a lot of rock shops selling gems, thunder eggs and things petrified. With a population teetering between slow growth and no growth, Holbrook doesn't offer much opportunity for the job seeker, although its small town atmosphere, modest home prices and relatively temperate climate may appeal to retirees.

Holbrook was founded in 1881 as a railroad terminal and provisioning center for area ranches. It was named for H.R. Holbrook, chief engineer of the Atlantic & Pacific Railroad. The town's original name was much more colorful—Horsehead Crossing. It was the commercial center for the Aztec Ranch, one of the largest spreads in America. It ran 60,000 head of cattle over a million acres of open range, and it was nicknamed the Hashknife outfit because of its spade-shaped brand. Bad management and falling beef prices shut down the huge operation at the turn of the last century.

The town managed to hang on, supported by other area ranches and, more currently, by tourists bound for Petrified Forest and other travelers along Interstate 40.

**Elevation** • 5,080 feet

**Location** • On I-40 and Highway 66 in Navajo County, 90 miles east of Flagstaff.

**Climate** • Warm summers; cool winters with cold evenings. July average high 94.3, low 60.4; January average high 47.4, low 18.5. Rainfall about 20 inches; some traces of snow.

**Population** • 4,930

**Population trend** • Gained about five percent in the past ten years.

**Property tax** • $11.11 per $100 assessed valuation.

**Economy** • There isn't a strong economic base here, except for tourism and the nearby Cholla Power Plant.

**Job prospects** • Other than summer tourist jobs, employment prospects aren't strong.

**Industrial facilities** • City-run business park with airport and freeway access.

**Real estate** • Average home price is $45,000 to $65,000.

**The media** • Bi-weekly *Holbrook Tribune* and cable TV.

**Medical services** • Three medical clinics.

**Transportation** • Holbrook Municipal Airport has a 6,700-foot lighted runway with general aviation facilities; no scheduled air service.

**Education** • Two private schools, branch campus of Northland Pioneer College; two public elementary, one middle and one high school.

**Local government** • Incorporated in 1917; mayor, six-member council and city manager.

**Places to stay** • Because of adjacent Petrified Forest National Park, it has more than 25 motels, two RV parks and camping at nearby Cholla Lake.

**Leisure facilities** • Five city parks, a county recreation complex with ball courts, a playground and picnic area.

*Tourist lures* ● Courthouse Museum is near downtown, Petrified Forest National Park is twenty miles east and the huge Navajo-Hopi Reservation is to the north, offering Canyon de Chelley and Navajo national monuments and historic Hopi pueblos.

*Contacts* ● Holbrook Chamber of Commerce & Holbrook Economic Development Department, 100 E. Arizona St., Holbrook, AZ 86025; (800) 524-2459 or (928) 524-6558; *www.azjournal.com;* e-mail: *holbrookchamb@cybertrails.com.*

City of Holbrook, 465 First Ave., Holbrook, AZ 86025, (928) 524-6225; *www.ci.holbrook.az.us.*

## ORO VALLEY

Cradled by handsome peaks north of Tucson, Oro Valley was the second fastest growing community in Arizona, according to the millennium census, with a ten-year gain of 345.3 percent. Only Marana just to the northwest exceeded it statistically, more than quintupling its size. However, it started from a much smaller base. Oro Valley offers an attractive mix of modern subdivisions, golf courses and the cactus gardens of the surrounding Sonoran Desert. All of this is within half an hour of Tucson.

The valley was settled as a farming area after World War II, was incorporated in 1974 and caught the growth bug as Tucson and the rest of Arizona began booming in the eighties.

*Elevation* ● 2,450 feet

*Location* ● In Pima County, six miles from north Tucson.

*Climate* ● Warm to hot summers; mild winters with cool evenings. July average high 100.3, low 70.6; January average high 66.6, low 32.4. Rainfall 15.68 inches; half an inch of snowfall.

*Population* ● Approximately 33,000

*Population trend* ● Gained 345.3 percent in the decade of the nineties.

*Property tax* ● $14.77 per $100 assessed valuation.

*Economy* ● This is primarily a commuter, retirement and resort community, so most of the economy is based on retail trade and the services sector.

*Job prospects* ● Honeywell has a facility nearby. Otherwise, employment is limited to retail resort jobs; many workers commute to Tucson.

*Industrial facilities* ● None.

*Real estate* ● Most homes are in modern subdivisions; median price of a three-bedroom detached home is $180,000.

*The media* • The daily *Oro Valley Territorial*, weekly *Oro Valley Explorer*; TV from Tucson, plus cable.

*Medical services* • Urgent care facility; many hospitals in Tucson.

*Transportation* • No airport or commercial transportation.

*Education* • Public and private elementary and high schools.

*Local government* • Incorporated in 1974; mayor, four-member council and town manager.

*Places to stay* • One large resort; many places in nearby Tucson.

*Leisure facilities* • Five public or private golf courses, several public parks, a public swimming pool and tennis and racquetball courts.

*Tourist lures* • The Santa Catalina Mountains offer hiking, picnicking and other outdoor pursuits; Catalina State Park is just east.

*Contact* • Town of Oro Valley, 11000 N. La Cañada Dr., Oro Valley, AZ 85737; (520) 229-4700; *www.ci.oro-valley.az.us.*

# PINETOP-LAKESIDE

We recommend these two towns only as retirement places, primarily because of their attractive forested settings. Both Pinetop and Lakeside are perched rather dramatically on the edge of the Mogollon Rim, just above the wooded White Mountain Apache Indian Reservation.

It gets cold here in winter since it's well over a mile high, although residents don't suffer Minnesota style blizzards. They do get occasional white Christmases. With a limited employment base, Pinetop and Lakeside offer little potential for relocating families. They are popular with retirees, however.

The two communities were founded by Mormons in the early 1880s. Lakeside was named because of its proximity to several small lakes. While there's no shortage of pine trees hereabouts, Pinetop actually as named for a saloon keeper who served the soldiers at Fort Apache. The two burgs were incorporated as a single town in 1984.

*Elevation* • 7,200 feet

*Location* • In Navajo County in east central Arizona, just above the White Mountain Apache Reservation.

*Climate* • Mild summers and rather cold winters. July average high 85.8, low 55.5; January average high 44.2, low 17.7. Rainfall 22.31 inches; snowfall 38.2 inches.

*Population* • 3,700

*Population trend* • Gained 47.9 percent in the past decade.

*Property tax* • $11.11 in Pinetop; $10.86 in Lakeside.

*Economy* • It's mostly tourism and recreation oriented, with a handful of jobs in light industry.

*Job prospects* ● A new Commerce Park offers a few jobs in light industry; most of the rest are in the service and retail sectors.

*Industrial facilities* ● A 90-park for light industry.

*Real estate* ● Woodsy chalet style homes are typical of the area and they're not terribly expensive, starting around $100,000.

*The media* ● Two biweeklies, the *White Mountain Independent* and the *Apache Scout.*

*Medical services* ● A small hospital in nearby Show Low.

*Transportation* ● A local firm provides bus service. The nearest airport is in Show Low.

*Education* ● Northland Pioneer College has a campus in Show Low; the usual public schools in Pinetop-Lakeside.

*Local government* ● Incorporated in 1984; mayor, six council members and a town manager.

*Places to stay* ● Numerous motels and rustic cabins, plus the large summer and winter Sunrise Resort on the Apache reservation.

*Leisure facilities* ● Three golf courses, a health center, two pools, a 70-acre recreation area, tennis and racquetball courts.

*Tourist lures* ● Thousands come to escape the desert heat and sniff the pine-scented air of the surrounding Apache-Sitgreaves National Forest. Adjacent White Mountain Reservation offers hunting, camping, hiking and a Native American casino. The Apaches' Sunrise Resort is one of the leading ski areas in the state and it also has an active summer program.

*Contacts* ● Pinetop-Lakeside Chamber of Commerce, P.O. Box 4220, Pinetop, AZ 85935; (800) 573-4031 or (928) 367-1247; *www.pinetoplakesidechamber.com; e-mail: info@pinetoplakesidechamber.com.*

Town of Pinetop-Lakeside, 1360 Niels Hansen Lane, Lakeside, AZ 85929; (928) 368-8696; *www.ci.pinetop-lakeside.az.us.*

White Mountain Regional Development Corporation, 1201 E. Cooley, Suite F, Show Low, AZ 85901; (800) 818-2520 or (928) 537-3777; *www.wmrdc.org; e-mail: wmrdc@cybertrails.com.*

# SAFFORD

A well-tended old farm town, Safford is an appealing community that may attract folks looking for a rural lifestyle. A modestly active economy offers some job prospects, a few housing developments are underway and prices are affordable.

Established as a farming community in 1872, Safford is the commercial and retail hub for about 65,000 people in the attractive Gila Valley in southeastern Arizona. Mount Graham, one of Arizona's tallest peaks at 10,713 feet, provides an imposing backdrop and its Coronado National Forest offers an abundance of outdoor lures. Sheltered from rainfall and sitting below 3,000 feet, Safford has a dry climate more akin to a desert than a farming valley. Hot summers provide the proper environment for cotton, one of the area's major crops. The seat of Graham County, Safford is a well-tended town with a middle America look. Sturdy brick and masonry buildings define the downtown area, while carefully kept old homes stand along tree-shaded streets.

A state-of-the-art Discovery Park and science center is on the edge of town, and adjacent Thatcher is home to Eastern Arizona College, which has a fine little anthropology museum.

**Elevation** • 2,900 feet

**Location** • In Graham County in southeastern Arizona.

**Climate** • Warm to hot summers and balmy winters with chilly evenings. July average high 99.7, low 70.2; January average high 61.1, low 29.1. Rainfall 8.3 inches; snowfall 1.3 inches.

**Population** • 9,600

**Population trend** • Increased by about 25.5 percent in the past ten years.

**Property tax** • $12.41 per $100 assessed valuation

**Economy** • Agriculture is the area's leading industry, with 35,000 acres of the Gila Valley under irrigation. Other important economic elements are services, light manufacturing, retailing and public employment, primarily at Eastern Arizona College.

**Job prospects** • There are needs in medical, professional and technical areas, according to the local chamber of commerce. The unskilled and semi-skilled job markets are rather limited, except in agriculture.

**Industrial facilities** • Two industrial parks. Local industries include several label-making factories, a solar pump plant and two cotton gins.

**Real estate** • Three-bedroom homes range from $90,000; a few housing developments are underway with new homes starting above $100,000.

**The media** • The weekly *Eastern Arizona Courier*; television via cable.

**Medical services** • A regional hospital and a few medical clinics.

**Transportation** • Served by Greyhound. Safford Regional Airport meets the area's general aviation needs; charter service is available.

**Education** • Eastern Arizona College (two year) in next-door Thatcher; both private and public elementary, middle and high schools.

**Local government** • The seat of Graham County; mayor, five-member council and a city manager.

**Places to stay** • Several motels, eight mobile home and RV parks, a guest ranch and numerous campsites in adjacent national forests.

*Leisure facilities* ● A community center and fine arts center, public pool, an 18-hole golf course, two health clubs, swimming pools, tennis and basketball courts and ball fields.

*Tourist lures* ● The 200-acre Discovery Park is popular with locals and visitors. There are two small museums downtown and a museum of anthropology on the Eastern Arizona College campus. Mount Graham offers outdoor pursuits and it's home to an international observatory. Nearby Roper Lake State Park offers camping, swimming and fishing.

*Contacts* ● Graham County Chamber of Commerce, 1111 Thatcher Blvd., Safford, AZ 85546; (888) 837-1841 or (928) 428-2511; *www.graham-chamber.com;* e-mail: *director@graham-chamber.com.*

City of Safford, 717 Main St., Safford, AZ 85546; (928) 348-3100; *www.ci.safford.az.us.*

# SHOW LOW

This is where the Pinetop-Lakeside folks come to shop. Show Low is the commercial center of this high mountain region of east central Arizona. Somewhat lower than Pinetop-Lakeside, it's a bit milder in winter.

Once the hub of a ranching area, Show Low got its unusual name from a low-ball poker expression. If you "show low"—have the lowest cards—you win. It seems that C.E. Cooley and Marion Clark had built up a 100,000-acre cattle spread in the 1870s. After six years, they decided to break up the partnership, and drew cards to see who would buy who out. Cooley drew the deuce of clubs; Clark moved on. Show Low's main drag is called Deuce of Clubs in honor of that curious event.

Despite is colorful roots and odd name, the town today has no historic flavor. The business district is basically three miles of strip malls along Deuce of Clubs. Most of the area's visual appeal comes from its location between wooded hills and high grasslands. The town *is* booming, gaining more than 50 in population in the nineties.

*Elevation* ● 6,300 feet

*Location* ● In the White Mountain foothills of Navajo County in east central Arizona.

*Climate* ● Warm summers; cool winters with cold evenings. July average high 85.8, low 55.5; January average high 44.2, low 17.7. Rainfall 23 inches; snowfall 35 inches.

*Population* ● Just over 8,000

*Population trend* ● Gained 53.3 percent in the past decade.

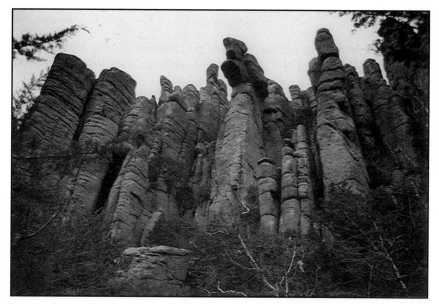

*Arizona's southeastern area contains several natural attractions, including Chiracahua National Monument east of Sierra Vista, with its fantastic rhyolite formations.*

**Property tax** ● $10.86 per $100 assessed valuation

**Economy** ● It's more diverse than Pinetop-Lakeside, with a mix of tourism and related services, retail trade, logging and forest products manufacturing.

**Job prospects** ● Limited; there isn't much beyond lumbering and tourist related services.

**Industrial facilities** ● Three small industrial parks; some with airport access.

**Real estate** ● It's a mix of older downtown homes, a few subdivisions on the fringes and chalet style homes among the trees. Prices start around $90,000 for a three-bedroom house.

**The media** ● Two bi-weeklies, the *White Mountain Independent* and the *Apache Scout.*

**Medical services** ● A small medical center and several clinics.

**Transportation** ● A local company offers bus service. The Show Low Airport has a 6,000-foot lighted runway, with commuter flights to Phoenix.

**Education** ● Show Low campus of Northland Pioneer Community College; elementary, middle and high schools.

**Local government** ● Incorporated in 1953; mayor, six council members and a city manager.

**Places to stay** ● About twenty motels, nine campgrounds and five RV parks.

**Leisure facilities** ● Two golf courses, public parks, a fitness center,soccer fields, tennis and racquetball courts.

*Tourist lures* • A repeat of Pinetop-Lakeside: People are drawn by the piney woods and the recreational lures of the White Mountain Apache Reservation.

*Contacts* • Show Low Chamber of Commerce, P.O. Box 1083, Show Low, AZ 85901; (928) 537-2326.

City of Show Low, 200 W. Cooley Rd., Show Low, AZ 85901; (858) 537-5724; *www.ci.show-low.az.us; e-mail: info@show-low.az.us*

White Mountain Regional Development Corporation, 1201 E. Cooley, Suite F, Show Low, AZ 85901; (800) 818-2520 or (928) 537-3777; *www.wmrdc.org; e-mail: wmrdc@cybertrails.com.*

# SIERRA VISTA

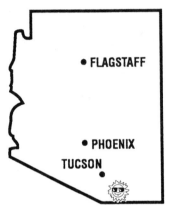

Started in 1956 as a retirement and vacation retreat, Sierra Vista has mushroomed to become the largest city in eastern Arizona. More than one in three Cochise County residents lives here. Rivaling neighboring Tucson in land area, it looks more like a well-planned suburb than a town. It's an expansive spread of shopping centers, subdivisions, service stations and stop lights.

Despite the suburban sprawl, it can appeal to relocating families and retirees. Surrounding mountains provide an impressive backdrop and it's close to Chiricahua National Monument, Coronado National Memorial and the legendary gunslinger town of Tombstone. National climate experts rate this area as one of the most temperate in the nation. With an average maximum high of 75 and low of 50, it's practically a room temperature community. Housing is inexpensive, with detached homes available for as little as $65,000. The area is decidedly pro-growth and it has extensive retirement facilities.

*Elevation* • 4,623 feet

*Location* • In Cochise County, 70 miles southeast of Tucson.

*Climate* • Warm summers; mild winters with cool evenings. July average high 88.6, low 66.4; January average high 58.4, low 43.2. Rainfall 14.64 inches; snowfall seven inches.

*Population* • 38,800

*Population trend* • Gained 14.5 percent in the past ten years.

*Property tax* • $12.46 per $100 of assessed valuation.

*Economy* • Once retirement oriented, Sierra Vista's economy is diversifying into light manufacturing, the services sector and expanding retail trade.

*Job prospects* • Employment possibilities are about average. Best bets are in retail sales and public administration. The largest employer is next-door Fort Huachuca, with more than 11,700 military and civilian personnel drawing government paychecks, although future cut-backs could reduce this.

**Industrial facilities** • Two industrial parks; Sierra Vista is a "Foreign Trade Zone Grantee."

**Real estate** • Three-bedroom home prices begin around $65,000 and range well beyond $100,000. The market is "moderately active," according to the Sierra Vista Association of Realtors.

**The media** • The daily *Sierra Vista Herald* and the weekly *Huachuca Scout*. Television feeds from Tucson, Nogales and Phoenix.

**Medical services** • A local hospital, a VA hospital at Fort Huachuca, two extended care facilities and several clinics.

**Transportation** • A local bus company has connections to Greyhound in Tucson. Sierra Vista Municipal Airport has three runways, with commuter service and charters.

**Education** • Cochise Community College; five public elementary, one middle and one high school.

**Local government** • Incorporated in 1956; mayor, six-member council and city manager.

**Places to stay** • About a dozen motels; several RV and mobile home parks, mostly in next-door Huachuca City.

**Leisure facilities** • A community center, nine public parks, four swimming pools, two golf courses and tennis and racquetball courts.

**Tourist lures** • Sierra Vista is near Coronado National Memorial, Chiricahua National Monument, Fort Bowie National Historic Site, historic Tombstone and Ramsey Canyon Nature Preserve. A fine military museum is located in Fort Huachuca.

**Contacts** • Greater Sierra Vista Chamber of Commerce, 21 E. Wilcox Dr., Sierra Vista, AZ 85635; (800) 288-3861 or (520) 458-6940; *www.sierravistachamber.org.*

Sierra Vista Economic Development Foundation, P.O. Box 2380, Sierra Vista, AZ 85636-2380; (520) 458-6948.

City of Sierra Vista, 1011 N. Coronado Dr., Sierra Vista, AZ 85635; (520) 458-3315.6; *www.ci.sierra-vista.az.us*

# SPRINGERVILLE & EAGAR

Although not generally regarded as retirement communities, Springerville and Eagar offer possibilities for pensioners who don't mind nippy winters. However, they have little job potential.

Springerville may appeal to those seeking the quiet life and perhaps a fine old home on a tree-lined street. Eagar is essentially a Springerville suburb, although it has twice the population and its own city government. Housing is inexpensive in both, the tax rate is low and the surrounding hills offer outdoor recreation and a couple of historic pueblo sites. It's a short drive to Sunrise Ski Area and other lures of the White Mountain Apache Reservation and Apache-Sitgreaves National Forest.

Eagar was named for brothers John, Joel and William Eager who donated land for a townsite, not for an ambitious beaver. The spelling was changed to 1892 to "Eagar" for reasons that are lost to historians; maybe there were too many beaver jokes. About the time the Eagers' Eagar was getting started, Henry Springer opened a trading post four miles north. It was granted a post office in 1879 and it has outpaced Eagar commercially to become the trading center of a large cattle ranching region.

The twin towns are in Round Valley, a grassy basin on the northeastern edge of the White Mountains.

**Elevation** ● 6,965 feet

**Location** ● In Apache County on U.S. Highways 60 and 191 in east central Arizona, near the New Mexico border.

**Climate** ● Warm summers; cool winters with cold nights. July average high 83.3 low 51.6; January average high 46.7, low 14.6. Rainfall about 23 inches; snowfall 36 inches.

**Population** ● Springerville, just over 2,000; Eagar, 4,800.

**Population trend** ● Springerville gained 9.4 percent in the last decade; Eagar was almost unchanged.

**Property tax** ● $7.47 in Springerville and $8.34 in Eagar.

**Economy** ● It's a mix of tourism, lumbering and agriculture and it's not particularly active.

**Job prospects** ● Limited opportunities are available in tourism, lumbering and retailing.

**Industrial facilities** ● An industrial park adjacent to the Springerville Municipal Airport, plus a few other small sites.

**Real estate** ● Most homes on the market are used although there is some new construction. Prices for a three-bedroom fixer-upper can be as low as $50,000; newer homes start around $80,000 and a few "ranchettes" on wooded acreages go considerably higher.

**The media** ● The bi-weekly *White Mountain Independent*; daily news comes from Phoenix and Albuquerque. TV relays bring in Phoenix, Tucson and cable channels.

**Medical services** ● A regional hospital and a few medical clinics.

**Transportation** ● Springerville Airport has two lighted runways; no scheduled air service.

**Education** ● Northland Pioneer College, plus public schools.

**Local government** ● Both incorporated in 1948; Springerville has four council members and Eagar has six; with town managers.

*Places to stay* • About half a dozen motels in Springerville and Eagar; nine RV parks in the area and several campgrounds in the national forest.

*Leisure facilities* • "Enosphere" at Round Valley High School is a multi-use dome hosting cultural and sports activities; other campus recreational facilities also are available to the public. Springerville has two parks and racquetball courts. Eager has a public pool, tennis courts, plus three parks and a large multi-purpose facility at its high school.

*Tourist lures* • The White Mountains offer the usual outdoor appeal, and it's a short drive to the Sunrise summer and winter resort on the White Mountain Apache reservation. Despite their small size and rural demeanor, Springerville and Eagar have several museums, focusing on local history, art and Native American archeology. Nearby is Casa Malpais Pueblo.

*Contacts* • Springerville-Eagar Regional Chamber of Commerce, P.O. Box 31 (318 E. Main St.), Springerville, AZ 85938-0031; (928) 333-2123.

Town of Springerville, P.O. Box 390, Springerville, AZ 85938; (928) 333-2656; *www.springerville.com.*

Town of Eagar, P.O. Box 1300 (174 S. Main St.), Eagar, AZ 85925; (928) 333-4128; *www.eagar.com.*

# TOMBSTONE

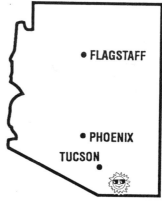

If you'd like to rub shoulders with history and you're attracted by mild climate and inexpensive housing, this may be the place. Don't expect any fancy subdivisions or golf courses. Tombstone is as funky as it sounds, with false front buildings, boardwalks and cowboy-style tourist trappings.

This rough-hewn frontier village has been called "the town too tough to die." Of course it can't die; Hollywood would never allow it. A few years ago, two more movies were added to the long list of films portraying the legendary gunfight at the O.K. Corral.

The town's roots can be traced to Ed Schieffelin, a prospector who decided to check out the rocky hills southeast of present-day Tucson in 1877. He was warned that the Apaches were on the warpath.

"All you'll find out there is your tombstone," a friend advised.

Ed found a big silver strike instead, and called it—appropriately— the Lucky Cuss. Word spread and other argonauts poured in. A town was platted two years later, two miles from Schieffelin's hillside mine. Tombstone soon became one of the largest, wildest and wickedest mining camps in the Southwest. It attracted such characters as Doc Holliday, Johnny Ringo, Bat Masterson and—of course—the Earp brothers. Wyatt was co-owner of the Oriental Saloon, where gunslinger Luke Short was a faro dealer.

By 1881, Tombstone boasted 10,000 citizens and it became the seat of Cochise County. In that same year, the Earps shot it out with the Clantons and McLaurys near the O.K. Corral. Actually, it was more of a blood feud than a police action. The Earps had accused the Clantons and McLaurys of cattle thievery and sheltering stage robbers at their ranches. The cowboys boasted openly that they would kill the Earps for besmirching their reputations.

"They tried to pick a fuss out of me," Wyatt testified at the hearing following the corral shootout.

After the excitement from the West's most publicized gun battle faded, Tombstone faded as well. Most of the downtown area burned in 1882. A few years later, water began seeping into its mines. Falling silver prices and labor problems closed the last one early in this century. The county seat was moved to Bisbee in 1931 and the town too tough to die was on the verge of doing it. Its population dropped to 150.

Then tourists began trickling in, lured by stories of the Earp brothers and the shootout. The town's old Western look, unchanged because nobody could afford to modernize, became an asset. However, that asset has been overdone. Tourists buy frozen yogurt and John Wayne posters and visit museums that are mostly fronts for souvenir shops. Still, there's an air of legitimacy about all of this. Tombstone is a national historic landmark and the courthouse is a state historic park. Visitors clunk along boardwalks shaded by overhangs from false front stores. They catch rides in horse-drawn surreys and watch reenactments of the shootout. These occur several times a day and according to local historians, they're probably more accurate than anything portrayed by Hollywood.

**Elevation** • 4,540 feet

**Location** • In Cochise County, seventeen miles northeast of Sierra Vista.

**Climate** • Warm summers; mild winters with cool evenings. July average high 93.7, low 65.4; January average high 61.4, low 33.6. Rainfall 12.77 inches; snowfall seven inches.

**Population** • About 1,500

**Population trend** • Gained 23.3 percent in the past ten years.

**Property tax** • $13.42 per $100 of assessed valuation.

**Economy** • Other than selling cowboy souvenirs and snow cones? Not much else. The economy is almost all tourist based.

**Job prospects** • There aren't any to speak of, other than working in tourist shops. Even the O.K. Corral shootout players are unpaid amateurs. However, commercial centers of Sierra Vista and Bisbee are nearby.

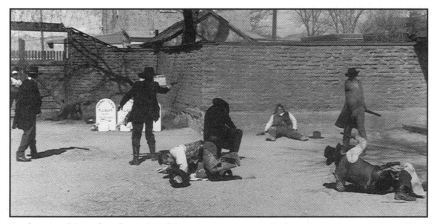

*Bad guys bite the dust in this reenactment of the shoot-out at the O.K. Corral, a 30-second gun battle that put Tombstone in the history books.*

**Industrial facilities** • None.

**Real estate** • Home prices outside the historic district start as low as $60,000; restored or restorable historic homes are rare and considerably more expensive. Some new subdivisions are rising between Tombstone and Sierra Vista.

**The media** • The legendary *Tombstone Epitaph* is still published although it's now a tourist paper; the news is more than a century old. There is a contemporary weekly called the *Tombstone Tumbleweed*.

**Medical services** • Small clinic available by appointment only; nearest hospital is in Sierra Vista, seventeen miles southwest.

**Transportation** • Tombstone has an unpaved landing field; the nearest air service is in Sierra Vista.

**Education** • Community college in Sierra Vista; the usual public schools in Tombstone.

**Local government** • Incorporated in 1881; mayor, four-member council and city clerk.

**Places to stay** • About a dozen motels and bed & breakfast inns; three RV parks.

**Leisure facilities** • Three public parks, a swimming pool and two tennis courts.

**Tourist lures** • Tombstone's rustic look and reputation are the only lures it needs. It has five historic museums and quasi-gift shop museums, many century-old buildings and of course, the O.K. Corral. The original Boot Hill cemetery on the edge of town is now a tourist attraction; visitors enter through a gift shop.

**Contacts** • Tombstone Office of Tourism, P.O. Box 248 (Allan and Fourth streets), Tombstone, AZ 85638; (800) 457-3423 or (520) 457-9317.

City of Tombstone, P.O. Box 339, Tombstone, AZ 85638; (520) 457-3562; *www.cityoftombstone.com;* e-mail: *tombstone@primenet. com.*

# TUBAC

Most historians say Arizona was born in Tubac. Established as a Spanish presidio in 1752, it's the state's oldest non-native settlement. It was built to protect missionaries and settlers after Pima Chief Oacpicagigua led a revolt against the intruders.

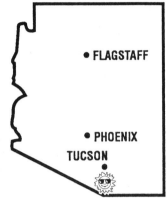

Tubac commander Juan Bautista de Anza left here in 1776 on his historic overland trek to establish the pueblos of San José and Yerba Buena (San Francisco) in California. After Mexico won its independence from Spain in 1821, troops were withdrawn from Tubac. The settlement—harassed by Apache raiders—was abandoned. The Gadsden Purchase brought the community under America's protection and it was resettled. In 1860, it was Arizona's largest town. Then the Civil War pulled U.S. troops away, and hostile Apaches again forced its abandonment. Resettlement came after the Apaches finally were subdued late in the nineteenth century.

Today, slightly weathered little Tubac is a serious art colony, with many galleries housed in a mix of old and new adobe and brick buildings. This is where "art and history meet," proclaims a sign at the edge of town. A dozen or more boutiques, import and curio shops sell native and Southwest crafts and assorted giftwares.

Statistically, Tubac is growing rapidly, gaining nearly 25 percent in the nineties. However, with a total population of only 2,000, it isn't a risk to become Arizona's next metropolis. Two thirds of its new residents are retirees.

*Elevation* ● Approximately 3,000 feet

*Location* ● Santa Cruz County, 40 miles south of Tucson on I-19.

*Climate* ● Warm to hot summers; mild winters with cool evenings. July average high 97.1, low 65.5; January average high 65.9, low 31.2. Rainfall about 10 inches; rare traces of snow.

*Population* ● About 2,000

*Population trend* ● Gained 24 percent in the last decade.

*Property tax* ● $16.49 per $100 of assessed valuation.

*Economy* ● It's based mostly on tourism and retirement.

*Job prospects* ● They're very limited; a few jobs may be available in retailing and tourist services.

*Industrial facilities* ● None.

*Real estate* ● There isn't much on the market; homes start around $80,000.

*The media* ● Nearest newspaper is the *Green Valley News & Sun* published twenty miles away. TV feeds from Tucson and Nogales.

**Medical services** • A small clinic; hospital in Nogales, twenty-three miles south.

**Transportation** • Served by Greyhound and a local bus line.

**Education** • One private elementary school; public schools in adjacent communities.

**Local government** • Unincorporated; services provided by Santa Cruz County.

**Places to stay** • A country club near Tubac, a few small motels in the area and the Rio Rico resort, ten miles south.

**Leisure facilities** • Tubac Center for the Arts, several galleries, boutiques and a community center.

**Tourist lures** • Visitors are drawn by the galleries, boutiques and Southwest style cafés. Tubac State Historic Park is located here and Tumacacori National Monument is a few miles south.

**Contacts** • Tubac Chamber of Commerce, P.O. Box 1866, Tubac, AZ 85646; (520) 398-2704, www.tubacaz.com.

Nogales/Santa Cruz County Economic Development Foundation, P.O. Box 1688, Nogales, AZ 85620; (520) 377-2055.

# WINSLOW

*"I'm standing on a corner in Winslow, Arizona; such a fine sight to see..."*

"Take It Easy," a 1970s song made popular by the Eagles, wasn't referring to Winslow itself, but to a pretty girl driving by in a flatbed Ford. It did bring fifteen minutes of fame to this quiet old prairie town, which is attractive in a homey sort of way. It may offer potential for retirees, assuming they don't mind rather cold winters.

Winslow is an old-fashioned community with a sturdy brick business district rimmed by tree-lined residential areas. Nearby are considerably older villages—the Homol'ovi ruins of the Anasazi. The town was established in 1882 as a railway division point, and named for General Edward F. Winslow, president of the St. Louis and San Francisco Railroad. Despite its remote location, it thrived as a cattle and freight center.

Folks who enjoy sightseeing may like the fact that Winslow is within a one or two-hour drive of several attractions, including Petrified Forest National Park, the Painted Desert and Meteor Crater. Flagstaff is 60 miles west.

**Elevation** • 4,850 feet

**Location** • On the western edge of Navajo County on I-40, just south of the Navajo Nation.

**Climate** • Warm summers, cool to cold winters. July average high 93.6, low 62.9; January average high 45.6, low 19.6. Rainfall 7.33 inches; snowfall 11.2 inches.

**Population** • About 1,000

**Population trend** • Very flat; gained 2.6 percent in the last decade.

**Property tax** • $11.89 per $100 assessed valuation.

**Economy** • Moderately active, with a balance of retail trade, services, rail shipping and area ranching.

**Job prospects** • About average despite rather slow growth. Major employers are the Santa Fe Railway and nearby Arizona State Prison. Some light manufacturing, lumbering and seasonal tourism work is available.

**Industrial facilities** • A few small industrial sites.

**Real estate** • Housing is quite inexpensive; three-bedroom home prices start around $50,000.

**The media** • The weekly *Winslow Mail* and *The Reminder*.

**Medical services** • A 42-bed hospital; native American outpatient clinic; convalescent home and three medical clinics.

**Transportation** • Served by Greyhound and Amtrak; Winslow Airport offers general aviation services.

**Education** • Winslow campus of Northland Pioneer College, plus the usual public schools.

**Local government** • Town founded in 1882 and incorporated in 1900; mayor, six-member council and city administrator.

**Places to stay** • Seventeen motels and two RV parks.

**Leisure facilities** • Golf course, public indoor and outdoor pools and community parks. McHood Park, five miles southeast, offers fishing, boating, swimming and picnicking.

**Tourist lures** • Homol'ovi Ruins State Park north of town, plus nearby attractions of Petrified Forest National Park, Painted Desert, Meteor Crater and the Hopi and Navajo reservations.

**Contacts** • Winslow Chamber of Commerce, P.O. Box 460 (300 W. North Rd.), Winslow, AZ 86047; (928) 289-2434 or 289-2435; *winslowarizona.org; e-mail: winslowchamber@cybertrails.com.*

City of Winslow, 21 Williamson Ave., Winslow, AZ 86047; (928) 289-2422; *www.winslowarizona.com.*

# PART THREE
# THE ATTRACTIONS

Once you've settled in your special corner of Arizona, you'll want to explore the rest of the state. But where to begin? You already know that it's an amazingly diverse place, with snow-clad pinnacles as well as cactus gardens.

In the chapters that follow, we've divided the state into six major tourist areas, and added a special section on exploring next-door Mexico.

If you'd like more detail than we list in these chapters, several statewide guidebooks are available, ranging from the rather staid but practical *AAA Arizona & New Mexico TourBook* to the more readable and almost encyclopedic *Arizona Handbook* by Moon Publications. (We published the *Arizona Discovery Guide* for several years, although it is no longer in print.) For a list of Arizona specialty guides and reference books, see Chapter Nineteen, starting on page 261.

The Arizona Office of Tourism will happily send you general travel information, including its free full-color *Arizona Travel Planner.* Contact the tourism office at 2702 N. Third St., Suite 4015, Phoenix, AZ 85004-4608; (888) 520-3434 or (602) 230-7733; *www.arizonaguide.com* or *www.arizonavacationvalues.com.*

## Chapter Twelve

# THE NORTHWEST
## GRAND CANYON AND VICINITY

**W**e begin our exploration with the state's most famous attraction—that magnificent 227-mile-long chasm across its northwest corner. Indeed, despite its fame as a sunbelt retirement haven, Arizona is officially known as the "Grand Canyon state." This is its most visited landmark, drawing more than four million people a year.

This high-country corner of Arizona contains other lures as well. Find time to explore the remote and intriguing Arizona Strip on the northern side of the canyon, and Glen Canyon National Recreation area adjacent to Page. South of the Grand Canyon, you can hike down to the isolated Havasupai village of Supai, deep in a scenic chasm and reached only by foot or horseback. Or you can catch a vintage steam train that runs between the Grand Canyon and the woodsy town of Williams.

***Grand Canyon National Park*** ● One of the world's most famous attractions, the Grand Canyon is not a single ravine but a vast network of hundreds of chasms carved deeply into the Kaibab section of the Colorado Plateau. Most people visit the South Rim, which has extensive facilities including lodges, restaurants, museums, gift shops, campgrounds and even an airport. The less visited yet equally spectacular North Rim is our favorite. It's uncrowded, drawing only a tenth as many visitors as the opposite side, and it offers complete—if scaled down—visitor facilities.

*The Grand Canyon's grandeur is best appreciated from below the rim; this view is from Horseshoe Mesa, reached by a South Rim trail.*

The best way to experience the canyon is to hike into its wild depths from either rim, or run the roller-coaster rapids of the Colorado River. You can book overnight accommodations at Phantom Ranch at the bottom of the canyon, or reserve spots at several campgrounds. This must be done well in advance; Phantom Ranch lodgings should be booked a *year* or more ahead. Whitewater rafting through the canyon is popular and you can send for a list of outfitters (see below).

The South Rim remains open the year around, while the North Rim—which is much higher—closes after the first serious snowfall, usually in late October.

**For information** • Superintendent, Grand Canyon National Park, P.O. Box 129, Grand Canyon, AZ 86023. Call (928) 638-7888 or (928) 638-7770 for South Rim information and (928) 638-7864 for North Rim information.

Backcountry Reservations office, P.O. Box 129, Grand Canyon, AZ 86023. (Backcountry camping and hiking reservations can be made only by mail or in person, and they must be made well in advance.) For a list of rafting companies, write to River Subdistrict Office at the address above.

Amfac Parks & Resorts (South Rim, Phantom Ranch and Trailer Village RV park reservations), 14001 E. Iliff, Suite 600, Aurora, CO 80014; (303) 297-2757.

Grand Canyon Lodge (North Rim reservations), North Rim, Grand Canyon National Park, AZ 86052; (928) 638-2389 in summer and (303) 297-2757 the rest of the year.

## Williams

Below the South Rim, the plateau slopes southwesterly through Kaibab National Forest, turning into a high prairie of Joshua trees and bunchgrass. If you follow U.S. Highway 180 and then State Route 64 south, you'll climb into more forest and hit the little town of Williams at Interstate 40. This wooded community is home to a steam train that will take you right back to the Grand Canyon.

**For area information** ● Williams-Grand Canyon Chamber of Commerce, 200 Railroad Ave., Williams, AZ 86046; (928) 635-4061.

**Grand Canyon Railway** ● *Grand Canyon Boulevard and Railroad Avenue, Williams; (800) 843-8724; www.thetrain.com* □ This firm offers historic train rides from Williams to the South Rim that began in 1901. It uses vintage steam trains in the summer and 1950 era diesel locomotives the rest of the year.

## Hualapai & Havasupai reservations

Northeast of Williams, much of the Grand Canyon is rimmed by the Hualapai and Havasupai Indian reservations. An eight-mile hike (or horseback ride) through pretty Havasu Canyon will take you to one of America's most remote villages.

**Havasu Canyon and the village of Supai** ● *For camping permits or overnight lodging and horseback trips, contact: Havasupai Tourist Enterprise, P.O. Box 160, Supai, AZ 86436; (928) 448-2121.* □ To reach the trailhead for the Supai hike, follow historic Highway 66 west from Williams and then go north on Indian Route 18 through the Hualapai Reservation to Hualapai Hilltop. From there, you can hike or ride down to Supai village, reached only by trail through Havasu Canyon, which is a tributary chasm of the Grand Canyon. Below the village are several camping areas and two beautiful waterfalls. Back at the top, a Native American casino perches near the edge of the canyon.

# THE ARIZONA STRIP & GLEN CANYON

If you visit the Grand Canyon's North Rim, you'll pass through the Arizona Strip. Isolated from the rest of the state by the great chasm, this high plateau covering 12,000 square miles is home to only a handful of people. Many are descendants of early Mormon pioneers who came down from Utah in the mid-1800s.

Towns in the area such as **Colorado City** and **Fredonia** are still predominately Mormon. Following State Route 389 southeast from Colorado City, you'll encounter one of Arizona's many national monuments. Not surprisingly, this one has Mormon roots:

**Pipe Spring National Monument** ● Fredonia, AZ 86022; (928) 643-7105. Visitor center/museum open daily 8 to 5. □ This small preserve contains the great fortified ranch headquarters of an early Mormon cattle spread. You can tour furnished rooms in the fortress-like ranch house and climb a low, steep bluff for a nice panorama of the Arizona Strip's grasslands. A Native American casino, not connected with Pipe Spring, is just above the national monument.

From here, the highway continues into **Fredonia**, where it merges with U.S. 89-A and swings southward. You can follow it and State Route 67 through Kaibab National Forest to the Grand Canyon's North Rim. Or continue east on 89-A to **Marble Canyon**, a steep walled ravine where the Colorado River begins slicing into this high plateau. Most river-runners put in at **Lee's Ferry,** just northeast of the hamlet of Marble Canyon. A part of Glen Canyon National Recreation Area, it has a campground and several historic exhibits.

## Page

If you continue following 89-A east and then take U.S. 89 north, you'll enter Page. Adjacent is Glen Canyon National Recreation Area, encompassing a mighty dam and a flooded canyon behind it.

*For area information* ● Page-Lake Powell Chamber of Commerce, P.O. Box 727, Page, AZ 86040; (928) 645-2741.

*Glen Canyon National Recreation Area* ● *P.O. Box 1507, Page, AZ 86040; (928) 608-640-4.* ☐ Within this area are Glen Canyon Dam, Lake Powell and a million acres of eroded desert sandstone. Glen Canyon, whose serpentine side ravines and fantastic formations rivaled those of the Grand Canyon, was inundated by the dam. You can see the tops of this geological wonderland by taking boat cruises in and out of the finger-like fjords of Lake Powell. They depart from Wahweap Marina near Page; call (602) 278-8888 or (800) 528-6154.

While you're in the neighborhood, take a guided or self- guiding tour of Glen Canyon Dam and stop at the Carl Hayden Visitor Center and Museum. It's open daily 8 to 7 in summer and 8 to 5 the rest of the year.

# FLAGSTAFF & SURROUNDS

During most of this northwestern Arizona exploration, you've been in huge Coconino County, which covers 18,629 square miles. If you head east on I-40, you'll encounter the county seat of Flagstaff. It's the gateway to some of Arizona's most varied attractions. Within a short drive are seven national parks and monuments (including some of America's finest Indian ruins), Arizona's largest ski area and highest peak, and the red rock beauty of Oak Creek Canyon.

*For area information* ● Flagstaff Chamber of Commerce, 101 W. Route 66, Flagstaff, AZ 86001; (928) 774-4505.

### Attractions in and near Flagstaff

*Arizona Snowbowl and Humphreys Peak* ● *Flagstaff; (928) 779-1951 for the Snowbowl.* ☐ Although primarily a ski area, the Snowbowl also is popular with summer visitors. You can take a sky tram to the dizzying heights of the San Francisco Peaks and hike into the Kachina Wilderness Area. A trail leads from the Snowbowl to the top of Humphreys Peak, tallest in Arizona at 12,633. It's not a technical climb; it's just a long, hard trudge.

**Lowell Observatory** • *1400 W. Mars Hill Rd., Flagstaff; (928) 774-2096. Daily 9 to 5 April-October and noon to 5 the rest of the year. Call for night sky show schedules.* □ Privately-endowed Lowell Observatory sits atop a pine-covered mesa less than a mile from downtown Flagstaff. Visitors can view celestial exhibits and join lecture tours or wander about the grounds on their own.

**Museum of Northern Arizona** • *3101 N. Fort Valley Rd., Flagstaff; (928) 774-5213. Daily 9 to 5.* □ Housed in a handsome fieldstone and timber complex, this museum three miles north of Flagstaff is "dedicated to the anthropology, biology, geology and fine arts of the Colorado Plateau." Remodeled and modernized several years ago, it's one of the state's finest archives.

**Riordan State Historic Park** • *Riordan Ranch Road downtown, Flagstaff; (928) 779-4395. Daily 8:30 to 5 May-October, 10:30 to 5 the rest of the year; tours on the hour.* □ Now surrounded by downtown Flagstaff, this state park contains the pioneer Riordan brothers' elaborate and unusual double-home, joined in the middle by a gaming room; it has been restored to its original rustic splendor.

**Sunset Crater Volcano National Monument** • *Twelve miles north of Flagstaff on U.S. 80, and then east; (928) 556-7042. Visitor center open daily 8 to 6.* □ The focal point of this park is an almost perfect volcanic cindercone with a burnt orange cast, particularly evident at sunset—and thus, the name. It's surrounded by the wild geological turmoil of eruptions that date back more than 700 years.

**Wupatki National Monument** • *Fourteen miles north of Sunset Crater; (928) 679-2365. Visitor Center open daily 8 to 5.* □ Wupatki is home to several ancient Indian ruins scattered about a high volcanic prairie. The largest and most elaborate is Wupatki Pueblo, a short walk from the visitor center. It's a four-story, 100-room condo built of sandstone blocks instead of the usual adobe.

## Flagstaff to Winslow

Eastbound from Flagstaff on Interstate 40, you'll discover several other attractions. One of them comes from the mysterious past; another from out of space.

**For area information** • Winslow Chamber of Commerce, 300 W. North Rd., Winslow, AZ 86047; (928) 289-2434.

**Walnut Canyon National Monument** • *Seven miles east on I-40, then three miles south; (928) 526-3367. Visitor center and ruins open daily 8 to 6 June-August, 8 to 5 September-November and 9 to 5 the rest of the year.* □ Steep-sided Walnut Canyon shelters an elaborate Sinagua cliff dwelling built about 800 years ago. Recessed into overhangs between the rim and canyon floor, the ruins can be reached by a 251-step trail from the visitor center. Save some of your energy for the return trip!

**Meteor Crater** • *Forty miles east of Flagstaff to Meteor Crater exit, then six miles south; (928) 289-2362. Tours depart daily 9:15 to 2:15.* ☐ Imagine this: a monster chunk of nickel and iron weighing millions of tons streaks earthward at 43,000 miles an hour. It slams into the ground with a force that buries fragments hundreds of feet deep. What you'll see is the massive hole that it left, plus an excellent museum with displays concerning meteorites, the universe and America's space program.

**Homol'ovi Ruins State Park** • *Just north of Winslow on State Highway 87; (928) 289-4106. Park open dawn to dusk; visitor center open daily 8 to 5,* ☐ In contrast to partially restored Wupatki and Walnut Canyon ruins, Homol'ovi Ruins State Park shelters several unrestored sites. These are remnants of thirteenth to sixteenth century Anasazi villages as they looked before the archaeologists and anthropologists arrived.

**Little Painted Desert County Park** • *Just off State Route 87, about thirteen miles north of Winslow; gates open 8 to 9.* ☐ This is a surprising jewel of a park—a mini badlands of softly contoured, pastel hued sandstone. From a parking area, you can drive or walk along rim roads in either direction for varied vistas of this fluted amphitheater of erosion. A trail from the north rim road takes you into this sensuously rounded landscape.

# SEDONA & THE VERDE VALLEY

If you head south of Flagstaff on U.S. 89-A, you'll enter a mosaic of natural beauty, upscale tourism and pre-history. You will discover the red ramparts of Oak Creek Canyon; the galleries, boutiques and elegant resorts of Sedona; the ancient Indian ruins of the Verde Valley and the rustic copper mining town of Jerome.

**For area information** • Camp Verde Chamber of Commerce, P.O. Box 3520, Camp Verde, AZ 86322; (928) 567-9294.

Jerome Chamber of Commerce, P.O. Box K, Jerome, AZ 86331; (928) 634-2900.

Sedona-Oak Creek Canyon Chamber of Commerce, P.O. Box 478, Sedona, AZ 86339; (928) 204-1123.

Cottonwood Chamber of Commerce, 1010 S. Main St., Cottonwood, AZ 86326; (928) 634-7593.

The road into **Oak Creek Canyon** is one of the prettiest drives in America. It twists down through thick ponderosa forests to the valley floor, where it follows sparkling Oak Creek. At the lower end, the canyon emerges into a stunning panorama of red rock pinnacles, buttes and fairy castles.

You'll shortly encounter **Sedona,** surrounded by this splendid red rock display. Take time to explore its upscale shops and galleries, particularly in Tlaquepaque, a Spanish colonial style complex just southeast of town on State Route 179.

Inquire at the Coconino National Forest office or the chamber of commerce about scenic drives and hikes in the area. Several operators offer jeep trips into the red rock formations and balloon flights above them.

Stop to admire the **Chapel of the Holy Cross;** it's tucked among red rock formations on Chapel Road off Highway 179, two miles south of town. With a huge cross forming its façade, it rivals the rocks themselves as one of the area's most appealing attractions.

## Sedona to Jerome

Back on Highway 89-A, head south into the Verde Valley and you'll encounter one of Arizona's newest state parks. Beyond the park are four more intriguing attractions. Two are remnants of the dim past and two are of more recent vintage.

**Red Rock State Park** ● *South of Sedona, to the left off Highway 89-A; (928) 282- 6907. Park open daily 8 to 6 May-September and 8 to 9 the rest of the year; visitor center 9 to 5.* ☐ A former millionaire's vacation retreat, this area backdropped by red rock ramparts was opened as a state park in 1991. It's a state-of-the-environment park, with a strong focus on the ecosystems of Oak Creek and nearby rock formations. Its Center for Environmental Education teaches visitors about the flora, fauna and history of the area.

**Tuzigoot National Monument** ● *Between Cottonwood and Clarkdale on Tuzigoot Road; (928) 634-5564. Daily 8 to 7 Memorial Day through Labor Day and 8 to 5 the rest of the year.* ☐ These extensive Sinagua ruins crown a low ridge north of Clarkdale. They were built around the thirteenth century, abandoned and then restored as a WPA project during the Depression.

**Montezuma's Castle National Monument** ● *Southeast of Clarkdale, just east of I-17; (928) 567-3322. Daily 8 to 7 Memorial Day to Labor Day and 8 to 5 the rest of the year.* ☐ It's not a castle and it was never visited by the Aztec chieftain Montezuma. It's a small yet dramatic ruin perched high in a cliff face. Nearby and equally interesting (and equally misnamed) is **Montezuma Well,** a limestone sinkhole rimmed by several pueblo ruins.

**Fort Verde State Historic Park** ● *In the town of Camp Verde, just south of Montezuma's Castle; (928) 567-3275. Daily 8 to 5.* ☐ The park preserves remnants of a frontier army post built in the 1870s to protect settlers from the people they had rudely displaced. A museum spotlights the native people and the white settlement history of the Verde Valley.

*Montezuma's Castle occupies a dramatic niche in a cliff face above the Verde Valley.*

# Jerome

If you follow 89-A southwest through the Verde Valley, you'll climb into the flanks of Mingus Mountain and enter the scruffy remnants of one of Arizona's most interesting old mining towns. Jerome isn't a ghost town but a lively tourist village with museums, nineteenth century homes, art galleries, curio shops and antique stores. From the late 1870s to the 1950s, billions of dollars in copper, gold and silver were gouged from Mingus Mountain's steep slopes. Several attractions here are worth stops:

**Jerome State Historic Park** ● *Off Highway 89-A, (928) 634-5381. Daily 8 to 5.* □ The park embraces the estate of James S. "Rawhide Jimmy" Douglas, owner of the Little Daisy Mine and one of Jerome's wealthiest copper barons. The mansion offers a mix of period furnishings, historic photos, videos and mining exhibits.

**Jerome Historical Society Mine Museum** ● 200 Main Street, Jerome; (928) 634- 5477. Daily 9 to 4:30. □ Although not professionally done, the museum is nicely arrayed with a series of tableaux about Jerome and its boom days.

**Gold King Mine Museum** ● *Just above town. Daily 9 to 5:30.* □ This scruffy clutter of early day mining equipment and nineteenth century memorabilia walks a fine line between a museum and a junkyard. And therein lies its character.

## Prescott

Continuing southeast from Jerome on Highway 89-A, you'll climb over the shoulders of Mingus Mountain, drop down into a grassy valley and begin climbing again—into the wooded Bradshaw Mountains of Prescott National Forest. Cradled among these trees is Prescott, one of our favorite Arizona towns. It has a New England look and a Western attitude, and it offers several museums and galleries.

**For area information** ● Prescott Chamber of Commerce, P.O. Box 1147 (117 W. Goodwin St.), Prescott, AZ 86302; (800) 266-7534 or (928) 445-2000.

### The attractions

**Phippen Museum of Western Art** ● *4701 N. Highway 89 (seven miles north); (928) 778-1385. Wednesday-Monday 10 to 4, Sunday 1 to 4, closed Tuesday.* □ This fine museum, named in honor of noted local artist George Phippen, exhibits paintings, bronzes, ceramics and other works of past and present Western artists.

**Sharlot Hall Museum** ● *415 W. Gurley St.; (928) 445-3122. Monday-Saturday 10 to 5 and Sunday 1 to 5 April-October; Monday-Saturday 10 to 4 and Sunday 1 to 5 the rest of the year.* □ Covering more than a city block, the Sharlot Hall complex contains a dozen furnished historic buildings, either original or reconstructed. The centerpiece is the governor's "mansion," a log cabin that served as the official residence when Prescott was the territorial capital in the late 1800s.

**Smoki Museum** ● *100 N. Arizona St.; (928) 445-1230. Monday-Saturday 10 to 4 and Sunday 1 to 4.* □ Pronounced "Smoke-Eye," this museum houses a significant collection of artifacts of Southwest Indians and other American tribes, including stone tools, baskets and pottery excavated from local sites.

**Yavapai County Courthouse and Plaza** ● *Gurley and Montezuma streets.* □ The Greco-Roman style courthouse and surrounding tree-shaded plaza give Prescott a typical New England look. However, the town is definitely Western, as evidenced by the nearby cowboy galleries and shops.

Across from the courthouse along Montezuma Street is "Whiskey Row," once the town's bawdy district and now a solid rank of old style store fronts. Most of the saloons are gone, replaced by gift shops and boutiques.

### Nearby attractions

Two lures are within a short drive of Prescott—one southeast and one southwest. Either direction will take you quickly from pines to cactus. If you head southeast on State Route 69, you will soon hit Interstate 40, bound for Phoenix. At Cordes Junction, you'll encounter a most curious complex:

**Arcosanti** • *Cordes Junction; (928) 632-7135. Daily 9 to 5; tours on the hour from 10 to 4 with a four-person minimum. Adjacent bakery-café; accommodations available.* □ Arcosanti is the creation of Italian architect and visionary Paolo Soleri. Seeking to solve many of the world's problems in one architectural swoop, he is trying—with eager young helpers—to build an idyllic, energy-efficient, space-saving and environmentally correct community. However, its geometric precast concrete shapes have begun to weather in the more than three decades since the project was started. It looks more like a scruffy space station that crash-landed in the desert.

## Wickenburg

If you take U.S. 89 southwest from Prescott, you'll discover a community of quite a different stripe. Wickenburg works to preserve its cowboy past instead of fretting about an Orwellian future. It calls itself the "Dude ranch capital of the world," a title well earned, since five guest ranches function in the attractive surrounding desert.

Wickenburg was first a gold rush boomtown and then an important ranching center. Today, it still looks like yesterday, with false front stores and boardwalks. And it proudly hosts one of the finest small museums in Arizona.

**For area information** • Wickenburg Chamber of Commerce, 216 N. Frontier St., Wickenburg, AZ 85390; (800) 942-5242 or (928) 684-5479.

### The attractions

**Desert Caballeros Western Museum** • *20 N. Old Railroad St. (at Wickenburg Way); (928) 684-2272. Monday-Saturday 10 to 4, Sunday noon to 4.* □ The focal point of this fine museum is a full scale old fashioned Western street scene. Excellent dioramas and artifacts recall the area's development from the Paleozoic to the present. An adjoining gallery displays Western art by such notables as Russell, Remington and Catlin.

**Hassayampa River Preserve** • *West side of Highway 60/93, three miles southeast town; (928) 684-2272. Wednesday-Sunday 8 to 5 from mid-September to mid-May; closed the rest of the year.* □ This is a fine example of a riparian woodland along the course of the Hassayampa River. Once a stage stop and guest ranch, it was opened as a preserve in 1987 by the Nature Conservancy.

## Chapter Thirteen
# THE WEST & SOUTHWEST
## THE COLORADO RIVER CORRIDOR

---

**W**e discussed the Colorado River's aquatic playground in Chapter Eight. A series of dams has turned it into a chain of lakes, disrupting the great stream's efforts to flow from the Grand Canyon into Mexico's Gulf of California.

Other than the stream itself, there aren't a lot of attractions along the river corridor, or elsewhere in southwestern Arizona. Away from the river, the region is mostly unpopulated desert. The area does have a few lures, however.

If you live elsewhere and plan to visit this region, we'd suggest coming in the spring or fall. Summers sizzle, with average daytime temperatures over 100 degrees. It's not uncommon for the mercury to crawl into the 120s. Winter nights, while pleasantly balmy, can get a bit cool. During spring and fall, temperatures are close to idyllic day and night.

As you approach these corridor communities, bear in mind that they aren't bastions of culture or architectural gems. Many, like Bullhead City, look hastily assembled. Few have significant tourist attractions other than their water play potential. Notable exceptions are Hoover Dam, Lake Mead National Recreation Area, the historic areas of Yuma and—well—there's that British bridge at Lake Havasu. Inland, you will discover Organ Pipe Cactus National Monument and Kitt Peak, both definitely worth a detour.

# HOOVER DAM & LAKE MEAD

Our tour starts in the north and wanders south to Yuma and then inland to Organ Pipe and Kitt Peak. We begin at the Arizona- Nevada border with Hoover Dam and Lake Mead. Visitor facilities for both are on the Nevada side. Just beyond is the attractive community of **Boulder City**, built in the 1930s as a construction town for the dam. Its nicely preserved art deco downtown area, Boulder Dam Hotel and Hoover Dam Museum are definitely worth a look. Boulder City is the only town in Nevada that prohibits gambling, although Hacienda Casino sits between the town and the dam. Don't spend all of your money before your tour along the Colorado River corridor begins!

*For area information* ● Boulder City Chamber of Commerce, 1305 Arizona St., Boulder City, NV 89005; (702) 293-2034.

*Hoover Dam and Lake Mead National Recreation Area* ● *601 Nevada Highway, Boulder City; (702) 293-8906. Hoover Dam Visitor Center open daily 8 to 5:15. Alan Bible Visitor Center open daily 8:30 to 4:30; (702) 293-8990.* □ A sparkling new visitor center was opened at Hoover Dam a few years ago, with exhibits, videos and a dramatic viewing platform. From the center, tours take visitors through the innards of one of the grandest engineering marvels of the world. Hoover Dam holds back the world's largest reservoir, **Lake Mead,** a major aquatic playground. Lake Mead and **Lake Mohave** below the dam comprise Lake Mead National Recreation Area. For details about its marinas, lodgings, campsites and water sports, continue west from the dam to the Alan Bible Visitor Center, a few miles into Nevada.

# SOUTH TO QUARTZSITE

*For area information (in order of appearance)* ● Kingman Powerhouse Visitor Center, 120 W. Andy Devine Ave., Kingman, AZ 86402; (928) 753-6106.

Bullhead Area Chamber of Commerce, 1251 Highway 95, Bullhead City, AZ 86429; (928) 754-4121.

Lake Havasu Tourism Bureau, 314 London Bridge Rd., Lake Havasu City, AZ 86403; (800) 242-8278 or (928) 453-3444.

Laughlin Chamber of Commerce, Box 77777 (1585 Casino Dr.), Laughlin, NV 89028; (800) 337-5245 or (702) 298-2214.

Parker Area Chamber of Commerce, 1217 California Ave., Parker, AZ 85344; (928) 669-2174.

Quartzsite Chamber of Commerce, P.O. Box 85 (1490 Main Event Lane), Quartzsite, AZ 85346; (928) 927-5600.

From Hoover Dam, you can choose between Arizona or Nevada for your southbound trip. Both routes miss the river until you reach Bullhead City. The Nevada route is the fastest, although we prefer the Arizona side, since it takes you to the interesting towns of Kingman and Oatman, and through the dramatic ramparts of the Black Mountains on historic Route 66.

To begin, follow U.S. 93 east from Hoover Dam through the dry Detrital Valley to **Kingman.** You'll want to poke about its weathered old downtown, check out historic Highway 66 monuments in Railroad Park and visit its fine museum:

**Mohave Museum of History and Arts** • *400 W. Beale St. (Grandview); (928) 753-3195. Weekdays 9 to 5 and weekends 1 to 5.* □ A cut above the typical small-town archive, this museum tells the story of this valley's settlement, from Native Americans through the silver and copper rush to the present. A major exhibit traces the life of gravel-voiced character actor Andy Devine, who was born in Flagstaff and grew up here.

From Kingman, take historic Route 66 west over the rugged Black Mountains toward Bullhead City. Take time to poke around funky **Oatman**, a mining camp turned tourist trap. Merchants will sell you feed for feral burros that hang around town waiting for handouts; don't let one of them follow you home. From here, the highway tilts downward and hits State Route 95 at the Colorado River's **Lake Mohave.** Turn north for the short drive into **Bullhead City.**

Most visitors find Bullhead interesting only for its water recreation. For retirees and Snowbirds, however, the greatest draw is its balmy winters. If you feel like pulling a few slot machine handles, you can drive across a bridge to Laughlin, or leave your car in a parking lot on the north end of Bullhead and catch a shuttle boat.

Heading south from Bullhead City, you'll stay rather close to the river until you bump into I-40. Drive eastward briefly and then head south on Highway 95 to **Lake Havasu City.** As we discussed in Chapter Eight, the attraction here is the **London Bridge**, brought stone-by-stone from England and reassembled over a peninsula of Lake Havasu. Promoters call it the second most visited attraction in Arizona, after the Grand Canyon. It *is* interesting, sitting in the desert, looking like a left-over Roman ruin in North Africa. Unfortunately, an "English village" built around its base is rather tacky.

From Havasu, continue south on Highway 95 to **Parker Dam**, which offers brief self-guided tours. If you turn west at the "business route" sign just below **Buckskin Mountain State Park**, you'll drive along the **Parker Strip**. It's a water recreation area lined with resorts, marinas and RV parks. The route takes you into **Parker,** an unassuming little town surrounded by the Colorado River Reservation. There's a Native American casino here, in case you didn't spend all of your quarters in Laughlin. The **Colorado River Indian Tribes Museum** on the south end of town is worth a pause; open weekdays 8 to 5; (928) 669-9211.

Below Parker, the highway swings away from the river, cuts arrow-straight through boring desert and hits I-10 at **Quartzsite**, which we have unkindly called the ugliest town in Arizona. You can stop by the little **Quartzsite Museum** on the north side frontage road if it's open; the hours are rather irregular. Before leaving town, stop by the local cemetery and visit a curious pyramidal monument to Haiji Ali. He was a Syrian who came over as part of a late nineteenth century experiment to use camels for Southwestern desert transport. The program flopped so "Hi Jolly" hung around Quartzsite and became something of a local character.

# YUMA TO ORGAN PIPE & KITT PEAK

Below Quartzsite, highway 95 stays away from *Rio Colorado* until it hits **Yuma**, the only town of substance along the river. With a population pushing 80,000, it offers a fine historic park, the "notorious" territorial prison and a museum fashioned from an elegant early day residence. From Yuma, you might want to swing west and follow I-8 into California, where you'll see sand dunes right out of a Lawrence of Arabia film.

**For area information** ● Yuma Convention & Visitors Bureau, 202 S. First Ave., Yuma, AZ 85364; (928) 376-0100; *www.visityuma.com.*

### The attractions

**Century House Museum** ● *240 Madison Ave.; (928) 782-1841. Tuesday-Saturday 10 to 4.* □ Italian pioneer E.F. Sanguinetti made his fortune as a Yuma merchant and developer, and he spent a lot of it on this spacious nineteenth century house and garden. The 1870s adobe is now a fine museum with exhibits concerning early Colorado River sternwheelers, mining, railroading, settlers and native cultures.

**Yuma Crossing State Historic Park** ● *100 N. Fourth Avenue at the Colorado River; (928) 329-0471. Daily 10 to 5.* □ This site preserves two important elements in Western history—a ford across the Colorado River that opened California to overland travelers from the east, and a major Army supply center. Several buildings survive from the original depot, which operated from 1864 until 1883. The original storehouse, office, commanding officers quarters and other structures have been refurbished and furnished to the period. A riverside trail links the historic park and Yuma Territorial Prison.

**Yuma Territorial Prison State Historic Park** ● *Prison Hill Road; (928) 783-4771. Daily 8 to 5.* □ Hollywood made this old prison more notorious than it really was. Actually, it was designed to be a model lockup with a library, schooling and even crafts classes. However, it had no air conditioning and summers were beastly, even if the guards weren't. It was closed in 1909 and what remains are a few cell blocks and the main guard tower built over a water tank. A museum constructed on the mess hall foundation displays prison artifacts, scowling photos of inmates and graphics concerning prisoners and the men who guarded them.

There's not much south of Yuma, other than the rather large and dusty Mexican border town of **San Luis**, which offers some handicraft and curio shops. If you head east on I-8 to **Gila Bend** and then swing south onto State Route 85, you'll hit the interesting old company mining town of **Ajo**. Check out its Spanish colonnade style shopping plaza. Also worth a pause are the small **Ajo Historical Museum** in a former Indian mission, and an overlook to the **New Cornelia** open pit copper mine. From Ajo, continue south to one of our favorite patches of desert.

*Organ Pipe Cactus National Monument* ● *Just south of Ajo; (520) 387-6849. Park open 24 hours; visitor center open daily 8 to 5.* ☐ Arizona's largest and most remote national monument preserves some of the world's most striking desert wilderness. It is named for a large cactus with multiple arms that reach upward from a common base, supposedly resembling organ pipes. This is but one botanical resident of this mountainous rock garden. It's busy with giant saguaro and hundreds of other desert plants, including 29 species of cactus.

Head briefly north from Organ Pipe and turn east at the oddly named town of **Why** onto State Route 86. You'll travel through the barren desert of the huge **Tohono O'odham Indian Reservation**. As you leave southwestern Arizona and approach Tucson, follow a winding road up to the world's largest astronomical facility.

*Kitt Peak National Observatory* ● *Off State Highway 86; (928) 318-8726. Daily 9 to 4; film and guided tours at 10, 11:30, and 1:30.* ☐ This busy complex offers extensive visitor facilities, including a reception center, astronomical museum and theater. Among its exhibits are artifacts and crafts of the Tohono O'odham people, whose land the observatory occupies. Self-guiding tours take you into structures that house three of the observatory's thirteen telescopes. A highlight attraction is the monster McMath solar telescope, built into an angular shaft thrusting 300 feet into the earth.

### Chapter Fourteen
# PHOENIX & SURROUNDS
## VALLEY OF THE SUN ATTRACTIONS

---

**I**t will come as no surprise that the greater Phoenix area is a major destination for tourists as well as for job-seekers, retirees and Snowbirds. Although Phoenix boasts several mountain and desert parks, most of the lures here are man-made—fine museums, huge air conditioned malls and elegant resorts. Phoenix has been rated second in the nation for visitor services, accommodations and dining by the Zagat Survey. Phoenix and Scottsdale have more Mobile Travel Guide five-star resorts and four and five-diamond AAA resorts than any other area in the country.

With all of this, it is still a remarkably economical city in which to play tourist. A survey revealed that it was the third least expensive major city in the country for lodging and meals. Los Angeles costs nearly twice as much and New York is nearly three times as pricey.

**For area information** ● Greater Phoenix Convention and Visitors Bureau, 400 E. Van Buren St., Suite 600, Phoenix, AZ 85004-2290; (877) CALL-PHX or (602) 254-6500; *www.phoenixcvb.com.*

### The attractions

**Arizona Hall of Fame Museum** ● *1101 W. Washington St. (near 11th Street, in the former Carnegie Public Library); (602) 255- 4675. Weekdays 8 to 5.* ☐ The museum features changing exhibits concerning Arizona's famous people. Only two exhibits are permanent—the Arizona Woman's Hall of Fame and some interesting cast-from-life statues representing typical people of the state's past.

***Arizona Military Museum*** • *5636 E. McDowell Rd.; (602) 267-2676. Tuesday and Thursday 10 to 4, weekends 1 to 4.* □ This unprofessional but nicely done museum is housed in the Depression era Arizona National Guard arsenal. Exhibits trace the history of the military as it relates to Arizona, starting with Francisco Vásquez de Coronado's 1540 quest for the fictitious golden cities of Cibola, and continuing through Arizona's involvement in contemporary conflicts.

***Arizona Mining and Mineral Museum*** • *1502 W. Washington St. (Fifteenth Avenue), (602) 255-3791. Weekdays 8 to 5, Saturday 11 to 4; free.* □ Appropriate to Arizona, this museum focuses on the mining end of minerals, with core samples, tools and mine models, plus an extensive collection of rocks and gems. No ordinary rock house, it features unusual exhibits such as "pseudo fossils"—minerals that have fooled even experts into thinking they were of fossil origin.

***Arizona Science Center*** • *Washington and Fifth in the new Heritage and Science Park; (602) 716-2000. Daily 10 to 5.* □ This is one of the most advanced science centers in America, with a focus on medical advances, space age technology and computers. The center has four floors of science displays, plus a planetarium, big-screen theater and an excellent science store.

***Arizona State Capitol Museum*** • *1700 W. Washington (17th Avenue); (602) 542-4675. Weekdays 8 to 5; longer hours during the January to May legislative session.* □ Arizona outgrew its copper domed state capitol in 1972 and moved to an adjacent highrise. Sitting in the shadow of its replacement, the old Grecian style tufa and granite relic has become a museum of the state's early government. Senate and house chambers are furnished as they appeared when Arizona gained statehood in 1912, with wooden desks, tulip chandeliers and spittoons. Other rooms serve as museums to the state's political past.

***Desert Botanical Garden*** • *1201 N. Galvin Parkway (in Papago Park); (602) 941-1225. Daily 7 to 8 May through September and 8 to 8 the rest of the year.* □ In Arizona's finest botanical garden, you'll see desert plants from around the globe, including more than half of the world's cactus varieties. March to May is the garden's peak blooming season. A special exhibit shows how the Hohokam and other Indians used plants to survive and thrive in this dry environment.

***Hall of Flame Museum of Firefighting*** • *6101 E. Van Buren St. (in Papago Park); (602) 275-3473. Monday-Saturday 9 to 5 and Sunday noon to 5.* □ Every kid of every age whose pulse is quickened by the shriek of a siren and the red flash of a fire engine will love this place. It's the world's largest museum of firefighting equipment, exhibiting glittering ranks of hand-drawn pumpers, early hook-and-ladder rigs and other smoke-chasing classics. More than 100 restored fire engines are on display.

***The Heard Museum*** • *2301 N. Central Ave.; (602) 252-8840. Daily 9:30 to 5.* □ Quite simply, the Heard is the finest museum in Arizona and probably the world's greatest monument to native people. Although it dates back to 1929, this treasury of American Indian cultures is a state-of-the-art facility. With more than 30,000 objects to draw from, its staff exercises artistic discipline in keeping displays both simple and topical. Major exhibits provide an enlightening study of Arizona's ancient and modern native cultures, with artifacts, graphics and mock-ups.

**Heritage Square** • *Sixth Street and Monroe (a block east of Civic Plaza); (602) 262-5029.* □ This is a scene from Phoenix yesterday—ten structures dating from the late nineteenth and early twentieth centuries. They're gathered around an attractive patio garden, shaded by a curved-wood lath house. Surprisingly, all but three are in their original locations.

**Phoenix Art Museum** • *1625 N. Central Ave. (McDowell Road); (602) 257-1222. Tuesday-Sunday 10 to 5.* □ The American West, contemporary art and old world classics are featured in this large, versatile art museum. A major renovation and expansion program was completed in 1996, nearly doubling its exhibit space. Permanent collections include a gallery of Western Art, galleries of early European and American art, an Asian gallery, costume displays and decorative arts.

**Phoenix Museum of History** • *105 N. Fifth Street at Washington; (602) 253-2734. Monday-Saturday 9 to 5 and Sunday noon to 5.* □ This museum in the Heritage and Science Park focuses on the region's history from the territorial era to the "Romantic Movement" of the 1920s. Exhibits include Hohokam artifacts, battleship Arizona mementos, an egg from a former Phoenix ostrich farm, a rifle collection and modern Kachina dolls.

**Phoenix Zoo** • *455 N. Galvin Parkway (in Papago Park); (602) 273-1341. Daily 9 to 5 Labor Day through April and 7:30 to 4 the rest of the year.* □ This would be a pleasant place to stroll even if it weren't stocked with 7,600 animals. Occupying 125 acres of Papago Park, the zoo encloses a fine slice of desert terrain. It's landscaped with giant eucalyptus trees, pools, trickling streams and shady patios. Among its more interesting animal enclosures are the Baboon Kingdom and Tropical Flights rainforest.

**Pioneer Arizona Living History Museum** • *Off Pioneer Road at I-17; (623) 465-1052. Tuesday-Sunday 9 to 5, hours may be shorter during the summer.* □ Since 1956, a non-profit group has been assembling an historic Arizona community on a chunk of desert 30 miles north of Phoenix. About two dozen buildings—either originals or reconstructions—occupy the site. It's a sampler town of Arizona from its earliest Spanish days to statehood. Although the site seems a bit disconnected and exhibits need sprucing up, it's worth the drive. To reach it, follow I-17 north and take exit 225 (Pioneer Road) west.

*Pueblo Grande Museum* • *4619 E. Washington St. (44th Street); (602) 945-0901. Monday-Saturday 9 to 4:45, Sunday 1 to 4:45; Ruins Trail closes at 4:30.* □ Surrounded by the expanding city, this site preserves a large Hohokam settlement. A Ruins Trail leads to the "Platform Mound" the size of a football field, which has been partially excavated. Ridges and depressions suggest the shapes of an ancient ball court and canal banks. Other exhibits include a reconstructed pit house and above-ground adobe dwelling.

# PHOENIX NEIGHBORS

Once a Western style town way out in the lonely desert, Scottsdale has become an upscale residential and commercial center, merging its expanding borders into Phoenix. Carefree and Cave Creek are two hamlets on the Valley of the Sun's fringe. Carefree is an attractive planned community while Cave Creek is a funky old mining town that draws folks to several "saloon restaurants" for cowboy steaks. Among Carefree's lures are the world's largest sundial, and El Pedrigal Marketplace, a shopping center that resembles a cross between Frank Lloyd Wright architecture and Tune Town.

Fountain Hills is a newly developing community in scenic desert slopes northeast of Scottsdale and southeast of Carefree. Its claims to fame are the world's tallest fountain, gushing from a downtown park, and a close-contact animal center called Out of Africa.

*For area information* • Carefree/Cave Creek Chamber of Commerce, 7207 E. Carefree Dr. (P.O. Box 734), Carefree, AZ 85337; (480) 488-3381; *www.carefree-cavecreek.com.*

Fountain Hills Chamber of Commerce, P.O. Box 17598, Fountain Hills, AZ 85268; (480) 837-1654; *www.fhchamberofcommerce.org.*

## The attractions

*Cave Creek Museum* • *Basin and Skyline, Cave Creek; (480) 488-2764. Wednesday-Sunday 1 to 4:30 October through May; closed the rest of the year.* □ This typically small town historical museum displays relics of Cave Creek's past as a mining and ranching center. A model pit house and Indian artifacts trace early Native American cultures in the area.

*Cosanti* • *6433 Doubletree Ranch Road (Invergorden), Scottsdale; (480) 948-6145. Monday-Saturday 9 to 5 and Sunday 11 to 5.* □ Paolo Soleri is a visionary working on an environmentally correct city called Arcosanti, 68 miles north of Phoenix (see Chapter Twelve). Cosanti is his home, workshop and art studio in Paradise Valley, north of Scottsdale. Here, he and his students create bronze and ceramic bells and wind chimes and other decorator items. Like Arcosanti, his Cosanti studio has an extra-terrestrial look with pre-cast concrete free-form shapes. It suggests melted geometry, with a kind of doughy primitive look. Yoda would feel right at home here.

***Fleischer Museum*** • *17207 N. Perimeter Dr., Scottsdale; (480) 585-3108. Daily 10 to 4; tours by appointment. Free; contributions accepted.* ☐ The imposing atrium lobby and second floor of the Franchise Finance Corporation building have been given over to a fine museum of American impressionistic art. Exhibits focus primarily on California and the West, although special shows are sometimes featured. Several bronze sculptures occupy a glass domed rotunda courtyard beyond the foyer.

***Out of Africa*** • *9736 N. Fort McDowell Rd. (near Beeline Highway), Fountain Hills; (480) 837-7779. Tuesday-Sunday 9:30 to 5 October through May; Wednesday-Friday 4 to 9:30 June through September; then Saturday 9:30 to 9:30 and Sunday 9:30 to 5 the rest of the year.* ☐ This small and rather snugly packed animal park features a variety of big cats and other animals. The cat population includes spotted, black and snow leopards; mountain lions; and Bengal and Siberian tigers. It's fun to watch the "Tiger Splash" when big cats, bears and other critters swim with handlers. Visitors can get snacks and meals at the Kalahari Cafe and buy African gifts and cultural artifacts at two gift shops.

***Rawhide*** • *23023 N. Scottsdale Rd. (Pinnacle Peak Rd.), Scottsdale; (480) 502-1880. Daily 11 to 10.* ☐ "How the West was fun," says the sign out front. Rawhide is the largest and best of several wanna-be cowboy towns in the area, with a couple of dozen false-front stores housing boutiques, curio shops, saloons and restaurants. Visitors can catch a stagecoach, witness a shoot-out, feed goats in a petting zoo and watch a "meller- drammer" in the Moonshine Theatre. An Old West museum boasts 5,000 items—from high-button shoes to antiques.

***Scottsdale Center for the Arts*** • *7380 E. Second St., Scottsdale; (480) 874-4610. Tuesday-Saturday 10 to 5 (until 8 Thursday) and Sunday noon 5* ☐ The Valley of the Sun's finest multiple arts complex, the Scottsdale Center houses a performing arts theater, the Scottsdale Museum of Contemporary Art and an excellent arts and museum shop. The facility was completed in 1999 as the cultural hub of Scottsdale.

***Scottsdale Historical Museum*** • *7333 E. Civic Center Mall; (480) 945-4499. Wednesday-Saturday 10 to 5, Sunday noon to 4.* ☐ Small and nicely done, this museum exhibits original furniture of Scottsdale pioneers Winfield and Helen Scott, along with artifacts and photos of the early days. Featured displays include an early American kitchen and a mock-up of a turn-of-the-last-century school room.

***Taliesin West*** • *114th Street at Cactus, Scottsdale; (480) 860-2700. Bookstore-visitor center open daily 8:30 to 5:30; various hours for tours.* ☐ The former winter home and studio of legendary architect Frank Lloyd Wright, Taliesin West is an intriguing mix of concrete and stone that seems fused into the desert instead of rising from it. The complex sits on a 600-acre alluvial fan, sweeping down from the McDowell Mountains. Wright's designs involved the repeated play of geometric forms, using natural materials to embody nature, man and architecture. Taliesin West is mostly triangular, with red sandstone and concrete wedges and desert stone sculpted into the sloping hill. Docents give comprehensive tours of the facility while discussing Wright's architectural and personal philosophies.

# TEMPE-MESA

These are essentially bedroom communities southeast of Phoenix. While not tourist centers, they offer some worthy attractions.

**For area information** ● Tempe Chamber of Commerce, P.O. Box 28500, Tempe, AZ 85285-8500; (480) 967-7891.

Mesa Convention & Visitors Bureau, P.O. Box 5820 (120 N. Center St.), Mesa, AZ 85211-5820; (800) 283-6372 or (480) 827- 4700; *www.mesachamber.com.*

## The attractions

**Arizona Historical Society Museum** ● *1300 N. College Ave., Tempe; (480) 929-0292. Weekdays 9 to 4, Saturday 10 to 4 and Sunday noon to 4.* ☐ This fine facility captures Arizona's yesterdays, from the coming of the Spanish, the Mexican era, cowboys and bad guys to the twentieth century irrigation projects that blossomed the desert. The structure is built around a sunny courtyard and gurgling stream.

**Arizona State University Campus** ● *Visitor Center at the southeast corner of the campus at Apache and Rural roads; (480) 965-3633. Weekdays 9 to 4:30.* ☐ Green lawns and palms create a park-like setting for ASU's imposing gathering of brick buildings. The centerpiece is Frank Lloyd Wright's Gammage Center for the Performing Arts, a dramatic sandstone pink structure of circles within circles. The campus contains several art museums, a planetarium, geology museum and gallery of design.

**Champlin Fighter Museum** ● *4636 Fighter Aces Dr. (Falcon Field, off McKellips Road), Mesa; (480) 830-4540. Daily 10 to 5 mid-September to mid-April and 8:30 to 3:30 the rest of the year.* ☐ Snoopy would love this place. You can fantasize dogfights with the Red Baron and other aces at this impressive gathering of fighter planes from the two world wars, Korea, Vietnam and Desert Storm. Three dozen planes, either restored originals or airworthy replicas, seem ready to take off into the wild blue yonder.

**Commemorative Air Force Museum** ● *2017 McKellips Road, Mesa; (480) 924-1940. Daily 10 to 4.* ☐ Operated by former World War II pilots and others with an interest in military aviation, this museum is devoted to collecting, restoring and flying military aircraft. The collection, while not large, is impressive. It includes an airworthy Flying Fortress, a C-26 Invader that fought in World War II, Korea and Vietnam; and a rare German Heinkel Blitz Bomber. (It originally was called the Confederate Air Force Museum until its members were asked to be more politically correct.)

*Mesa Southwest Museum* • *53 N. MacDonald St. (First Street), Mesa; (480) 644-2230 or 644-2169. Tuesday-Saturday 10 to 5, Sunday 1 to 5.* ☐ One of the best museums in the state, this excellent archive effectively captures the area's history and pre-history. Visitors pass through a gem and mineral exhibit and arrive at "Dinosaur Mountain," an imposing display of life-sized animated creatures on terraces of a large red rock formation. Other exhibits include "Dineh: Life and Cultures of the Navajo," mockups of several territorial prisons, a Sonoran Desert walk, plus artifacts from Arizona's Spanish colonial period. A really fun exhibit, "Arizona and the Movies," focuses on the many films shot here.

# PHOENIX-TUCSON CORRIDOR

Interstate 10 that runs diagonally between Phoenix and Tucson is Arizona's busiest freeway. Highway 79, just to the northeast, is a much more genteel route. Several tourist lures can be encountered along each route.

*For area information* • Apache Junction Chamber of Commerce, P.O. Box 1747, Apache Junction, AZ 85217-1747; (480) 982-3234; *www.apachejunctioncoc.com.*

Greater Casa Grande Chamber of Commerce, 575 N. Marshall St., Casa Grande, AZ 85222-5244; (800) 916-1515 or (520) 836-2125; *www.casagrandechamber.org.*

The U.S. 60 freeway running southeast from Phoenix will take you to **Apache Junction**. It's a growing community in an attractive desert setting, below the grimly fascinating ramparts of the **Superstition Mountains**. You've probably heard the tale of the Lost Dutchman Mine. A German prospector named Jacob Waltz supposedly found a rich gold cache in the Superstitions in the 1860s, although he died without revealing its whereabouts.

You can explore the foothills of these rough-hewn mountains and indulge in a bit of water sports by following State Route 88 northeast from Apache Junction. Known locally as the Apache Trail, it takes you to **Lost Dutchman State Park** with camping, picnicking and hiking. Farther along the "Trail" is the old mining town of **Goldfield**, which now functions as a rustic tourist attraction.

Continuing east, you'll pass the tiny and touristy hamlet of **Tortilla Flat** and then enter rugged **Salt River Canyon**, where dams of the Salt River Project have created several reservoirs. A rough but passable road continues through the canyon's scenic and rocky ramparts to **Theodore Roosevelt Dam** and **Tonto National Monument** which preserves a small native cliff dwelling. It's open daily 8 to 5, with a nicely done interpretive center and a short trail leading through an impressively thick forest of saguaro cactus to the ruin; (928) 467-2241.

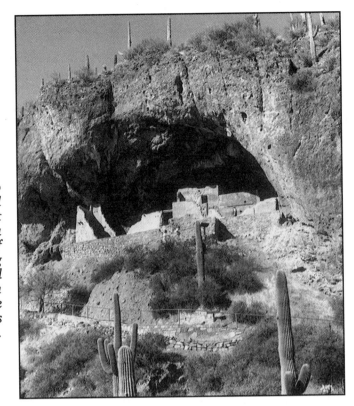

*Tonto National Monument preserves a small cliff dwelling surrounded by an attractive cactus garden.*

## Florence

If you drive south from Apache Junction on Highway 79, you'll encounter the attractive Western style town of Florence. Check out the **Florence Townsite National Historic District** and the gingerbread trimmed **Pinal County Courthouse.** And save an hour or so for an interesting historical museum:

**McFarland State Historic Park** • *Main Street and Ruggles Avenue; (520) 868-5216. Thursday-Monday 8 to 5.* □ This adobe functioned as Pinal County's courthouse, sheriff's office and jail from 1878 to 1891. Among its exhibits are the old courtroom with its jury box, wooden pews and judge's bench. A special display focuses on local boy-makes-good Ernest W. McFarland. He authored the G.I. Bill of Rights as a U.S. senator and served as chief justice of the Arizona Supreme Court.

As you continue south toward Tucson, Highway 79 becomes the **Pinal Pioneer Parkway**, passing through attractive desert gardens. Signs identify the roadside flora, so think of it as a 55-mile-an-hour nature trail. The highway eventually skirts the Santa Catalina Mountains and enters the northern portal of Tucson.

Interstate 10 is a much faster route between Arizona's two metropolitan centers, although it's considerably less interesting. However, it does offer three visitor lures:

*Gila River Cultural Center* • *Casa Blanca Road, Sacaton; (520) 315-3411. Daily 8 to 5.* ☐ More than 30 different tribes and 2,000 years of Native American history are represented in this modern cultural center on the Gila River Indian Reservation. It's actually a blend of four facilities—the Gila River Museum, with historical exhibits; the Arts and Crafts Center; Heritage Park, with reconstructions of Indian dwellings; and a restaurant serving fry bread and other typical Native American fare.

*Casa Grande Ruins National Monument* • *1100 Ruins Dr., Coolidge; (520) 723-3172. Daily 8 to 5* ☐ Covered by a metal roof to keep it from melting back into the earth, this is the tallest and perhaps most mysterious of Arizona's many pueblos. It's four stories high with four-foot thick walls at the base to support its 2,800-ton mass. The structure was the centerpiece of a Hohokam village, occupied for about a century, until 1450 A.D. Archaeologists don't know why Casa Grande was built, or why it was abandoned.

*Picacho Peak State Park* • *Near the town of Picacho, off I-10; (520) 466-3183. Daily 8 to 5.* ☐ This park at the base of a peak shaped like a fat thumb has picnic areas and hiking trails, including a path to the 1,400-foot summit of the stone upcropping. Confederate and Union forces clashed near here in 1862 in the westernmost battle of the Civil War. These weren't regular troops, but members of the Texas Volunteers and California Volunteers. Although the Texans won the first skirmish, killing four Californians, they realized that reinforcements would soon arrive in this pro-Union territory, so they hightailed it back to Texas.

## Chapter Fifteen

# TUCSON & BEYOND

## TOURING "THE OLD ADOBE" & SURROUNDS

---

**A**rizona's second largest city rivals its big sister in both the quality and quantity of its tourist attractions. It offers a fine mix of indoor culture and outdoor recreation. Five mountain ranges rim Tucson's high desert basin and a 17,000-acre slice of this terrain has been preserved in Tucson Mountain Park. This vast swatch of desert shelters several major attractions.

One of Arizona's oldest cities, Tucson is an appealing blend of cosmopolitan, old pueblo and the great outdoors. All of this—and it claims to have more days of sunshine than any other major American city.

**For area information** • Metropolitan Tucson Convention & Visitors Bureau, 110 S. Church Ave., Suite 9100, Tucson, AZ 85701; (800) 638-8350 or (520) 624-1817; *www.visittucson.org.*

### The attractions

**Arizona Historical Society Museum** • *949 E. Second St. (Park Avenue); (520) 628-5774. Monday-Saturday 10 to 4, Sunday noon to 4; free.* ☐ Located just outside the University of Arizona campus, it covers the area's settlement from the arrival of the Spanish to the development of modern Arizona. Uncluttered, informative exhibits tell the state's story with cattle brands, Bull Durham pouches, highwheeler bicycles and period costumes.

***Arizona-Sonora Desert Museum*** • *2021 N. Kinney Rd. (in Tucson Mountain Park); (520) 883-2702. Daily 7:30 to 5 March through September and 8:30 to 5 the rest of the year.* ☐ Planners re-invented the museum when they created this outstanding indoor-outdoor complex. It is the finest natural history museum in Arizona and Tucson's most-visited attraction. The museum takes its name from the states of Arizona, U.S.A., and Sonora, Mexico. Its primary focus is ecological, telling the story of the plants, animals and geology of the Sonoran Desert that covers much of these two states. Particularly impressive is the Earth Sciences Center, an elaborate grotto with an elaborate mock-up of a limestone cavern and displays explaining the formation of the earth.

***Arizona State Museum*** • *University Avenue at Park Avenue; (520) 621-6302. Monday-Saturday 10 to 5 and Sunday noon to 5.* ☐ Occupying two buildings just inside the University of Arizona's main gate, this museum focuses on prehistoric and modern Indian cultures of the area. An outstanding exhibit, "Paths of Life: American Indians of the Southwest," features the ten major tribes of Arizona, depicting their origins, history and present-day lives. A mezzanine is stuffed with stuffed animals indigenous to Arizona, along with a gemstone and Hohokam exhibit.

***De Grazia Gallery in the Sun*** • *6300 N. Swan Rd. (Skyline Drive); (800) 545-2185 or (520) 299-9191. Daily 10 to 4.* ☐ The late Ted De Grazia developed a large following with his impressionistic, whimsical style of painting. Simple, quick brush strokes created color-splashed Indians, Mexicans, roadrunners and other Southwestern subjects. After his death, a foundation was created to continue operating his rustic gallery and gift shop. Exhibits are changed periodically, drawn from his extensive collection, and replicas of his art is on sale.

***El Presidio Historic District*** • *Bounded by Pennington, Church, Washington and Main.* ☐ Although its adobe walls have long since melted back into the sand, the site of Tucson's original walled city retains some of its yesterday flavor. Many of its nineteenth century adobes house galleries and restaurants. Signposts and plaques relate the history of homes, many dating back nearly two centuries.

***Flandrau Science Center and Planetarium*** • *Northwest corner of University and Cherry; (520) 621-STAR. Monday-Saturday 9 to 5 and Sunday noon to 5, plus Wednesday-Saturday evenings 7 to 9 for public telescope viewing.* ☐ This is a science museum as well as a planetarium. Push assorted buttons and levers to learn about holography, radio waves and Light Amplification by Stimulated Emission Radiation—and now you know that LASER is an acronym. A large mineral museum downstairs displays hundreds of specimens from around the world.

***Fort Lowell Museum*** • *Craycroft and Fort Lowell roads; (520) 885-3832. Wednesday- Saturday 10 to 4.* ☐ Part of a large city park and recreation center, Fort Lowell Museum is a reconstruction of a military camp established in 1873. Structures include the commanding officers quarters with period furnishings and historical displays, and the "kitchen building," with exhibits of the fort's development and excavations of early Indian sites.

**International Wildlife Museum** • *4800 W. Gates Pass Rd. (Camino de Oeste); (520) 617-1439. Weekdays 9 to 5 and weekends 10 to 6.* ☐ The museum is enclosed in a curious architectural blend of feudal castle and French Foreign Legion fort. It's focus supposedly is on conservation, and to "promote wildlife appreciation." It does have some fine educational displays on these subjects. However, some exhibits defend hunting and one large room is filled with more than a hundred trophies. Bodyless Cape buffalo, rhinos, elephants and assorted antelopes stare morosely from the walls.

**Mission San Xavier del Bac** • *San Xavier Road (nine miles south, off I-19); (520) 294-2624. Church, museum and gift shop open daily 7 to 5. Daily mass at 8:30 a.m., Saturday vigil at 5:30 p.m. and Sunday masses at 8, 11 and 12:30.* ☐ With its Spanish-colonial architecture, gleaming white walls and brown façade, the "White Dove of the Desert" is perhaps Arizona's most beautiful structure. Its roots reach back to the earliest days, when Spanish mission builder Father Eusebio Kino ministered to the people of the village of Bac. Located on the San Xavier Reservation, it still serves Native Americans. Its handsomely restored sanctuary, chapel, a small museum and other rooms are open to visitors.

**Mount Lemmon Recreation Area** • *Reached via the Catalina Highway from northeast Tucson. For information: Santa Catalina Ranger District, 5700 N. Sabino Canyon Rd., (520) 749-8700.* ☐ The Catalina Highway spirals quickly from the saguaro-thick foothills of the Catalina Mountains to the piney forests of Mount Lemmon. Along the way, you'll see fantastic roadside rock formations that look like misplaced Easter Island statues. In winter, you can hit the slopes at Mount Lemmon Ski Valley. One of its lifts operates the year around for the benefit of sightseers; call for hours—(520) 576-1400

**Old Tucson Studios** • *201 S. Kinney Rd. (Tucson Mountain Park); (520) 883-0100. Daily 10 to 6.* ☐ Old Tucson is Universal Studios with hay bales—a working memorial to all those shoot-outs that have blazed across the Arizona landscape. It began in 1939 when Columbia Pictures built a set to produce one of the first big movie epics, *Arizona.* An entrepreneur later bought the old set, added more weather-worn buildings and created a permanent Western movie set. It suffered considerable damage in a 1995 fire although much of it has been rebuilt. Visitors can watch shoot-outs on Main Street, pan for gold and sip suds in the Royal Oak Saloon.

**Pima Air and Space Museum** • *6000 E. Valencia Rd. (Wilmot); (520) 574-0462. Daily 9 to 5.* ☐ If you've ever wanted to soar on fanciful wings of eagles, you'll love this place. More than 150 aircraft are on display, from a realistic full-scale model of the Wright brothers craft to a mach-3 Lockheed SR-71 Blackbird and several Russian MiGs. Exhibits trace the development of aviation from pre-Wright brothers attempts to space flight.

**Reid Park Zoo** ● *1100 S. Randolph Way (enter Lakeshore Drive off 22nd Street); (520) 791-4022. Daily 9 to 4.* ☐ This fine little zoo, landscaped with green lawns shaded by eucalyptus and palm trees, has a busy collection of giraffes, lions, tigers, hippos, primates and more. Some of its critters are housed in modern open-air enclosures; birds flit around a large aviary. About 500 critters occupy the zoo, which conducts ongoing conservation, educational and research programs.

**Sabino Canyon** ● *5700 N. Sabino Canyon Rd.; (520) 749-8700. Visitor center open 8:30 to 4:30 weekdays and 8 to 4:30 weekends. Trams depart frequently for Sabino Canyon and adjacent Bear Canyon.* ☐ Just minutes from downtown, steep- walled Sabino and Bear canyons cut deeply into the flanks of the Santa Catalina Mountains. Forests of saguaro cactus march up rugged canyon walls. Ultimately, they give way to forests of pine. Hiking trails lead into the more remote heights. Access is limited to trams, which make 45-minute round trips for sightseeing or to drop the more ambitious at various trailheads.

**Saguaro National Park** ● *Tucson Mountain section is off Sandario Road in Tucson Mountain Park; (520) 733-5153; park gates open daily 7 to 10; visitor center open 8:30 to 5. Rincon Mountain section is off Old Spanish Trail east of Tucson; (520) 733-5158; gates open 6 to dusk, visitor center 8:30 to 5.* ☐ The two sections of Saguaro National Park serve the same function—to preserve and exhibit their giant cactus namesake, plus other desert flora. Saguaro West, the Tucson Mountain section, has more bountiful cactus gardens than its eastern counterpart, although it doesn't have the elevation range. Saguaro East, off Old Spanish Trail, climbs through five climate zones from the desert to conifer ramparts of the Rincon Mountains, offering a rich cross-section of desert topography.

**Tohono Chul Park** ● *7366 N. Paseo del Norte (northwest corner of Ina and Oracle); (520) 742-6455. Park open daily 7 to sunset, Tea Room 8 to 5, and gift gallery 9:30 to 5.* ☐ Privately endowed Tohono Chul preserves a patch of desert landscape in the middle of spreading Tucson. Nature trails, patios, shade ramadas, two gift shops, an exhibit center and the Southwest style Teas Room provide refuge from the growing city.

**Tucson Botanical Gardens** ● *2150 N. Alvernon Way (Grant); (520) 326-9255. Daily 8:30 to 4:30.* ☐ Once the estate of a local nurseryman, the garden rambles over five and a half acres, with pleasant paths leading through lush plant life. Among its displays are an Australian garden, herb garden, historical garden with English ivy and such, and a Tohono O'odham garden with crops typical of early Native Americans.

**Tucson Mountain Park** ● *Eight miles west of downtown; (520) 749-2690. Daily 7 a.m. to sunset.* ☐ This huge Pima County park sprawls over 17,000 acres of the rough-hewn Tucson Mountain foothills. It provides instant desert wilderness to residents of the nearby city. Within the park's boundaries are three other attractions—the Tucson Mountain section of Saguaro National Park, Arizona-Sonora Desert Museum and Old Tucson Studios. Park facilities include picnic areas, hiking and riding trails and a campground.

**Tucson Museum of Art** ● *140 N. Main Ave. (Alameda, next to El Presidio Historic District); (520) 624-2333. Monday-Saturday 10 to 4 and Sunday noon to 4.* ☐ Galleries are arranged along downward spiraling ramps in this contemporary museum on the edge of El Presidio Historic District. The complex also includes a sculpture garden and five houses built between 1850 and 1907. Galleries display large collections of Western art and pre- Colombian artifacts.

**University of Arizona campus** ● *Visitor Center at Cherry and University open Monday-Friday 7:30 to 5 and Saturday 9 to noon; (520) 621-5130.* ☐ Located in the heart of Tucson, the university's expansive campus is a major cultural resource as well as an important learning center. Eight museums and galleries occupy its sturdy red brick buildings. Three major public attractions—Flandrau Science Center, Arizona State Museum and Arizona Historical Society Museum—appear above on this list.

# SOUTH TO NOGALES

Interstate 19 provides a fast link between Tucson and the twin border towns of Nogales, Arizona and Mexico. The first substantial habitat you'll encounter, other than dusty little Sahuarita, is the planned community of **Green Valley**. Nearby is the Titan Missile Museum, a grimly fascinating reminder of the cold war.

Twenty miles south of Green Valley is dusty little **Tubac**. Arizona's oldest Spanish community, it's now a haven for artists, individualists and retirees. Slices of Arizona's history are preserved in a state park here, and in a national historic park a few miles south.

Continuing below Tubac, you'll soon hit Mexico at **Nogales**, which offers the best *Latino* shopping of any Arizona border town. On the Arizona side, Nogales offers an interesting historical museum that's worth a pause.

**For area information** ● Green Valley Chamber of Commerce, P.O. Box 566, Green Valley, AZ 85622; (520) 625-7575; *www.greenvalleyazchamber.com.*

Tubac Chamber of Commerce, P.O. Box 1866, Tubac, AZ 85646; (520) 398-2704, www.tubacaz.com.

Nogales-Santa Cruz County Chamber of Commerce, 123 W. Kino Parkway, Nogales, AZ 85621; (520) 287-3685.

## Attractions, in order of appearance

***Titan Missile Museum*** • *Green Valley Road (Exit 69, then west), Green Valley; (520) 625-7736. Guided tours from 9 to 4, daily from November through April and Wednesday-Sunday the rest of the year.* ☐ This is one of the most fascinating tours in Arizona, through a decommissioned Titan missile silo. The tour begins with a video about the history of the Titan and its deadly nuclear delivery capability. Then visitors are taken deep into the "hardened" command center and to the silo itself, where a 110-foot-tall Titan is aimed skyward. Of course, it has been rendered harmless.

***Tubac Presidio State Historic Park*** • *Downtown Tubac; (520) 398-2252. Daily 8 to 5.* ☐ Little remains of the presidio that was built here in 1752, although an exhibit center effectively traces its history. Nicely done displays take you from Tubac's days as a seventeenth century Pima Indian village through its Spanish, Mexican and American periods. Exhibits include a set of wrist irons tied to a post that served as the town's jail, plus period weapons, religious art and friars' frocks.

***Tumacacori National Historic Park*** • *In the town of Tumacacori; (520) 398-2341. Daily 8 to 5.* ☐ Father Kino erected a small adobe here in 1691 and began preaching to the natives. Half a century later, construction began on a more elaborate structure. Today, Tumacacori Mission is a noble ruin, standing forlornly on a grassy field. An adjacent interpretive center has a diorama of the mission in its heyday, relics from the old church and an artistically-produced video of missionaries ministering to the Indians.

***Pimeria Alta Historical Society Museum*** • *136 N. Grand Avenue and Crawford Street, Nogales; (520) 287-4621. Thursday-Sunday 10 to 4.* ☐ This museum personifies the close ties between the twin towns of Nogales. Photos, documents and pioneer artifacts trace the history of both communities. Although not professionally done, it's quite interesting, with exhibits such as a hand-drawn fire pumper, a pictorial history of the twin towns and archeological artifacts.

## Chapter Sixteen
# EASTERN ARIZONA
## THE LAND OVERLOOKED

**M**ost visitors to Arizona, preoccupied with the Grand Canyon, the Red Rock country and the desert resorts of Phoenix and Tucson, overlook the eastern third of the state. This is a pity, since this remote, thinly populated area contains some of Arizona's most interesting attractions and some of its most varied terrain.

We begin with the state's southeastern wedge, where the traveler will discover Arizona's earliest roots.

## THE COWBOY CORNER

What we've chosen to call the Cowboy Corner is Cochise County, a history-laden 90-mile by 70-mile rectangle. It could as well be called the Cochise Corner in honor of the Chiricahua Apache warrior, or the Copper Corner, for the great copper mines around Bisbee.

Some of America's most dramatic historical pageants were played out here. Francisco Vásquez de Coronado passed through in 1540 on his quest for the Seven Cities of Cibola. Cochise made a futile stand against intruding whites from 1858 until 1869, and then Geronimo took up the lance of resistance until his final surrender in 1886. On October 26, 1881, in a dusty alley in Tombstone, three men died in the most celebrated gun battle of Western history.

These events are recorded in a variety of historic sites and monuments scattered about this intriguing corner of Arizona. The drive outlined here will hit the high spots.

# Tombstone

To approach the Cowboy Corner, drive east from Tucson on I-10, then turn south on U.S. 80 and follow it to Tombstone, the "town too tough to die." The town itself is the main attraction, with a mix of museums, boutiques, restaurants and saloons in old Western style buildings. They stand alongside boardwalks where the boots of Wyatt Earp, Doc Holliday, Johnny Ringo and Bat Masterson once clunked. The town has several museums and gift shops thinly disguised as museums. Only a few are serious attractions, which are listed below.

**For information** ● Tombstone Office of Tourism, P.O. Box 248 (Allan and Fourth streets), Tombstone, AZ 85638; (800) 457-3423 or (520) 457-9317.

## The attractions

**Bird Cage Theater** ● *Sixth and Allen streets; (520) 457-3421. Daily 8 to 6.* ☐ This should be one of Tombstone's better attractions, for it's the town's only original and intact gambling hall-theater-saloon. However, the museum is cluttered with many items unrelated to the theater's lively history. Among authentic relics are dusty four-by-six foot bird cage "cribs" suspended from upper walls, where fallen angels entertained their gents.

**Boothill Cemetery and Gift Shop** ● *Highway 80; (520) 457-9344. Daily 7:30 to 6.* ☐ You don't often find a cemetery that accepts Visa and MasterCard. Of course, that's only in the gift shop, through which you must pass to view the graves of Tombstone's fallen. Frank and Tom McLaury and Billy Clanton—victims of the O.K. Corral shootout—lie side by side on this sloping hill. More than 250 other citizens are buried here. Grave markers remind you that life was often short and death was quick in the Wild West. One poor soul was "hanged by mistake," according to his grave marker.

**Tombstone Courthouse State Historic Park** ● *219 E. Toughnut St. (Third Street); (520) 457-3311. Daily 8 to 5.* ☐ This imposing brick structure served as the Cochise County Courthouse from 1882 until neighboring Bisbee snatched away the county seat in 1931. It's now a museum of Cochise County yesterdays, with a restored sheriff's office, courtroom and various exhibits. Assorted versions of the O.K. Corral shootout hang on the courthouse walls.

**The O.K. Corral and Camillus Fly Photo Studio** ● *Allen Street (between Third and Fourth); (520) 457-3456. Daily 9 to 5; shootout reenactments several times daily in summer, less frequently in the off season.* ☐ The O.K. Corral has been corralled into a major tourist attraction. Among its exhibits are Camillus S. Fly's photo studio and several nineteenth century rigs, including a hearse that once toted unfortunate cowboys to Boothill. Near the scene of the shootout, beside Fly's studio, mannequins mark the position of the combatants when their guns started blazing.

# Sierra Vista & Fort Huachuca

The most direct route from Tombstone to Sierra Vista is a number-less road across the desert. To find it, head south on Tombstone's Sumner Street and just keep going. It becomes Charleston Road as it approaches **Sierra Vista**. This burgeoning community offers no specific tourist lures, although next-door **Huachuca City** is home to the West's oldest still-active Army fort. And there, you'll discover a fine military museum. To get there, head west through Sierra Vista on Fry Boulevard. It leads to the Fort Huachuca gate, where you'll need to get a pass for entry. It comes with a map of directions to the museum.

From Fort Huachuca, take Fry Boulevard back to the Highway 90-92 junction in Sierra Vista and turn right, following 92 south toward Bisbee. If you'd like to check out a sheltered canyon woodland, turn right onto Ramsey Canyon Road and follow it into **Ramsey Canyon Preserve**, a sanctuary operated by the Nature Conservancy. As you continue along Highway 92, watch for a sign to the right that will steer you into mountain woodlands and **Coronado National Memorial**.

*For area information* ● Greater Sierra Vista Chamber of Commerce, 21 E. Wilcox Dr., Sierra Vista, AZ 85635; (800) 288-3861 or (520) 458-6940; *www.sierravistachamber.org.*

## The attractions

*Fort Huachuca Museum* ● *U.S. Army Garrison, Fort Huachuca; (520) 533-5736. Weekdays 9 to 4, weekends 1 to 4.* ☐ This is one of Arizona's great surprises, an outstanding museum sitting among the barracks of an old Army fort. It has a dual focus—the history of the Southwest and the history of the fort, which are frequently linked. The museum's best feature is a large open exhibit portraying a patrol at evening's rest in the lonely desert. Tents are pitched, a campfire crackles, a distant coyote howls and a mannequin soldier strums a guitar.

*Coronado National Memorial* ● *4101 E. Montezuma Canyon Rd., Hereford; (520) 366-5515. Visitor center open daily 8 to 5.* ☐ This small preserve in the wooded flanks of the Huachuca Mountains honors Francisco Vásquez de Coronado's entry into present-day Arizona in 1540. However, he missed this spot; his trek took him about ten miles to the east. However, this land was available so, what the heck, the National Park Service took it. The interpretive center offers fine exhibits on Coronado's wanderings and the settling of this part of the American West. After checking out Coronado, visitors can follow hiking trails into the wooded slopes of Montezuma Canyon.

# Bisbee

From Coronado Memorial, follow Highway 92 east and then Route 80 briefly north to Bisbee. It's a yesteryear mining town whose outskirts are marked with headframes and tailing dumps. The sturdy downtown area is busy with nineteenth century brick buildings, and Victorians grace steeply-sloped neighborhoods.

*For area information* ● Greater Bisbee Chamber of Commerce, P.O. Drawer BA, Bisbee, AZ 85603; (520) 432-5421.

## The attractions

*Bisbee Mining & Historical Museum* ● *Five Copper Queen Plaza; (520) 432-7071. Daily 10 to 4.* ☐ This imposing brick building originally housed the Phelps Dodge mining company headquarters. Exhibits weave the story of the people and mines that transformed a frontier town into a sophisticated mini-city. Displays include photos of early mining activity, equipment and a make-believe shaft with cutaways of mining methods as they evolved through the years.

*Lavender Pit* ● *Adjacent to Highway 80, immediately south of town.* ☐ Tours aren't necessary to visit this gigantic brown, yellow and pale green hole in the ground. You simply park and walk to the fenced-off edge. A sign advises that the great terraced pit is more than a mile long, three- fourths of a mile wide and 950 feet deep. More than 380 million *tons* of material came out of this hole.

*Queen Mine Tour* ● *118 Arizona St.; (520) 432-2071. Tours daily at 10:30, noon, 2 and 3:30.* ☐ Tours of this now- closed copper mine, usually led by former miners, lead deep into the side of a mountain. There, participants learn about old and new mining techniques and the history of this operation.

## Bisbee to Willcox

Continue east from Bisbee toward **Douglas,** which sits on the Mexican border. It was a smeltering center for the Bisbee mines, and offers none of Bisbee's hilly charm. If you like old buildings, head downtown to the impeccably restored **Gadsden Hotel** at 106 G Avenue. If you don't, head north from Douglas on U.S. 191 (shown on some older maps as U.S. 666). Follow it about 25 miles through a high prairie to its junction with State Route 181. This takes you to **Chiricahua National Monument,** which preserves a slice of Arizona history and some of its most impressive geological formations.

As you depart the monument, turn north from the access road onto State Route 186. If you don't mind dust and bumps, turn left about nine miles above the Chiricahua junction and follow a dirt road to **Fort Bowie National Historic Site**. Otherwise, stay on 186 and follow it to the ranching town of **Willcox,** sitting astride Interstate 10. Appropriately, this dusty old town is home to the **Rex Allen Cowboy Hall of Fame.**

*For area information* ● Willcox Chamber of Commerce, 1500 N. Circle I Rd., Willcox, AZ 85643; (800) 200-2272 or (520) 384-2272.

## The attractions

*Chiricahua National Monument* ● *State Route 181 (13063 E. Bonita Canyon Rd.); (520) 824-3560, extension 104. Visitor center open daily 8 to 5.* ☐ This pocket-sized preserve, covering only 12,000 acres, shelters some incredibly complex rock formations and five of the seven North American life zones. Wind and rain have eroded a 27-million-year- old volcanic rhyolite deposit into fantastic shapes, and several hiking trails wind among them. These rocky ramparts were the refuge of the Chiricahua Apaches during their 25-year war with the Army.

**Fort Bowie National Historic Site** • *P.O. Box 158, Bowie; (520) 847- 2500. Visitor center open 8 to 5.* □ Reaching this remote site requires an eight-mile drive on a dirt road and then a 1.5-mile hike. Fort Bowie was built in 1862 to protect the vital Apache Pass during the army's war with the Chiricahuas. All that remains now are weathered ridges of adobe and stone walls—and a lot of history. Signs mark the sites of the former buildings and describe their uses.

**Rex Allen Arizona Cowboy Museum** • *Railroad Avenue near Malley Street, AZ 85644; (520) 384-4583. Daily 10 to 4.* □ They called him the "Arizona Cowboy," and he was that before he became a movie, TV and rodeo star. Rex Allen grew up on a homestead ranch near Willcox. After achieving fame and certainly fortune, he returned home to finance this small museum. Exhibits trace his rise to stardom, with movie posters, some of his gaudy boots and cowboy clothes, sheet music and even a badly-done oil painted by Rex.

# THE EASTERN MOUNTAINS

We now leave the Cowboy corner and travel to the far reaches of eastern Arizona. If you head east from Willcox on I-10 and turn north on U.S. 191, you'll shed the high prairie and climb into the foothills and forests of the White Mountains. You then enter an agricultural valley where—surprisingly—cotton is the main crop. Two towns serve as its commercial center.

## Safford-Thatcher

Although not tourist towns, Safford and next-door Thatcher offer a couple of tourist surprises. Safford's **Discovery Park** is an excellent science and history center. The campus of Eastern Arizona College in Thatcher contains the fine little **Museum of Anthropology.** Outdoor lovers may want to follow State Route 366 (the Swift Trail) south of Safford and then up into the ramparts of **Mount Graham**, one of Arizona's highest peaks, at 10,713 feet.

**For area information** • Safford-Graham County Chamber of Commerce, 1111 Thatcher Blvd., Safford, AZ 85546; (928) 428-2511; *www.chamber.safford.az.org.*

### The attractions

**Discovery Park** • *C/o Mt. Graham International Science and Culture Foundation, 1651 32nd St., Safford; (928) 428-6260. Tuesday-Saturday 1 to 10.* □ A focal point of this museum is an planetarium operated in conjunction with the nearby Mount Graham International Observatory. Museum exhibits feature the history, agriculture, flora and fauna of the area. Other Attractions include the Shuttlecraft Polaris ride and Discovery Park Railroad.

**Museum of Anthropology** • *On the campus of Eastern Arizona College, Church at College Avenue, Thatcher; (928) 428-8233. Weekdays 9 to noon and 1 to 4 during the school year.* □ Missed by most visitors, this is an impressive little museum featuring the early peoples of central Arizona. Its focal points are two remarkably detailed dioramas—one showing life here as it was 11,000 years ago when giant bisons and ground sloths roamed about, and another depicting a typical pueblo of 300 A.D.

# North to Clifton/Morenci & Springerville

From Safford, head east about twelve miles on Highways 70/191 and then branch northeast. Follow 191 through rocky desert foothills to the twin mining towns of Clifton and Morenci. This is a booming copper area and your drive will take you through a moonscape of tailing dumps and other unearthly gouges. You'll first travel through tired old **Clifton**, a blue collar town with a sagging Main Street that forks to the left off the highway. Its tattered old buildings are worth a browse, and it has a small historical museum.

From there, Highway 191 makes a wide sweeping turn up through terraced mining pits and tailing dumps to the neatly arrayed company town of **Morenci**. It's neatly arrayed because the original Morenci was dismantled and moved to this spot after rich copper or was found beneath it.

North of here, U.S. 191 becomes the **Coronado Trail,** winding steeply through more tailing dumps and then through the alpine beauty of Apache-Sitgreaves National Forest. Several turnouts along the way will help you appreciate the scenery.

You'll eventually wind up in another pair of towns, **Eagar** and **Springerville.** Quite different than Clifton-Morenci, these are commercial centers in a farming and ranching valley surrounded by wooded mountains. Although remote, this area is worth the drive for a fascinating archaeological site.

**For area information** • Greenlee County Chamber of Commerce, P.O. Box 1237, Clifton, AZ 85533; (928) 865-3313.

Round Valley Chamber of Commerce, P.O. Box 31 (318 E. Main St.), Springerville, AZ 85938-0031; (928) 333-2123.

**Casa Malpais Pueblo** • *Museum at 318 Main Street in Springerville; (928) 333-5375. Museum open weekdays 8 to 6 and weekends 8 to 4; pueblo tours depart the museum at 9, 11 and 2.* □ A downtown storefront visitor center contains a few relics from Casa Malpais Pueblo. From here, visitors are taken to the pueblo site, several miles away. It was occupied for about 200 years and abandoned around 1400 A.D. Although not large, it's one of the most intriguing in the Southwest, with a huge ceremonial kiva and a remarkably intact complex of adobe buildings.

*The author sits like a bump on a petrified log on the Giant Logs Trail, at Petrified Forest National Park.*

## North to the Petrified Forest

Drive three miles northwest of Springerville and take the Highway 180/191 fork north toward Holbrook and Petrified Forest National Park. You'll pass **Lyman Lake State Park** with swimming, boating and camping, and then the small prairie town of **St. Johns**. Go west and then northwest on U.S. 180 and you'll encounter the southern entrance to **Petrified Forest National Park**. Drive through the park, loop over I-40 through the **Painted Desert** and then take the freeway west to Holbrook.

*For area information* ● Holbrook Chamber of Commerce, 100 E. Arizona Street, Holbrook, AZ 86025; (800) 524-2459 or (928) 524-6558.

*Petrified Forest National Park* ● *Holbrook; (928) 524-6228. Park gates and visitor centers open daily 8 to 5.* ☐ This park in a high, windy prairie is full of trees, although they've all turned to stone. Petrified logs are scattered like broken columns of fallen temples over the preserve's 93,533 acres. Driving northwest on Highway 180, enter the park's southern gate, follow a 27-mile scenic drive and exit the northern gate, at Interstate 40 about 25 miles east of Holbrook. You actually get two attractions for the price of one. The drive takes you through a section of the **Painted Desert** north of the park. This multi-chromatic desert stretches for 200 miles across Arizona, along the northern edge of the Little Colorado River.

## Holbrook to Globe-Miami

The town of Holbrook is comprised mostly of motels and restaurants that serve visitors to nearby Petrified Forest. It does offer one lure, the small **Courthouse Museum** in the town's still-active courthouse at Arizona and Navajo Streets. It has the usual pioneer relics, and the Chamber of Commerce office is located here. Both are open weekdays 8 to 5.

From Holbrook, a long drive through mixed terrain will take you nearly half the length of the state to the mining towns of Globe and Miami. To begin, follow signs from Holbrook's Main Street to Highways 180 and 77 south, and then continue straight ahead on State Route 77. It cuts a direct line through bunchgrass prairie, and then begins climbing into the White Mountains as it passes through hamlets of **Snowflake** and **Taylor.**

As pine trees replace bunchgrass, you'll hit **Show Low.** It's a mountain vacation retreat, although it offers no specific visitor lures. Pick up U.S. 60 here and take it south into the huge **White Mountain Apache Reservation.** After winding through pretty pine forests, it drops downhill through the adjacent **San Carlos Indian Reservation**, where the trees begin to thin out. Leaving the reservation, you follow a dramatic spiral through spectacular **Salt River Canyon**, which is rimmed by jagged peaks, buttes and fluted ridges.

After ten miles of twisting canyon and another twenty miles of rocky mountainous terrain, you hit **Globe** in the arid Cobre Valley. Copper marks its past, present and future. The great open pits were abandoned several years ago, then mining resumed recently, bringing a bit of prosperity to this old brick-front town. It offers a few items of visitor interest, including impressive vistas of multi-colored tailing dumps.

**For area information** ● Greater Globe-Miami Chamber of Commerce, P.O. Box 2539 (1360 N. Broad), Globe, AZ 85502; (800) 804-5623 or (928) 425-4495.

## The attractions

**Besh-Ba-Gowah Archaeological Park** ● *Near Globe Community center, a mile southwest of town, off Jesse Hayes Road; (928) 425-0320. Daily 9 to 5.* ☐ Archaeologists and craftsmen have re-created Arizona's most realistic ancient Indian dwellings at Besh-Ba-Gowah. Climb a rough wooden ladder and peer into a second floor room where pottery, gourds, ears of corn and a plant fiber whisk broom are arranged as they might have been 600 years ago. The adjacent museum has fine graphics and implements of the ancient Salado people who occupied this pueblo.

**Historic downtown Miami** ● *Town Hall information desk is on Keystone Avenue.* ☐ Next door Miami, considerably more sleepy than Globe, is a virtual museum of weathered nineteenth century structures. A walking map available at the Town Hall will direct you past its more interesting buildings.

From Globe, you can follow State Route 77 south to Tucson, thus completing an ambitious loop of southeastern and far eastern Arizona.

### Chapter Seventeen
# FOUR CORNERS COUNTRY
## NAVAJO-HOPI LAND

The large Navajo and Hopi reservations in northeastern Arizona encompass some of the state's most interesting terrain, from starkly beautiful canyons to netherworld sandstone spires. They also provide an opportunity to witness two proud nations in transition—working to preserve their old ways while embracing many of our new ones.

The combined reservations cover about 29,000 square miles, encompassing all of northeastern Arizona and spilling over into Colorado, Utah and New Mexico. That's nearly as big as New Hampshire, Vermont, Massachusetts and Connecticut combined.

The Navajo reservation, largest in America, covers 25,000 square miles. The Hopi Nation is much smaller, about 4,000 square miles. By an unfortunate whim of the federal government, Hopi turf is entirely surrounded by the Navajo Nation. The Hopi reservation does, however, encompass some of the tribe's ancestral lands. One pueblo, Old Oraibi, has existed for more than 800 years. Dating from 1150 A.D., it may be the oldest continually occupied settlement in America.

Navajos are America's largest native tribe, numbering about 150,000 on the reservation, with several thousand more living elsewhere. Hopi population on the reservation is around 10,000. Navajos tend to live on their ranches and farms, while the Hopi prefer village life in the pueblos—commuting to the their agricultural lands.

# VISITOR TIPS

**Sovereign nations** • When you enter reservation lands, you technically leave Arizona and enter sovereign nations. You don't need a passport, of course, and both tribes welcome visitors. However, they are self governing and some of their laws differ from those outside. Alcohol is prohibited in Hopi-Navajo land; you cannot buy a drink at any reservation establishment or a can of beer in a market.

**Permits** • As on other reservations, permits are required for hunting or fishing, and you don't need Arizona licenses. These permits are readily available through tribal offices and at some trading posts and stores; fees are modest.

**Driving laws** • Safety belt use is required on the dual reservations, as it is in the rest of the state. Navajo police use radar to enforce the speed limit, although they aren't fanatics about it.

**What time is it?** • Here's a point of minor confusion: Arizona does not switch to daylight saving time, and neither does the Hopi Nation, but the Navajo Nation does.

**Photography** • The Hopi forbid kind of photography—still, movie or video camera. Photography is permitted in Navajo lands.

**Dining** • The Hopi, more traditionalist than the Navajo, have several distinctive dishes. The best place to find traditional Hopi fare—in fact, one of the *only* places—is the Tunosvongya Restaurant at the Hopi Cultural Center. Try the *chil-il ou gya va*, a spicy blend of pinto beans, beef and chilies, or *nok qui*, a stew with lamb, baked green chilies and Indian fry bread.

**Shopping** • Navajos have long been noted for their artistry with hand-woven wool blankets and turquoise and silver jewelry—particularly the squash blossom necklace. The Hopi produce fine basketry, pottery, silver jewelry and detailed, brightly-colored *kachina* (or *katsina*) dolls, carefully whittled out of cottonwood. Traditional *kachinas* are regarded as spiritual messengers. Navajo and Hopi artistry, like all native crafts, has been altered by the tourist market. The Navajo turquoise and silver jewelry trade actually was created in the late 1800s by the Fred Harvey Company. And don't be surprised to see a Levi-clad Hopi *kachina* in a craft shop, or one toting a camera.

Scores of roadside stands offer a bewildering variety of Navajo crafts, particularly in the western part of the reservation. Prices generally are better than those in the shops, although quality control may be better in some of the trading posts. Both Navajo and Hopi officials work to ensure that anything sold on the reservation is authentic.

**For area information** • Navajoland Tourism, P.O. Box 663, Window Rock, AZ 86515; (928) 871-6436, extension 7371.

Hopi Cultural Center, Second Mesa, AZ 86043, (928) 734-6650; or Hopi Tribal Headquarters, Kykotsmovi Village, AZ 86039, (928) 734-2441.

# NAVAJO-HOPI DRIVE

The Hopi-Navajo terrain may surprise you. Much of it is barren grassland, punctuated by startling scenery. Canyon de Chelly (pronounced *shay*) is one of the most interesting chasms we've ever seen. Monument Valley looks even more dramatic than it appears in photos, although it's smaller than one might think. After you've driven for hours across the reservation, seeing nothing but an occasional farmhouse, a great redwall butte may appear on the horizon or a cathedral-like spire may crop up in a pasture. Although the Hopi are famous for their distinctive pueblos, don't expect to see quaint Indian villages on the Navajo reservation. You'll see occasional log and mud hogans and some modern ones made of lumber. However, most Navajo towns differ little from ours.

Natural and historic lures of Navajo-Hopi land are widespread so we've again devised a driving route. Our starting point is **Page**, which is notched into the far northwestern tip of the Navajo Nation.

Drive south on U.S. 89, and then turn east onto U.S. 160. Look for a small sign indicating **dinosaur tracks**, which are imprinted into hardpan on a side road just north of the highway. Several locals usually are there to point out the tracks and tell you a bit about them. They'll splash them with water to accent them for photos. A small gratuity will be appreciated.

You soon enter **Tuba City**, the largest town on the Navajo reservation. Mormons settled here in 1877, and then sold out to the government when they realized that they were on native land. Tuba City was the reservation's administrative center until it was moved to Window Rock on the far eastern side in 1930. The town offers an interesting architectural mix—old cut sandstone government buildings, ordinary bungalows, mobile homes and typical octagonal hogans.

## THE HOPI NATION

Follow Highway 264 south from Tuba City into the Hopi Nation. Most of their celebrated pueblos occupy three mesas, simply called First, Second and Third. Some are true cliff dwellings, perched on shelves and niches high above the valley floor.

These pueblos, while intriguing, are not models of neatness. The earthy style of these ancient dwellings does not blend well with non-biodegradable objects such as car parts and tin cans. The gentle Hopi are more into spiritual things than landscaping. Look beyond the litter and realize that you are seeing dwellings that were here before Columbus set sail, before the Spanish began their intrusions into this peaceful land. The Hopi may have occupied this area for as long as man has wandered in the Southwest. Most anthropologists agree that they're descendants of the Anasazi.

Among the more interesting pueblos you'll encounter on this drive are **Old Oraibi** (*oh-RYE-bee*), **Kykotsmovi** (*Kee-KOTS-mo-vee*),

**Shungopovi** (*Shung-O-PO-vee*), **Shipaulovi** (*Shih-PAW-lo-vee*) and **Mishongnovi** (*Mih-SHONG-no-vee*). Did you get those pronunciations? Note that the accent is on a middle syllable.

To learn more about the people and their ancient pueblos, visit the fine cultural complex on Second Mesa in the heart of the Hopi Nation. Coming from the west, it's to the left on the main highway:

*Hopi Cultural Center and Museum* ● *Second Mesa; (928) 734-6650. Museum and cultural center open weekdays 8 to 5 and weekends 9 to 3; gift shops generally open 9 to 5.* □ This handsome sandstone colored pueblo style complex includes a museum, gift shops, the Tunosvongya Restaurant and a motel. The nicely done museum has collections of modern and ancient pottery, murals portraying traditional villages, a hand-woven bridal robe and other things Hopi. A diorama depicts Keet Seel, a ruin in Navajo National Monument, as it would have appeared in 1200 A.D.

*Hopi dances* ● The Hopi still perform centuries-old ceremonial dances in traditional dress. Some are private while others may be witnessed by visitors, and these are usually held on weekends. Although schedules aren't usually posted in advance, you can check with the cultural center to see if a dance is planned in the area. Photography, video taping and recording are forbidden at the dances.

# BACK TO THE NAVAJO NATION

Leaving Hopi land, follow Highway 264 east until you approach the Navajo village of **Ganado**. Watch for signs on the right to an interesting historic complex:

*Hubbell Trading Post National Historic Site* ● *P.O. Box 150, Ganado, AZ 86505; (928) 755-3475. Daily 8 to 6 in summer and 8 to 5 the rest of the year. Free.* □ The oldest active trading post on the reservation, Hubbell was established in 1876. It's both an historic landmark and an active trading post. You can buy canned goods, bolts of cloth or harnesses, or curios, souvenirs and books. A large barn next to the venerable stone store once housed the post's livestock. Several old wagons are on display out back. At the visitor center museum, you'll learn about the vital role of the Western trading post, which provided a commercial and cultural link between Indians and whites.

## Window Rock

Pressing eastward on Highway 264, you'll next hit Window Rock, right on the New Mexico border. It looks like a typical American community, although the culture is definitely Navajo, as you'll learn at the museum and crafts center, on the main highway near the border.

*Navajo Tribal Museum* ● *In the Arts and Crafts Center, Window Rock; (928) 871-4090. Weekdays 9 to 6 and Saturday 9 to 5.* □ This well-planned museum exhibits the skeleton of a 180-million-year-old *dilophosaurus,* plus displays tracing native occupation of the region

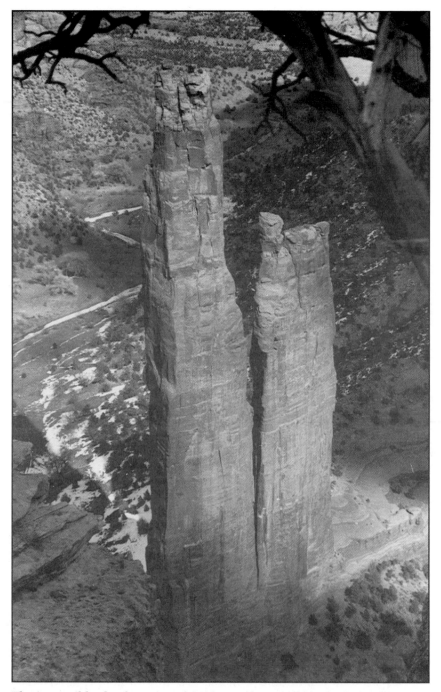

*The impossibly slender spire of Spider Rock rises from the bottom of Canyon de Chelley, one of several attractions on the huge Navajo and Hopi reservations.*

from the basketmakers of 50 A.D. to the present. Artifacts include pottery, projectile points, metates and such.

From the tribal museum, go back to the town's only traffic signal and turn north onto Highway 12. After half a mile, watch on the right for a sign pointing toward the community's namesake, **Window Rock**. A few blocks off the highway, it's a natural arch sculpted by wind and rain through Kayenta sandstone. It occupies a small, nicely landscaped park. As you approach the park, you'll pass the 1930s style masonry buildings of Navajo tribal headquarters.

## North to Canyon de Chelly

From Window Rock Tribal Park, press northward on Route 12, which takes you through imposing beige and red rock formations. When you reach the town of **Fort Defiance**, stay alert for a right hand turn at a service station to stay with the highway. Otherwise, you'll continue straight ahead into the town.

Pressing northward, you'll dip into New Mexico (marked by a sign) and then back into Arizona (not marked). This is an appealing drive into the pines of the Chuska Mountain foothills, offering picnic sites, campgrounds and a couple of fishing lakes. As further enhancement, the area is marked with occasional sandstone cliffs, buttes and spires. Particularly dominant to the east is a thick, towering butte with a wide alluvial skirt, called Black Pinnacle. Beyond small **Tsaile Lake**, you'll see the campus of Dené College on your left. It has a fine little museum worthy of pause:

*Hatathli Museum ● Dené College (Navajo Community College), just inside the east entrance of campus; (928) 724-3311. Weekdays 8:30 to 4:30.* □ This all-Navajo museum is housed in the octagonal Hatathli Center. Exhibits trace Navajo and other Native American cultures. Handicrafts and artwork are available at a sales gallery.

Just beyond the college, you'll reach the hamlet of **Tsaile**. From here, Highway 64 leads westward into the side door of Canyon de Chelly National Monument, about 25 miles west. However, before heading in that direction, we suggest that you continue another ten miles north on Route 12 to see a spectacular proscenium of red rock cliffs above the town of **Lukachukai**. Having done so, return to Tsaile Junction and head west toward the national monument.

*Canyon de Chelly National Monument ● P.O. Box 588, Chinle, AZ 86503; (928) 674-5500. Visitor center open 8 to 6 from May to September and 8 to 5 the rest of the year. Small museum in the center with graphics tracing canyon occupation from basketmakers to Anasazi cliff dwellers of the twelfth and thirteenth centuries.* □ Canyon de Chelly and its adjoining Canyon del Muerto are unexpectedly beautiful steep-walled ravines, dropping a thousand feet to neat patchwork farms on the valley floor. Lining the banks of a meandering stream, these lands are still being tilled, as they have been since the 1300s. Coming from Tsaile, you'll first encounter Canyon del Muerto, following the North Rim Drive. Continue to the visitor center and then take the South Rim Drive along Canyon de Chelly. Both scenic drives have turnouts with graphics describing the splendid canyon vistas.

## Four Corners, Monument Valley & Navajo National Monument

From Canyon de Chelly, drop down into the small town of **Chinle** and head north, following Highway 191 past several imposing free-standing red rock mesas. At U.S. 160, go east through **Mexican Water,** following signs to **Four Corners** where the borders of Arizona, New Mexico, Colorado and Utah merge. It's interesting mostly for its geographic oddity; a flat concrete monument with the four state seals marks the spot. It's in a Navajo tribal park and the monument is rimmed with dozens of crafts and souvenir stalls and small cafés.

Retrace your route on U.S. 160 through more imposing red rock formations and stay with the highway until you reach the town of **Kayenta**. Turn north for a visit to the Navajo Nation's most famous attraction:

**Monument Valley Tribal Park** ● *Monument Valley, Utah; (435) 727-3827. Daily 7 to 7 May through September and 8 to 5 the rest of the year; last admission 30 minutes before closing.* ☐ A small visitor center perched on a ridge offers great views of the famous Monument Valley. From here, an extremely rough road leads down to the famous buttes, spires, pinnacles and fins of Monument Valley. Should you not want to abuse your vehicle, a dozen or more tour operators are parked nearby, waiting to take you down by jeeps, flatbed trucks with seats affixed to the bed, or other improvised rigs. These are some of the most imposing formations on earth, although you may be surprised that the legendary valley is actually rather small.

From Monument Valley, return to Kayenta and continue west on U.S. 160 for the last major attraction of Navajo-Hopi land:

**Navajo National Monument** ● *HC 71, Box 3, Tonalea, AZ 86044; (928) 672-2700. Interpretive center open 8 to 5; lookout trail open during daylight hours.* ☐ This preserve shelters three of the most complete Anasazi ruins and one of the finest small museums in the state. Betatakin Ruin can be seen from an overlook near the visitor center museum, and you can visit it on ranger walks. Keet Seel, the most splendid of the Southwest's Indian ruins, is eight miles away and can be seen only with an advance permit. Its Inscription House is so fragile that it's closed to visitors. Back at the interpretive center, the excellent museum features stone tools, pottery and other artifacts found at the three ruins. You can crawl inside a reconstructed living unit that's so realistic the occupants appear to have just stepped out.

# OTHER INDIAN NATIONS

If you'd like to learn more about native people, Arizona is the ideal place to do so. The Navajo and Hopi nations offer good previews of contemporary Indian life. However, these are only two of twenty reservations in the state, and each tribal homeland has its own characteristics, arts and crafts.

Native American lands occupy 27 percent of Arizona—more than any other state. Further, Arizona has America's largest native population—around 200,000. It's one of the few places where Native Americans have the land and resources to maintain their own identity as members of viable communities. They are a major force in the state, both culturally and politically. Most reservations welcome visitors and many have fine natural attractions, and hunting and fishing areas.

Some reservations encompass lands that have been with the same tribes for centuries. Several Hopi villages, for instance, are among the oldest continually occupied settlements in America.

About three-fourths of Arizona's native people live on reservation land. It is communally owned and those who occupy it do not pay property taxes. As American citizens, they pay other state and federal tariffs, except some sales taxes.

## Indian gaming

Because reservations are sovereign nations, they are allowed to go into the gaming business, one an agreement is reached with the host state. Native casinos are scattered throughout Arizona and much of the rest of the country. Interestingly, there's also a tribal-owned casino in Nevada, where gambling is legal statewide; it's near Laughlin on the Colorado River. Tribes also have taken advantage of sales tax exemptions to operate smoke shops, where they can sell discounted cigarettes. You won't find many liquor sales, however, despite a potential savings on this heavily taxed product. Most reservations in Arizona prohibit the sale of alcohol—to their own people or anyone else.

More than a century has passed since the last Native American tribe yielded to white settlement and moved to reservations. Yet, they were not granted citizenship until 1924, and they weren't given the right to vote until 1948. This must have been particularly galling, since many of them fought in World War II, including the Navajo code-talkers who used their native language to the Japanese from deciphering messages, and Iwo Jima flag-raiser Ira Hayes, a member of Arizona's Pima tribe.

**For more information** ● Arizona Commission of Indian Affairs, 1400 W. Washington St., Suite 300, Phoenix, AZ 85007, (602) 542-3123.

## Chapter eighteen
# DOWN MEXICO WAY
### EXPLORING SOUTH OF THE BORDER

---

**A**rizona shares a long border and many ethnic ties with Mexico. Indeed, Southwestern cooking, architecture and even cowboying are heavily influenced by our neighbors to the south. One out of five Arizonans trace their roots to Mexico.

Visiting the Mexican state of Sonora through any of the six border crossings is a simple matter. At most points, you can merely walk across the international boundary to nearby shopping areas, restaurants and cantinas. Bear in mind that these aren't typical Mexican cities, any more than Arizona border towns are typically American. Each is influenced by the presence of the other. With the exception of Sasabe, these towns cater heavily to tourists, with an inordinate number of curio shops and restaurants. While you won't experience a typical slice of Mexico, you'll enjoy browsing through these bordertown shops. They offer bewildering selections of leather goods, ceramics, costume jewelry, turquoise and silver, onyx and wood carvings, embroidered clothing and glassware. Also, some of the simpler and more traditional Mexican Indian handicrafts are quite nice.

Most Mexican border towns are many times larger than their Arizona counterparts. A major reason for this is the "twin plant" program in which American-owned plants take advantage of inexpensive Mexican labor. Hundreds of thousands have flocked to the border towns, since—by Mexico's standards—wages paid at these plants are high.

Since most towns have shopping areas right next to the border, we recommend parking and walking across. U.S. Customs officials are more picky than their Mexican counterparts, and you might get stuck in a long line of cars, trying to get back into Arizona. Also, American car insurance policies aren't recognized in Mexico. Incidentally, it's best to avoid weekend visits, when most border crossings are extremely busy.

**Health matters** ● We've traveled extensively in Mexico without getting anything worse that diarrhea. However, that's awfully unpleasant, so take precautions. Follow a few simple rules and your trip across the border should be both happy and healthy:

**1.** Although no specific shots are required for entry into Mexico, we'd recommend getting hepatitis inoculations, particularly if you plan to spend some time there. Vaccines now offer long-term protection against both hepatitis A and B, so you no longer have to cope with that uncomfortable and short-term gamma globulin shot. Check with your physician for details.

**2.** Drink the beer, not the water. Most Mexican cities don't have adequately treated public water supplies. Tap water is safe for bathing and cooking if it's boiled, but not for drinking or brushing your teeth. Most hotels will furnish you with bottled water and it's readily available in stores and street stalls.

**3.** In restaurants, particularly out-of-the-way ones that don't cater to tourists, avoid rare meat, poultry and fish. Also avoid salad vegetables that may have been rinsed with untreated water or handled by unwashed hand. And steer clear of iced drinks, since freezing doesn't kill the bacteria that can bring havoc to visiting intestines. The best rule is to eat only cooked food that's served while it's still hot. If it has been allowed to cool, it can be re-contaminated by careless handling.

**4.** Never eat food offered by street vendors; you don't know where it's been. If you buy fruit from a public market or street vendor, eat only what you have peeled yourself, such as oranges or bananas.

**5.** Since freezing doesn't kill most infectious bacteria, ice cream may not be safe unless you can confirm that the milk used has been pasteurized. The same is true for milk you drink or pour on breakfast cereal. (Cereal? We always have tortillas for breakfast in Mexico.)

**Entry formalities** ● If you're an American or Canadian citizen, you need only to declare your citizenship for visits of 72 hours or less, if you aren't going beyond a border town. If you plan to stay longer and/or go deeper, you'll need a Mexican Tourist Card and an automobile permit. These can be obtained quickly at the border, or from the Mexican Consulate, 553 S. Stone Ave., Tucson, AZ 85701; (520) 882-5596. The office is open weekdays from 8 to 2. You'll need proof of citizenship such as a birth certificate, passport, voter's registration certificate or military ID. A driver's license won't work. For a vehicle permit, you *must* carry proof of ownership, such as the registration slip.

**Auto insurance** ● Don't drive anywhere in Mexico without Mexican auto insurance. Although insurance isn't mandated by law, your vehicle might be impounded if you're involved in an accident. Few American insurance policies extend coverage to Mexico and even if they do, Mexican officials won't recognize them. If you have a rental car, make sure your rental agreement permits driving into Mexico, and get proper insurance coverage. Mexican auto insurance is available on both sides of the border. Rates are similar to American premiums.

*Shopping* ● American money is widely accepted in border towns, so don't bother with currency exchanges unless you're going into the interior. Expect to haggle over prices in curio shops. The rule of thumb is to counter with a third of what they ask, then meet somewhere in the middle. Don't embarrass the poor shopkeeper and take all the fun out of haggling by paying full price. Because of lower labor costs and a favorable exchange rate, you'll find many good buys. Booze is cheap because of the lack of tax, and Mexican-made liquor such as tequila and brandy are less than half the U.S. price. However, there are limits on what you can bring back; see below.

*"Se habla Ingles?"* ● You won't have to resort to your high school Spanish in the border towns; English is spoken at virtually every shop, motel and restaurant.

*Driving the interior* ● It's generally as safe as driving around California, although there's a major difference. Once you get away from the border, service facilities are scarce and car parts even scarcer. For an extended trip into Mexico, take spare parts such as fan belts, water pumps and such—things that might likely conk out. And don't forget the tools needed to install them. Also, take plenty of bottled water in case you're stranded for a while.

Paved Mexican roads are usually narrower than ours and sometimes in need of repair. Watch out for potholes, tractors and cows who seem oblivious to the risk of colliding with a car. Because of open ranges in the Baja, we never drive after dark. In the more remote towns, you may want to filter gasoline through a fine sieve or cloth.

*Returning to Arizona* ● You can bring back $400 worth of duty-free goods per family member, plus one liter of liquor per adult. Mexico enjoys favored nation status with the U.S. and certain handicrafts can be imported in excess of the $400 limit. Check with a Customs office to see what's currently on the list. Bear in mind that some items can't be brought into the U.S., including ivory and certain animal skins and sea turtle oil. Also, there's a limit on the amount of American brand perfume that you can bring in from Mexico. For customs information, call (602) 914-1400; *www.customs.gov/travel/travel.htm*

# THE BORDER TOWNS

While none of the border towns are cool in summer, Nogales and Agua Prieta—at nearly 4,000 feet elevation—are a bit more bearable. San Luis, below Yuma, is near sea level; expect to sizzle if you plan a summertime visit.

**Agua Prieta** • This is Mexico's twin to Douglas. The two towns rub shoulders at the border, and Mexican shops are less than a block away. With more than 70,000 inhabitants—ten times as many as Douglas—Agua Prieta offers fair shopping variety. It's not as abundant as Nogales or San Luis, however. Downtown here is more of a conventional mix of businesses, with gift shops tucked among department stores, *farmacias* and professional offices. Paved highways lead from here into the interior; it's the most direct driving route to Mexico City.

**Naco** • A hamlet south of Bisbee, Naco is one of our favorite border towns. If there's such a thing as scruffily cute, this is it. Naco is more like an interior village—uncrowded, with little Mexican shops behind dusty pastel store fronts. You won't find much of a shopping selection here, although there's one good-sized liquor store. The wide—although pot-holed—streets with center dividers give the place a nice colonial charm.

**Nogales** • Opposite Nogales, Arizona, it's the largest of the border towns, with a population exceeding 200,000. Predictably, it's also the best place to shop. Scores of curio shops and liquor stores are crowded into the Calle Obregon, a shopping area that starts just a block from the border. Narrow arcades are stuffed with stalls. Some carry a variety of crafts, curios and general junk while others specialize in leather goods, fabric, glassware and such. You'll find an abundance of shops within a few blocks of the border, so it's best to park and walk in. Several lots on the Arizona side offer all-day parking for a few dollars.

**San Luis** • South of Yuma, San Luis is booming on both sides of the border because of is active "twin plant" program. Arizona's San Luis was the fifth fastest growing city in the state in the millennial census, leaping by 264 percent from 4,212 to 15,322 in just ten years. The weathered business district of Mexico's San Luis offers several shops within two blocks of the border. Selections are fairly good, although it's a distant second to Nogales for shopping variety.

**Sasabe** • At the bottom of Highway 286 southwest of Tucson, this is the smallest, least crowded and most typically Mexican of all the Arizona border towns. There are few tourist shops or other facilities here, or in its Arizona twin. Only dirt roads lead south from here, so Sasabe obviously gets very little through traffic. Incidentally, the border station is closed between 8 p.m. and 8 a.m.

**Sonoita** • Opposite Lukeville below Organ Pipe Cactus National Monument, Sonoita is about three miles from the border. A few shops are within walking distance of Lukeville although there isn't much of a selection. You might like to drive 63 miles south to **Rocky Point** (Puerto Peñasco), where you can swim, snorkel and fish in the clear waters of the Gulf of California. It has several tourist hotels and restaurants. Remember that you need a Mexican Tourist Card and vehicle permit to go south of Sonoita. The Sonoita-Lukeville border station is closed between midnight and 8 a.m.

## Chapter Nineteen

# AFTERTHOUGHTS

## OUR ARIZONA FAVORITES

**J**ust for the fun of it, after our lengthy examination of Arizona, we've compiled "Ten Best" lists of our favorite things here. The first selection on each list is our top pick, followed by the next nine in alphabetical order. In this manner, we have no losers among the ten best, only winners and runners-up.

### Arizona's ten best towns & cities

***1. Tucson*** • It has it all—urban conveniences, varied cultural offerings, a world class university, interesting attractions and fine climate—except for peak summer heat. Surrounding mountains and deserts offer lures for outdoor enthusiasts.

***2. Bisbee*** • This venerable copper mining town has found new life as a tourist and art center. We like the sturdy old downtown and steeply tiered residential areas. The mining scars aren't pretty although they add drama to the setting.

***3. Carefree/Cave Creek*** • Take your pick of modern (Carefree) or Old West (Cave Creek). They're beyond the Valley of the Sun's congestion, in an attractive desert setting, yet within half an hour's drive of the urban action of Phoenix and Scottsdale.

***4. Flagstaff*** • Think of it as a mini Tucson, with colder winters but milder summers. Northern Arizona University and several fine museums give it cultural depth. It's surrounded by natural attractions, and within a short drive of the Grand Canyon and several native ruins.

**5. Fountain Hills** ● The best of Arizona's new planned communities, Fountain Hills offers modern conveniences and beautiful homes in a rugged desert setting.

**6. Mesa** ● This is where we'd live if we lived in the Valley of the Sun. It's on the outer edge of congestion, yet within a short drive of Arizona State University, Phoenix and other lures. We like its nicely preserved old fashioned downtown area.

**7. Prescott** ● It's an appealing, self-contained little community tucked against forested mountains. Several colleges, galleries, a handsome old downtown area and a friendly Western attitude make this one of Arizona's most desirable communities.

**8. Safford** ● Tucked off by itself in southeastern Arizona, Safford is a prim little town in an agricultural valley. A fine science and history center and an adjacent college give it some cultural depth, and nearby Mount Graham offers outdoor pursuits.

**9. Sedona** ● We'd retire here in a minute if we could afford it, and spend every evening watching the sundown light and shadow show against those fantastic red rock formations.

**10. Wickenburg** ● If you wanna play cowboy, this is the place, dude. A pretty desert setting, an excellent museum, an old style downtown and guest ranches make this the best little cowtown in Arizona.

## Arizona's ten best retirement towns

**1. Tucson** ● With extensive retirement facilities, affordable housing and the attractions we've already mentioned, the Old Pueblo again tops our list.

**2. Apache Junction** ● The rugged backdrop of the Superstition Mountains, water play lures of the nearby Salt River Canyon and affordable housing make this a fine place to retire.

**3. Catalina** ● The town itself isn't much more than a widening of Highway 77 asphalt. What we're really recommending is the two nearby retirement villages of Sun City Vistoso and Saddlebrooke with their extensive amenities.

**4. Green Valley** ● The surrounding desert is rather bland, although careful planning has created a good place for the good life. Green Valley offers ample shopping, reasonable prices and the nearby lures of Tucson.

**5. Fountain Hills** ● Home prices are on the high side. If you can afford them, Fountain Hills provides a fine retirement environment with its nicely planned housing developments and robust desert setting.

**6. Florence** ● Mix an historic downtown area with modern housing in the suburbs and a convenient location between Phoenix and Tucson, and you have an excellent retirement community.

**7. Pine/Strawberry** ● Folks who need pine trees with their retirement will like these two woodsy communities tucked under the Mogollon Rim north of Phoenix. Winters are nippy but certainly warmer than in North Dakota.

**8. Prescott** ● In addition to its cultural lures, ample shopping, collegiate atmosphere and nice setting, Prescott offers extensive senior programs and good medical facilities. One of four residents is retired.

**9. Sedona** ● We again select Sedona for its stunning red rock backdrop. With warm summers and rather mild winters, it's a great place to be at leisure—if you can afford it.

**10. Yuma** ●The largest city outside the Phoenix and Tucson metropolitan areas, Yuma is an Arizona surprise. Its revitalized downtown and riverfront has been designated as a National Heritage Area. A good selection of inexpensive homes and mobile home parks, ample shopping and interesting historic sites make Yuma very attractive for retirees. It gets hotter than the hinges of Hades in summer but what the heck. You're retired; be a Sunbird and fly north!

## Arizona's ten best snowbird roosts

**1. Apache Junction** ● Both alphabetically and preferentially, it tops our list of Snowbird retreats. Although it isn't on the popular Colorado River corridor, it offers water sports in the nearby Salt River Canyon. The lures of Phoenix are a short drive away.

**2. Bullhead City** ● It ain't pretty, but it can be fun. Bullhead has an abundance of RV and mobile home parks, and the gaming centers of Laughlin, Nevada, are just across the Colorado River.

**3. Lake Havasu City** ● The best planned of the Colorado River corridor communities, Lake Havasu offers lots of water sports, good shopping and—oh, yes—that misplaced bridge.

**4. Lake Mead National Recreation Area** ● This isn't a community, although it's certainly a Snowbird roost. RV parks at Lake Mead marinas offer water play, and the casino action of Las Vegas is less than an hour away.

**5. Parker** ● This friendly little town is ideal for Snowbirds on a budget and those who love water play. The adjacent Parker Strip is lined with RV and mobile home parks.

**6. Phoenix-Scottsdale** ● This is your roost if you want to be in the middle of the action, with cultural pursuits and plenty of shopping. If you're a sports fan, look no further. The Valley of the Sun hosts seven Cactus League spring training baseball teams and Phoenix offers major league baseball, football, basketball and hockey.

**7. Mesa-Tempe** ● These two Valley of the Sun bedroom communities offer similar advantages as Phoenix and Scottsdale, with a greater selection of mobile home parks and cheaper space rent.

**8. Quartzsite** ● So all right, it's rather barren and unattractive. However, if you want *really* inexpensive RV parking, join the legions that descend on this sunbaked patch of desert. The gem shows and swap meets are a blast.

**9. Tucson** ● For all of the reasons we listed above, this is a great place to spend a winter or a lifetime. Tucson has a good assortment of RV parks and resorts, apartments and condos.

**10. Yuma** • Snowbirds double Yuma's population in winter, so why not join them? Ample shopping, interesting historic sites and the Colorado River playground make this a good choice.

## Arizona's ten best places to find jobs

**1. Phoenix** • Hands down, Phoenix is the job center of Arizona. With a generally low unemployment rate and a broad employment base, this is where we'd start knocking on doors.

**2. Buckeye** • This small town on the western fringes of the Valley of the Sun is actively promoting light industry and it's far from the congestion of metropolitan Phoenix.

**3. Chandler** • Fast growing Chandler offers a good mix of space-age firms, high tech, general manufacturing, construction and retail.

**4. Flagstaff** • This dynamic western Arizona city's job count increased by more than 30 percent in the past decade. Tourism, high tech manufacturing and education are leading job sources.

**5. Gilbert** • It was Arizona's fourth fastest growing city in the nineties, increasing by 277 percent, and its job market expanded with it. Gilbert and its neighboring communities offer a diversified job base.

**6. Glendale** • Like its booming neighbors, Glendale has a constantly increasing job base. Its varied employment picture includes manufacturing, high tech, construction, retailing and services.

**7. Goodyear** • The first of several West Valley towns started by the Goodyear Tire and Rubber Company, it is host to such firms as McKesson, Rubbermaid, Southwest Specialty Foods and Lockheed-Martin.

**8. Litchfield Park** • Another of the Goodyear towns, this attractive planned community offers access a growing job base while it remains relatively stable. While it grew only by fifteen percent in the last decade, tens of thousands of new jobs are within a short commute.

**9. Sierra Vista** • This prairie town offers the best job market in Arizona's southeast, which admittedly isn't as good as the Valley of the Sun. However, Sierra Vista is working to attract more light industry and it should appeal to those seeking a slower pace.

**10. Tucson** • The Old Pueblo isn't growing as fast as Phoenix, and most folks here like that. However, as Arizona's second largest city, it offers a large and varied employment base.

## Arizona's ten best tourist attractions

**1. Grand Canyon National Park** • Well, of course it tops our list! We might even call this incredible gorge *America's* best attraction. The pity is that most people see it only from the rim. To really love the canyon, you should hike down into it or run the wild rapids of the Colorado River.

**2. Arizona-Sonora Desert Museum** • If we had time to visit only one museum in Arizona, it would be this one on the outskirts of Tucson. You'll receive a thorough education about the flora, fauna and history of the state's great desert reaches.

**3. Canyon de Chelly National Monument** ● Located on the Navajo reservation, this steep-walled gorge with ancient pueblos tucked into its sheer flanks is often overlooked by visitors. Of Arizona's natural attractions, only the Grand Canyon surpasses its grandeur.

**4. The Heard Museum** ● If we had time to visit only two museums in Arizona, this would be the other one. Devoted exclusively to the study of native people, this outstanding Phoenix archive contains the world's best treasury of Indian culture.

**5. Hoover Dam/Lake Mead National Recreation Area** ● When Hoover Dam was completed in 1935, it was the world's highest, holding back the world's largest reservoir. It's still an awesome thing, and Lake Mead is a grand place to play on the water.

**6. Mission San Xavier del Bac** ● The "White Dove of the Desert" near Tucson is one of America's most beautiful Spanish missions. And it's one of the few still serving native people.

**7. Monument Valley Tribal Park** ● This is where they film those great car commercials. Although smaller than most people think, this park on the Arizona-Utah border has some of America's most dramatic sandstone buttes, spires and fins.

**8. Oak Creek Canyon** ● Awesome red rock shapes, a sparkling stream and thick forest combine to create one of Arizona's most beautiful settings—and one of its favorite playgrounds.

**9. Organ Pipe Cactus National Monument** ● Arizona's largest national monument is a striking microcosm of the great Sonoran Desert that covers much of southern Arizona and northern Mexico.

**10. Wupatki National Monument** ● This large preserve north of Flagstaff shelters scores of pre-Colombian ruins. It's the best of several ancient pueblos in the area.

# OTHER USEFUL ARIZONA BOOKS

Now that you've purchased this book and we've gotten your money—assuming you aren't still thumbing through it in the bookstore—we will recommend further reading. Some of these books may be out of print or difficult to find. Try your local library or internet sites such as *www.amazon.com, www. bn.com* and *www.borders.com.*

## General travel information

*Arizona Milepost Guide* by William Hafford; Arizona Highways Books. A milepost-pegged guide to fifteen driving tours.

*The Arizona Guide* by Judy Wade; Fulcrum Publishing, 16100 Table Mountain Parkway, Suite 300, Golden, CO 80401; (800) 992-2908 or (303) 277-1623; *www.fulcrum-books.com.* This comprehensive book, busy with color illustrations, covers attractions, activities, nightlife, shopping, restaurants, history, scenic drives and more.

*Arizona Off the Beaten Path* by Scott Barker; Globe- Pequot Press, P.O. Box 480, Guilford, CT 06437; *www.globe-pequot.com.* The author takes readers to less-visited areas of the state.

***Arizona Scenic Drives*** by Stewart Greene; Falcon Press, P.O. Box 279, Billings, MT 59103. This book features a series of descriptive drives through the state.

***Arizona Travel Planner*** distributed free by the Arizona Office of Tourism, 1100 W. Washington St., Phoenix, AZ 85007, call (800) 842-8257 or (602) 542-TOUR. A concise guide to the state, section by section, listing attractions, mileages, campgrounds, chambers of commerce, tour operators and other essentials.

***Day Trips from Phoenix, Tucson Flagstaff*** by Shifra Stein; current edition by Pam Hait. Globe-Pequot Press, P.O. Box 480, Guilford, CT 06437; *www.globe-pequot.com.* The lengthy title says it all. This guide to outings from Arizona's metropolitan areas is handy for visitors with spare time and residents seeking weekend getaways.

***Travel Arizona II: An Arizona Highways Guide to the Best Tourism Sites***; Arizona Highways, 2039 W. Lewis Ave., Phoenix, AZ 89009. Filled with the typically gorgeous color photos from the archives of *Arizona Highways,* this book has a detailed section on Phoenix and the Valley of the Sun. In addition to the pretty pictures, it has useful information on some of the area's popular visitor attractions.

***Roadside Geology of Arizona*** by Halka Chronic; Mountain Press Publishing Company, P.O. Box 2399, Missoula, MT 59806. Scholarly yet highly readable guide to geological formations that visitors see as they travel Arizona's highways.

***RVing America's Backroads: Arizona*** by Kitty Pearson and Jim Vincent; Trailer Life Books, Agoura, Calif. A full color, attractively illustrated guide to Arizona, oriented to the RV set, with suggested driving tours in various areas of the state.

***Travel Arizona: The Back Roads*** by Joseph Stocker; Arizona Highways, 2039 W. Lewis Ave., Phoenix, AZ 85009. Sixteen tours, with illustrations, maps and color photos.

***What Is Arizona Really Like: A Guide to Arizona's Marvels*** by Reg Manning; Reganson Cartoon Books, P.O. Box 5242, Phoenix, AZ 85010. Humorously written insider's look at Arizona with cartoon illustrations, by the former Pulitzer Prize-winning cartoonist for the *Arizona Republic.*

## Relocation & retirement

***The Book of Lists,*** published annually by the *The Business Journal,* 2910 N. Central, Phoenix, AZ 85012; (602) 230-8400. Although it doesn't provide specific job listings, it publishes names, phone numbers and addresses of the area's largest firms.

***Doing Business in Arizona*** by the University of Arizona Press, Tucson, AZ 85721. This scholarly book details the specifics of setting up a business in the state, covering laws, regulations, employment availability and such.

*The Phoenix Job Bank;* Adams Media Corp., 260 Center St., Holbrook, MA 02343; (800) 872-5627; *www.careercity.com.* A "how-to" book for job- seekers, with lists of major Phoenix and Tucson employers, job descriptions and techniques for successful job-hunting.

*StartSmart: Your Arizona Business;* Oasis Press, Box 3727, Central Point, OR 97502; (800) 228-2275; *www.psi- research.com.* This book lists detailed startup information, current state and federal laws affective business and other useful data.

## History, ghost towns & reference

*Arizona Almanac* by Dean Smith; WestWinds Press, P.O. Box 10306, Portland, OR 97210; (503) 226-2402; *www.gacpa.com.* Encyclopedic is the word for this book, covering state statistics, events and fairs, parks, rivers, native peoples, lists of state officials and more.

*Arizona: An Illustrated History* by Patrick Lavin; Hippocreme Books, 171 Madison Ave., New York, NY 10016; *www.hippocreme-books.com.* This comprehensive historical treatment is busy with old photos and drawings.

*Arizona Place Names,* re-print of a 1935 edition by Will C. Barnes, University of Arizona Press, Tucson. Thorough, comprehensive guide to the origin of Arizona's geographic names.

*Arizona's Best Ghost Towns* by Byrd Howell Granger; Northland Press, P.O. Box N, Flagstaff, AZ 86002. A helpful guide with maps and nice sketches.

*Arizona Trails & Tales: True Adventures of the Old West* by Charles Lauer; Golden West Publishers, 4113 N. Longview Ave., Phoenix, AZ 85014; (602) 265-4392; *www.goldenwestpublishers.com.* This book offers a light look at Arizona's history, focusing on its characters and offbeat historical events.

*History of Arizona* by Robert Woznicki, PH.D.; Messenger Graphics, 110 S. 41st Ave., Phoenix, AZ 85009. A highly-readable treatment of the state's history; not comprehensive, but filled with interesting vignettes and personality sketches.

*Roadside History of Arizona* by Marshall Turnbull; Mountain Press Publishing Co., P.O. Box 2399, Missoula, MT 59806; (406) 728-1900. This thick book is a milepost type guide to the state's history, with maps, photos and specific directions to historic sites.

*The Story of Superstition Mountain and the Lost Dutchman Mine* by Robert Joseph Allen; Pocket Books, New York. A readable narrative of the Dutchman mine mystery, with some very questionable suppositions.

## Hiking, camping & other outdoor activities

*Arizona Day Hikes* by Dave Ganci; Sierra Club Books. It describes a hundred day hike trails throughout the state.

*Arizona Wildlife Viewing* by John N. Carr; Falcon Press, P.O. Box 279, Billings, MT 59103. This small full-color book advises hikers and strollers where to see what kind of wildlife in the state's parks and recreation areas; compiled in cooperation with park and recreation departments.

*Best Hikes with Children in Arizona* by Lawrence Letham; The Mountaineers, 101 SW Klikitat Way, Suite 201, Seattle, WA 98134; *www.mountaineers.org*. This book outlines fifty Arizona hikes that are gentle enough for kids, including several in the Valley of the Sun's extensive mountain parks system.

*Desert Wildflowers*; Arizona Highways, 2039 W. Lewis Ave., Phoenix, AZ 85009. Gorgeous photos of desert blossoms, with descriptions and times to catch peak blooming periods.

*Guide to Arizona's Wilderness Areas* by Tom Dollar and photos by Jerry Seive; Westcliffe Publishers; *www.westcliffepublishers.com*. This comprehensive full color book covers 63 wilderness areas, featuring 158 one-day destinations.

*A Hiker's Guide to Arizona* by Steward Aitchison and Bruce Grubbs; Falcon Press, P.O. Box 279, Billings, MT 59103. A well-written guide with maps and black and white photos.

*Hiker's Guide to the Superstition Wilderness* by Jack Carlson and Elizabeth Stewart; Clear Creek Publishing, P.O. Box 24666, Tempe, AZ 85285. A fine little guide to trails in the Superstitions, brightened by the history and legends of the Lost Dutchman mine.

*Mountain Biking in Arizona* by Sarah Bennett; published Falcon Press, P.O. Box 279, Billings, MT 59103. This book details several mountain bike trails in the state's hinterlands.

*Outdoors in Arizona: A Guide to Camping* by Bob Hirsch; Arizona Highways, 2039 W. Lewis Ave., Phoenix, AZ 85009. A good mix of campsite listings, color photos and history and vignettes about the state's out-of-doors.

*Outdoors in Arizona: A Guide to Hiking and Backpacking* by John Annerino; Arizona Highways, 2039 W. Lewis Ave., Phoenix, AZ 85009. Suggested hikes from desert to mountain to prairie, with maps and photos.

## Native peoples

*A Clash of Cultures: Fort Bowie and the Chiricahua Apaches* by Robert M. Utley; for sale by the Superintendent of Documents, U.S. Government Printing Office, Washington, DC 20402. Also at national monuments and historic sites.

*American Indians of the Southwest* by Bertha P. Dutton; University of New Mexico Press. A good general guide to present and past Southwestern Indians.

*The Complete Family Guide to Navajo-Hopi Land* by Bonnie Brown and Carol D. Bracken; Bonnie Brown and Carol Bracken, P.O.

Box 2914, Page, AZ 86040. It's a bit unprofessionally done, but helpful, with lists of attractions, places to dine and sleep; several children's pages to amuse the youngsters.

***Geronimo: A Man, His Time, His Place*** by Angie Debo; University of Oklahoma Press, Norman, OK 73019. An award-winning biography of the famous Apache warrior; probably the most comprehensive Geronimo study ever written.

***Southwestern Indian Tribes*** by Tom Bahti; KC Publications, Inc., Box 14883-A, Las Vegas, NV 89114. Attractive guide to Arizona and New Mexico tribes with maps and color and black and white illustrations; nicely detailed photos of artifacts.

***Visitor's Guide to Arizona's Indian Reservations*** by Boye De Mente; Phoenix Books/Publishers, P.O. Box 32008, Phoenix, AZ 85064. A thorough, well-written guide with lots of detail and maps.

# HOW TO TALK LIKE AN ARIZONAN

Well, of course Arizonans speak English, although there's a generous sprinkling of Spanish and Indian words in there. Many Arizona place names have Spanish and Indian roots. This pronunciation guide—prepared with the aid of Brian C. Catts of the University of Arizona's Office of Public Service—will help you talk like a native.

**Ajo** *(AH-hoe)* — Town in southern Arizona; the word means "garlic" in Spanish.

**Anasazi** *(Ana-SAH-zee)* — Early Arizona Indian tribe; the name means "the ancient ones."

**Apache** *(Ah-PAH-chee)* — Central and southeastern Arizona tribe.

**Athabaskan** *(A-tha-BAS-kan; "a's" pronounced as in apple)* — Canadian Indian tribe; ancestors of the Navajo and Apache.

**Bowie** *(BOO-ee)* — Fort in southeastern Arizona, now a national historic site; also a tiny town on Interstate 10.

**Canyon de Chelly** *(du SHAY or day SHAY)* — Arizona national monument, whose name is often mispronounced.

**Canyon del Muerto** *(MWAIR-toh)* "Canyon of Death," a ravine adjacent to Canyon de Chelly.

**Carne** *(CAR-nay)* — Meat.

**"Cerveza fria, por favor"** *(Sehr-VE-sa FREE-ah, por fah-VOR)* — "Bring me a cold one, please."

**Chemehuevi** *(Tchem-e-H'WAY-vee)* — Southern Colorado River tribe of Yuman origin. Meaning of tribal name is unknown.

**Chinle** *(Chin-LEE)* Navajo town, the gateway to Canyon de Chelly.

**Chiricahua** *(Cheer-i-COW-wa)* — Southeastern Arizona Apache tribe made famous by Cochise and Geronimo's rebellions.

**Cholla** *(CHOY-ya)* — Large family of Arizona cactus.

**Coconino** *(Co-co-NEE-no)* — Arizona place name, given to a national forest, county and plateau south of the Grand Canyon.

**Colorado** *(Coh-lo-RAH-doh)* — Red.

**El Tovar** *(El To-VAR)* — Historic hotel at the Grand Canyon's South Rim.

**Gila** *(HEE-la)* — A river in southern Arizona.

**Guadalupe Hidalgo** *(Wa-da-LU-pay Hee-DAL-go)* The treaty ending the Mexican War, signed in 1848.

**Havasupai** *(Hah-vah-SOO-pie)* — "Blue-green water people" who occupy beautiful Havasu Canyon; also called Supai.

**Hohokam** *(Hoe-hoe-KAHM)* — Prehistoric tribe occupying deserts of Southern Arizona about AD 200 to 500; "those who have gone."

**Huachuca** *(Hwa-CHOO-ka)* — Army fort in southern Arizona with an historic museum; also the name of a mountain range.

**Hopi** *(HOE-pee)* — Indian tribe, most likely Anasazi descendants.

**Hotevilla** *(HOAT-vih-la)* — Hopi village on Third Mesa. The name means "skinned back" or cleared off.

**Hualapai** *(HWAL-a-pie or WAH-lah-pie)* — Western Arizona Indian tribe; the name means "pine tree people."

**Huevos Rancheros** *(WHEY-vose ran-CHER-ohs)* — Popular Spanish style breakfast with eggs and picante sauce.

**Kykotsmovi** *(Kee-KOTS-mo-vee)* — Hopi administrative center, on Third Mesa below Oraibi, also called New Oraibi. It means "the place of the mound of ruins."

**Maricopa** *(Ma-ri-KOH-pah)* — A name given to the Pipa tribe, which shares a reservation with the Pima.

**Mescalero** *(Mess-kah-LAIR-o)* — Arizona-New Mexico Apache tribe. The name is Spanish, referring to mescal cactus, a traditional food source.

**Moenkopi** *(Mu-en-KO-pee)* —Third Mesa Hopi village; "place of running water."

**Mogollon** *(MUGGY-yon)* — Ancient Indian tribe occupying eastern Arizona about AD 200 to 500; also Mogollon Rim, the abrupt southern edge of the Colorado Plateau.

**Mohave** *(Mo-HA-vay)* — Very common Arizona place name, referring to Indian tribe and a county in western Arizona. It's spelled "Mojave" in California.

**Navajo** *(NAH-VAH-hoe)* — America's largest Indian tribe, descended from the Athabascan band of Canada.

**Nogales** *(No-GAH-less)* Twin Arizona-Mexico border towns; the word is Spanish for "walnuts."

**Ocotillo** *(O-co-TEE-yo)* — Tall, skinny and spiney-limbed desert plant with red blossoms.

**Oraibi** *(Oh-RYE-bee)* — Hopi settlement on Third Mesa; the name means "place of the Orai stone."

**Paloverde** *(PAW-lo-VAIR-day)* — Desert tree distinctive for the green bark of its limbs.

**Papago** *(PAH-pa-go)* — Spanish word for "bean eaters," referring to a Southern Arizona Indian tribe, which has since re-adopted its traditional name of "Tohono O'odham."

**Pima** (PEE-mah) — Central and southern Arizona tribe. The name was a Spanish mistake. When questioned by early explorers, they responded *"Pi-nyi-match,"* which means "I don't understand." The Spanish thought they were identifying themselves.

**Prescott** *(PRESS-kit)* — The proper way to pronounce the name of that town in central Arizona.

**Quechan** *(KEE-chan or KAY-chan)* — Indian tribe near Yuma area; also known as Yuma Indians.

**Saguaro** *(Sa-WHA-ro)* — Large cactus; its blossom is Arizona's state flower.

**San Xavier** *(Sahn Ha-vee-YAY)* — Spanish mission south of Tucson; some locals pronounce it *Ha-VEER.*

**Sichomovi** *(si-CHO-MO-vee)* — Hopi settlement on First Mesa; means "a hill where the wild currants grow."

**Sinagua** *(Si-NAU-wa)* — Ancient north central Arizona tribe; lived in the area about 900-1000 A.D. It comes from the Spanish words *sin agua*—"without water."

**Shungopovi** *(Shung-O-PO-vee)* — Hopi settlement on Second Mesa; means "a place by the spring where tall reeds grow."

**Tempe** *(Tem-PEE)* — City east of Phoenix.

**Tohono O'odham** *(To-HO-no Ah-toon)* — Traditional Papago tribal name; it means "people of the desert who have emerged from the earth."

**Tubac** *(TU-bahk)* — Arizona's first settlement; below Tucson.

**Tumacacori** *(Too-mawk-ka-COR-ee)* — Spanish mission below Tucson.

**Tusayan** *(TU-sigh-yan or TUSSY-yan)* — Sinagua Indian ruin near Desert View in Grand Canyon National Park; also a town outside the south entrance station.

**Ute** *(Yoot)* — Large Great Basin Indian tribe; few members are in Arizona. It means "the tribe" in the Shoshoni and Comanche language.

**Verde** *(VAIR-day)* — Spanish for "green."

**Wahweap** *(WAH-weep)* — Ute Indian for "bitter water"; the name of a large marina at Glen Canyon National Recreation Area.

**Wupatki** *(Wu-PAT-key)* — National monument northeast of Flagstaff. The word is Hopi for "tall house."

**Yaqui** *(Ya-KEE)* — Small Indian tribe southwest of Tucson, near Tohono O'odham Reservation. Origin of name unknown; it might simply mean "the people," a self-reference used by many early tribes.

**Yavapai** *(YA-va-pie)* — Central Arizona tribe. The name might mean "crooked mouth people" or "people of the sun."

**Yuma** *(YOO-mah)* — Large tribal group near the city of Yuma; the name is derived from *lum,* which means tribe. The original name is Quechan (see above), which the tribe is again using.

# INDEX: main listings indicated by *bold face italics*

# Remarkably Useful DISCOVERGUIDES
## By Don & Betty Martin

Critics praise the "jaunty prose" and "beautiful editing" of travel, wine and relocation guides by authors Don and Betty Martin. They are recent winners of a gold medal for best guidebook of the year in the annual Lowell Thomas Travel Writing Competition. Their DISCOVERGUIDES are available at bookstores throughout the United States and Canada, or you can order them on line at **www.amazon.com, bn.com** or **borders.com.**

### ARIZONA IN YOUR FUTURE

It's a complete relocation guide for job-seekers, retirees and "Snow-birds" planning a move to Arizona. It provides essential data on dozens of cities, from recreation to medical facilities.  — *272 pages; $16.95*

### THE BEST OF DENVER & THE ROCKIES

Discover the very finest of the Mile High City, from its Ten Best attractions, museums and parks to its leading restaurants and lodgings, and then explore attractions of the nearby Rockies.  — *256 pages; $16.95*

### THE BEST OF PHOENIX & TUCSON

Head for the Sunbelt to explore Arizona's two largest cities. Discover their Ten Best attractions, desert parks, walking and biking trails, restaurants, resorts, dude ranches and much more!  — *272 pages; $16.95*

### THE BEST OF SAN FRANCISCO

Our perennial best seller takes you through the streets of everybody's favorite city, helping you discover its best attractions, museums, hidden lures, restaurants, cheap eats & sleeps and more!  — *280 pages; $16.95*

### THE BEST OF THE WINE COUNTRY

Where to taste wine in California? More than 350 wineries are featured, along with nearby restaurants, lodging and attractions. Special sections offer tips on storing and serving wine.  — *352 pages; $16.95*

### CALIFORNIA-NEVADA ROADS LESS TRAVELED

This is a "Discovery guide to places less crowded." It directs travelers to interesting yet uncrowded attractions, hideaway resorts, scenic campgrounds, interesting cafes and other discoveries.  — *336 pages; $15.95*

### HAWAII: THE BEST OF PARADISE

Discover the best of Hawaii in this guide to America's tropical paradise. The book lists the top attractions, restaurants and resorts of Honolulu, then it features the lures of the outer islands.  — *272 pages; $16.95*

---

**MORE BOOKS AND ORDERING INFORMATION ON NEXT PAGE**

## LAS VEGAS: THE BEST OF GLITTER CITY

This impertinent insiders' guide explores the world's greatest party town, with expanded Ten Best lists of casino resorts, restaurants, attractions, buffets, shows, pubs, clubs and more!    — *296 pages; $16.95*

## NEVADA IN YOUR FUTURE

It's a complete relocation guide to the Silver State, with useful information for job-seekers, businesses, retirees and winter "Snowbirds." A special section discusses incorporating in Nevada. — *292 pages; $16.95*

## SAN DIEGO: THE BEST OF SUNSHINE CITY

Winner of a Lowell Thomas gold medal for best travel guide, this lively and whimsical book features the finest of sunny San Diego, featuring its Ten Best attractions, restaurants and much more.  —*236 pages; $16.95*

## SEATTLE: THE BEST OF EMERALD CITY

This upbeat and opinionated book directs visitors to the very best of Emerald City's attractions, restaurants and lodgings, with interesting side trips to the rest of Western Washington.    —*236 pages; $15.95*

## THE ULTIMATE WINE BOOK

This great little book covers the subject in three major areas—Wine and Heath, Wine Appreciation and Wine with Food. And it does so with good humor, poking harmless fun at wine critics    —*194 pages; $10.95*

## WASHINGTON DISCOVERY GUIDE

This handy book steers motorists and RVers from the Olympic Peninsula to Seattle to the Cascades and beyond, with details on attractions, restaurants, lodging, camping and more.    —*464 pages; $17.95*